365 Baked Cheese Appetizer Recipes

(365 Baked Cheese Appetizer Recipes - Volume 1)

Peggy Ervin

Published on December, 02 2020

Content

365 Awesome Baked Cheese Appetizer Recipes

***

1. 4 Cheese Mexican Tortilla Appetizers Recipe

Serving: 12 | Prep: | Cook: 10mins |Ready in:

Ingredients

- 6 (6-inch) fajita-size flour tortillas
- 1 3/4 cups (1-pound can) refried beans
- 1/2 cup Thick & Smooth taco sauce
- 1/2 cup chopped green bell pepper
- 1/2 cup chopped red bell pepper
- 1/2 cup (about 3) sliced green onions
- 1/4 teaspoon crushed red pepper (optional)
- 2 cups (8 ounces) 4 cheese Mexican Blend Shredded cheese

Direction

- PREHEAT oven to 400° F.
- Place tortillas on baking sheet(s).
- BAKE for 3 to 4 minutes or until crisp.
- SPREAD refried beans evenly on tortillas.
- Spread 1 tablespoon taco sauce over beans.
- Top with bell peppers, green onions and crushed red pepper. Sprinkle with cheese.
- BAKE for 7 to 8 minutes or until cheese is melted.
- Cut into wedges.

2. A Touch Of Southwest Cheese Cake Dip Recipe

Serving: 6 | Prep: | Cook: 45mins |Ready in:

Ingredients

- 1 cup finely crushed tortilla chips
- 3 tablespoons melted butter
- 16 ounces cream cheese
- 2 large eggs
- 10 ounces colby/jack cheese, shredded
- 1-4 ounce can chopped green chilies, drained
- 1 cup sour cream
- 1/2 cup diced scallions
- 1/2 cup diced tomatoes
- 1/2 cup sliced black olives
- 1 cup chopped yellow peppers and orange peppers, mixed
- tortilla chips to serve

Direction

- Preheat oven to 325°.
- Mix crushed tortilla chips and butter and press into a springform pan.
- Bake for 15 minute.
- In a bowl, beat cream cheese and eggs with a mixer until well blended.
- Mix in cheese and chilies.
- Pour over crust and bake 30 minutes.
- Cool slightly.
- Spread sour cream over cheesecake.
- Loosen cake from rim of pan. COOL BEFORE removing the rim of the springform pan.
- Cover and refrigerate overnight.
- When ready to serve, top with scallions, tomatoes, black olives and yellow and orange peppers.
- Serve with tortilla chips.

3. Almond Double Crunch Nachos Recipe

Serving: 4 | Prep: | Cook: 10mins | Ready in:

Ingredients

- 6 pita bread rounds
- 1-1/2 cups grated pepper jack cheese
- 1/2 cup sliced green olives
- 1/2 cup sliced green onions
- 1/2 cup toasted slivered almonds
- 1 cup bottled salsa

Direction

- Cut each pita bread open to make 2 circles.
- Cut each circle into 8 wedges.
- Spread in a single layer on 2 baking sheets.
- Toast under broiler turning to toast both sides of chips approximately 1 minute per side.
- Transfer all chips to 1 baking sheet.
- Sprinkle evenly with cheese, olives, onions and almonds.
- Broil 2 minutes or until cheese melts.
- Serve with a bowl of salsa.

4. Alouette Caramel Apple Brie Recipe

Serving: 8 | Prep: | Cook: | Ready in:

Ingredients

- 2 tbsp. caramel fruit dip
- 1 pkg. (13.2 oz. or 8 oz.) Alouette Baby Brie, Original
- 2 apples, sliced
- lemon juice to brush on apples

Direction

- Spread caramel over the top of Alouette Baby Brie.
- Brush apples with lemon juice to prevent browning.
- Arrange apples on top of the Alouette Baby Brie.
- Serve at room temperature.

5. Alouette Cranberry Brie Recipe

Serving: 6 | Prep: | Cook: 5mins | Ready in:

Ingredients

- 1 pkg. (13.2 oz. or 8 oz.) Alouette Baby Brie, Original
- 1 cup Ocean Spray® Cran-fruit Cranberry orange Sauce
- 2 tbsp. packed dark brown sugar
- 3 tsp. rum or orange extract
- 1/8 tsp. ground nutmeg
- 2 tbsp. chopped pecans

Direction

- Preheat oven to 450° F.
- Remove top rind of Alouette Baby Brie leaving a 3" rim around the circumference of the cheese.
- In a small bowl combine Cran-Fruit, brown sugar, extract and nutmeg.
- Top Alouette Baby Brie with cranberry mixture and sprinkle with 2 tbsp. chopped pecans.
- Place in an ovenproof dish and bake in a 450° F oven for 4-5 minutes.
- Serve warm with assorted crackers or apple slices.

6. American Buffalo Wings With Bleu Cheese Dip Recipe

Serving: 6 | Prep: | Cook: 45mins | Ready in:

Ingredients

- 24 chicken wings disjointed
- 1 stick butter melted
- 8 tablespoons hot pepper sauce
- 1/4 teaspoon cayenne pepper
- 4 tablespoons soy sauce
- 1 cup brown sugar
- 6 cloves garlic minced
- Dip:
- 6 ounce package cream cheese softened
- 1/2 cup sour cream
- 2 tablespoons mayonnaise
- 1/2 teaspoon salt
- 1 teaspoon white pepper
- 4 ounces bleu cheese crumbled

Direction

- Preheat oven to 400.
- Place wings in baking pan.
- In mixing bowl combine remaining ingredients then coat wings on both sides.
- Bake 45 minutes basting frequently.
- Just before serving pour remaining sauce over wings and broil 1 minute.
- In bowl of a food processor combine all dip ingredients except bleu cheese.
- Process until creamy then add bleu cheese but do not process to keep dip chunky.
- Spoon into a bowl and refrigerate until ready to use.

7. Apache Cheese Dip Recipe

Serving: 6 | Prep: | Cook: 60mins | Ready in:

Ingredients

- 1 round loaf adobe bread
- 16 oz. sharp grated cheese
- 1 block (8oz) cream cheese
- 1 tub (8 oz) sour cream
- 1/2 cup of green onions, chopped
- 1 tablespoon worcestershire sauce
- 2 4 1/2 oz cans of chopped green chilies
- 1 lb game sausage; chopped

Direction

- After cutting the top off the round loaf of bread, clean out the inside.
- Although we use native adobe bread any hard crusted round loaf (9 1nches) can be used. Mix together in a bowl all of the other ingredients. We have used both elk and buffalo sausage. If no game sausage can be found you can substitute any dry sausage or good smoked ham. After placing the bread on a cookie sheet, fill the cavity of the bread 'bowl' and replace the bread lid. Bake for 1 hour at 350°. The 'bowl' will be very stiff. Remove the lid and stir the ingredients. Serve with fry bread or the bread taken from inside the loaf.

8. Apple And Feta Pan Fried Pizzas Recipe

Serving: 24 | Prep: | Cook: 30mins | Ready in:

Ingredients

- 6 1/2 ounces dry pizza crust mix
- 1/2 cup hot water
- 5 tablespoons olive oil
- 8 ounces crumbled feta cheese
- 1 red onion, thinly sliced
- 1 tablespoon chopped fresh thyme
- 1/2 tablespoon butter
- 4 apples, cored and chopped
- ground black pepper to taste

Direction

- In a medium bowl, combine contents of the pizza dough package and 1/2 cup hot water. Stir vigorously, about 25 strokes.
- Set the bowl in a warm place (about 85 degrees F, or 35 degrees C) for 5 minutes.

- Turn dough onto floured board, divide the dough into 8 small sections. Knead the dough and shape it into rounds.
- Preheat the oven to 300 degrees F (150 degrees C).
- In a large skillet, heat the olive oil.
- Add the dough and fry until the dough is lightly browned, flipping once to brown on both sides.
- Once cooked, place the circles on a cookie sheet.
- Sprinkle the feta, red onion, and thyme on top of the circles.
- Bake the pizzas until the feta begins to brown, about 10 to 12 minutes.
- While the pizzas bake, in the previously used skillet, heat 1/2 tablespoon of butter and a few sprigs of thyme.
- Mix the apples into the skillet, and cook until the apples are soft and golden.
- Lay the apples on top of the pizzas, season with pepper, and serve.

9. Apricot Baked Brie Recipe

Serving: 10 | Prep: | Cook: 30mins | Ready in:

Ingredients

- 1 - 8oz wheel of brie cheese (I usually use the president's brand)
- 3 TBSP apricot preserves
- 1 - 17.5 oz package frozen puff pastry, thawed (you will only used one of the two sheets in the box)
- 1 egg white

Direction

- Preheat oven to 350 degrees
- Lightly grease cookie sheet
- Slice the wheel of brie in half so you have 2 circles of cheese
- Spread apricot or peach preserves on the cut side
- Make a sandwich out of the two halves so the preserves are in the centre
- Wrap the entire wheel of brie with one sheet of puffed pastry and flip the folded side down
- Brush pastry with egg white
- Bake 30 minutes or until the pastry is golden brown
- Serve Immediately

10. Apricot Rosemary Crostini With Brie Recipe

Serving: 15 | Prep: | Cook: 5mins | Ready in:

Ingredients

- 3/4 cup apricot Spread
- 1 lb . Brie, trim rind off
- 30 rosemary Crostini
- apricot SPREAD
- 3 cups apricot, thawed
- 1 sprig rosemary, leaves minced
- 1 tsp. lemon zest, thawed
- Combine the apricot puree, lemon zest puree and minced rosemary in a saucepot.
- Bring to a boil, reduce to simmer and cook until reduced to 3/4 cup. Remove from the stove. Cool.

Direction

- Preheat oven to 350 degrees.
- Spread one side of the rosemary croutons with the All Apricot Spread.
- Top with a small 1/2 oz. slice of Brie and bake in oven to lightly melt the cheese. Serve.

11. Apricot Pecan Camembert Recipe

Serving: 8 | Prep: | Cook: 25mins | Ready in:

Ingredients

- I wheel of camembert cheese, 8 ounces
- 1/4 cup of apricot preserves
- 1 tablespoon of chopped nuts. toasted
- a few sprigs of fresh thyme leaves

Direction

- Heat oven to 350 degrees.
- Place cheese in a shallow ovenproof serving dish.
- Bake for 20 minutes until the cheese is very soft.
- Remove from oven and top with preserves of choice, and pecans.
- Bake another 3 minutes.
- Top with thyme.
- Serve with crackers or cocktail bread slices. You know those little square ones.

12. Artichoke Cheese Dip Recipe

Serving: 12 | Prep: | Cook: 30mins |Ready in:

Ingredients

- 1/2 cup mayonnaise
- 1/2 cup shredded cheddar cheese
- 1/2 cup shredded pepper jack cheese
- 1/8 teaspoon onion salt
- 1 teaspoon dill weed
- 1/8 teaspoon lemon pepper
- 6-1/2 ounces marinated artichoke hearts drained

Direction

- Preheat oven to 350.
- Combine all ingredients in a 2 quart baking dish.
- Bake uncovered for 30 minutes.

13. Artichoke Parmesan Strudel Recipe

Serving: 24 | Prep: | Cook: 32mins |Ready in:

Ingredients

- 1 (17.3 oz) box frozen puff pastry
- 2 (8 oz) packages cream cheese, softened
- 1 1/4 c freshly grated parmesan cheese, divided
- 5 large eggs, divided
- 1/4 c chopped fresh parsley
- 2 T fresh lemon juice
- 2 t dried thyme
- 1/4 t salt
- 1/4 t fresh ground black pepper, or white pepper
- 2 (14 oz) cans artichoke hearts, drained and chopped

Direction

- Preheat oven to 400
- Grease a 13x9 inch baking pan, set aside
- On a lightly floured surface, roll each puff pastry sheet into a 14x10 inch rectangle
- Place one sheet in bottom of prepared pan and prick with a fork
- Bake for 8 minutes, set aside to cool slightly
- In a medium bowl, combine cream cheese, 1 c parmesan, 4 eggs, parsley, lemon juice, thyme, salt and pepper
- Beat at medium speed with an electric mixer until smooth
- Stir in artichokes until well combined
- Spread artichoke mixture on bottom crust in pan and top with remaining puff pastry sheet
- Lightly beat remaining egg and gently brush over top of crust
- Bake for 15 minutes, sprinkle with remaining 1/4 c Parmesan cheese and bake 10-12 minutes, or until lightly browned
- Cool in pan for 10 minutes, and cut into squares

14. Asparagus And Parmesan Cheese Puddings Sformati Di Asparagi E Parmigiano Recipe

Serving: 8 | Prep: | Cook: 60mins | Ready in:

Ingredients

- 1/2 cup fresh breadcrumbs made from crustless Italian bread
- 2 pounds asparagus, trimmed
- 2 tablespoons unsalted butter
- 1 medium onion, finely chopped
- 1 cup freshly grated parmesan cheese (about 3 ounces)
- 1/2 cup whole-milk ricotta cheese
- 1/4 cup all purpose flour
- 4 large eggs

Direction

- Butter eight 3/4-cup custard cups or soufflé dishes.
- Coat with breadcrumbs.
- Cut off asparagus tips. Cook tips in large saucepan of boiling salted water until crisp-tender, about 3 minutes.
- Drain; reserve tips and 1 cup cooking liquid. Coarsely chop asparagus stalks.
- Melt butter in large non-stick skillet over medium heat.
- Add onion; sauté until tender, about 6 minutes.
- Add stalks; sauté until crisp-tender, about 5 minutes.
- Add reserved asparagus cooking liquid. Cover; simmer until stalks are tender, about 12 minutes.
- Uncover; cook until liquid is absorbed, stirring often, about 5 minutes.
- Transfer to food processor; puree.
- Add Parmesan cheese, ricotta and flour. Using on/off turns, process just until blended. Season with salt and pepper.
- Whisk eggs in bowl to blend.
- Add asparagus puree; whisk to blend.
- Stir in all but 16 asparagus tips.
- Divide custard among cups.
- Place cups in roasting pan. (Can be made 6 hours ahead. Cover; chill puddings and remaining asparagus tips.)
- Preheat oven to 350°F.
- Pour hot water into pan to come 1 inch up sides of cups.
- Bake puddings until set, about 35 minutes.
- Let stand 10 minutes. Invert onto plates.
- Garnish with asparagus tips. .
- That's it! Buon Appetito...enjoy!

15. Asparagus Gruyere Tart Recipe

Serving: 8 | Prep: | Cook: 35mins | Ready in:

Ingredients

- flour, for work surface
- 1 sheet frozen puff pastry
- 5 1/2 ounces (2 cups) gruyere cheese, shredded
- 1 1/2 pounds medium or thick asparagus
- 1 tablespoon olive oil
- salt and pepper

Direction

- Preheat oven to 400 degrees. On a floured surface, roll the puff pastry into a 16-by-10-inch rectangle. Trim uneven edges. Place pastry on a baking sheet. With a sharp knife, lightly score pastry dough 1 inch in from the edges to mark a rectangle. Using a fork, pierce dough inside the markings at 1/2-inch intervals. Bake until golden, about 15 minutes.
- Remove pastry shell from oven, and sprinkle with Gruyere. Trim the bottoms of the asparagus spears to fit crosswise inside the tart shell; arrange in a single layer over Gruyere, alternating ends and tips. Brush with oil, and season with salt and pepper. Bake until spears are tender, 20 to 25 minutes.

16. Avacodo And Goat Cheese Dip Recipe

Serving: 10 | Prep: | Cook: 20mins | Ready in:

Ingredients

- 2 large avacodos
- 1 large pkg goat cheese (8 oz.)
- 1/4 large red onion fine choped
- 3 cloves garlic fine chopped
- 1 shallot chopped
- 1 tsp cajun spice
- 1 tblspn garlic salt
- 3oz cilantro fine chopped
- sliced almonds
- juice of 1 lime
- fresh ground black pepper
- 2 tblspn olive oil
- (optional 1 hot red chili pepper or more)
- 1 pkg mixed color bell peppers or 3 red bell peppers
- raspberry balsamic vinegar

Direction

- Allow cheese to come to room temp
- Peel and seed avocado and cut to smaller pieces
- Add everything else except bell peppers and balsamic vinegar
- Combine in bowl, mash and mix until a smooth consistency is achieved
- Blanch bell peppers in boiling water for 2 min
- Slice and core peppers
- Place pepper strips on cookie sheet
- Roast in oven 20 min at 400
- Remove from oven drizzle with raspberry balsamic vinegar
- Serve with your favourite crackers
- A little dip a little pepper.

17. BAKED BRIE WITH PRESERVES Recipe

Serving: 8 | Prep: | Cook: 30mins | Ready in:

Ingredients

- 1 large sheet of puff pastry dough or 1 tube of refrigerated crescent dinner rolls
- 1 round or wedge of brie cheese (do not remove rind)
- raspberry jam, or other sweet jam
- brown sugar
- 1/4 cup of maple syrup

Direction

- Preheat oven to 350 degrees F.
- On a stick-free cookie sheet, lay out the puff pastry or the crescent rolls flat; put brie round or wedge on top.
- Spread jam on brie, fold dough over top, cutting off excess dough. Drizzle maple syrup and place a handful of brown sugar on top.
- Bake at 350º for 25-30 minutes, pastry should be golden brown. Let cool for 10 minutes before serving.
- Serve with crackers and apple slices.

18. BAKED PARMESAN DIP Recipe

Serving: 12 | Prep: | Cook: 30mins | Ready in:

Ingredients

- 1 package (10 oz.) frozen chopped spinach, thawed, or 1 13.75 oz. can water-packed artichoke hearts, drained and chopped
- 1 cup reduced-fat or regular mayonnaise
- 1 package (3 oz.) cream cheese
- 1 onion (6 oz.), peeled and minced
- 1 clove garlic, pressed or minced

- 1 cup plus 2 tbsp. Shredded parmesan cheese
- 1/8 tsp. pepper
- 1/2 tsp. paprika
- 2 Artisan baguettes (8 oz.), thinly sliced

Direction

- Squeeze spinach to remove liquid. With a mixer, beat spinach, mayonnaise, cream cheese, onion, garlic, 1 cup of the parmesan cheese, and pepper until thoroughly combined.
- Mound mixture in a 3- to 4-cup baking dish. Sprinkle evenly with 2 tbsp. parmesan cheese and paprika.
- Bake in a 350° oven until hot in centre and lightly browned on top, 25 to 30 minutes.
- Serve hot to spread on baguette slices.

19. Bacon Cheddar Chestnut Cheesecake Recipe

Serving: 12 | Prep: | Cook: 25mins | Ready in:

Ingredients

- 1 pound Philly cream cheese, softened
- 2 large eggs
- 2 teaspoons lemon juice
- 3 strips bacon, cooked crisp, drained, crumbled
- 1/4 teaspoon pepper
- 1/2 cup chestnuts, roasted, chopped fine
- 1/2 cup sharp cheddar cheese, shredded

Direction

- Spray the bottom and sides of 6 or 8 inch spring-pan with cooking spray
- Swirl 1/2 cup of bread crumbs or crushed crackers (Ritz) to dust sides and bottom of pan.
- Set in fridge.
- Blend cream cheese until smooth.
- Add eggs one at a time.
- Add lemon juice and pepper.
- Fold in bacon, chestnuts, and cheese, mixing thoroughly.
- Pour into prepared pan.
- Bake at 325^ for 45-50 minutes.
- Let cool and serve at room temperature.
- Leftovers can be refrigerated or frozen in a tight wrapping of plastic.

20. Bacon Cheese Dip Recipe

Serving: 10 | Prep: | Cook: 80mins | Ready in:

Ingredients

- 1 two lb. loaf of round sturdy bread
- cut off lid and hollow out, reserving insides in large chunks
- 1 lb. of bacon (fried and crumbled)
- 1 cup of white cheddar cheese
- 1 cup of monterey jack cheese
- 1 cup of parmesan cheese shredded
- 1 small onion grated fine
- 1 large glove of garlic, minced
- 1 cup of mayonnaise

Direction

- Scoop out bread. Reserve insides for dipping.
- Combine ingredients from the bacon to the mayonnaise.
- Mix well.
- Spoon into hollowed out bread.
- Double wrap in foil, with the lid back on top.
- Bake at 325 degrees for one hour.
- Carefully unwrap and serve on a heatproof platter surrounded with bread cubes, pretzels or crackers.

21. Bacon Wrapped Cheddar Apple Puffs Recipe

Serving: 16 | Prep: | Cook: 20mins | Ready in:

Ingredients

- 1 granny smith apples -- cut into 16 (1/4-inch) slices (1 to 2)
- 1 tablespoon packed brown sugar
- 1 Dash salt
- 1 can Pillsbury® refrigerated crescent dinner rolls
- 8 slices extra-sharp cheddar cheese -- (1/4 inch) cut in half (from 8-oz block)
- 16 slices packaged precooked bacon

Direction

- Heat oven to 375°F. Line cookie sheet with non-stick foil, parchment paper or silicone baking mat. (Some cheese will melt out during baking so this will make clean-up easier.)
- 2 In medium bowl, toss apple slices with brown sugar; sprinkle with salt.
- 3 On cutting board, unroll dough; separate dough into 8 triangles. From center of longest side to opposite point, cut each triangle in half, making 16 triangles.
- 4 Place 1 cheese slice on shortest side of each dough triangle; top each with 1 apple slice. Fold sides of dough triangle up slightly; wrap dough around apple and cheese.
- 5 Wrap 1 bacon slice around outside of each dough roll-up, making sure ends of bacon are on bottom and slightly tucked in. Place on cookie sheet.
- 6 Bake 12 minutes or until golden brown. Immediately remove from cookie sheet. Serve warm.

22. Bacon And Garlic Blue Cheese Dip Recipe

Serving: 12 | Prep: | Cook: 35mins | Ready in:

Ingredients

- 8 slices bacon
- 2 cloves garlic, minced
- 1 (8 ounce) package cream cheese, softened
- 1/4 cup milk
- 4 ounces blue cheese, crumbled
- 2 tablespoons chopped fresh chives

Direction

- Preheat oven to 350 degrees F.
- Cook bacon over medium high heat until evenly brown. Remove bacon from skillet, drain on paper towels and crumble.
- Place garlic in hot bacon grease. Cook and stir until soft, about 1 minute. Remove from heat.
- Place cream cheese and milk in a medium bowl. Beat with an electric mixer until blended. Stir in bacon, garlic, blue cheese and chives. Transfer mixture to a medium baking dish.
- Bake 30 minutes, or until lightly browned.

23. Bacon, Cheese Dip Recipe

Serving: 0 | Prep: | Cook: 45mins | Ready in:

Ingredients

- thx to:
- Prego & Mommy Chat with Peggy Cook Tucker-Roe on facebook
- bacon, cheese Dip
- Ingredients
- 8 ounces cream cheese, softened
- 2 cups sour cream (I used light)
- 1 1/2 cups shredded cheddar cheese...
- 6 slices bacon, cooked and crumbled
- 1/2 cup sliced green onion

Direction

- Instructions
- Preheat oven to 400 F.
- Combine softened cream cheese, sour cream, cheddar cheese, bacon and green onion. Spoon mixture into a 1-quart baking dish and bake for 25-30 minutes, or until cheese is bubbling and hot.

24. Bacon Cheddar Puffs Recipe

Serving: 8 | Prep: | Cook: 8mins | Ready in:

Ingredients

- 1/2 - cup milk...........
- 2- tablespoon butter...........
- 1/2 -cup all-purpose flour..........
- 2- eggs........
- 1/2- cup shredded cheddar cheese..........
- 4- slices bacon , crisply cooked and crumbled.........
- 1/4- cup green onion , chopped...........
- 1/4- teaspoon garlic salt.............
- 1/4- teaspoon pepper...............

Direction

- Bring milk and butter to a boil over medium heat...........
- Add flour, stirring until mixture forms a ball......
- Remove from heat and add eggs, one at a time.................
- Blend until smooth
- Add cheese, bacon, green onion, garlic salt, and pepper
- Mix well
- Drop by teaspoonfuls on a greased baking sheets
- Bake at 350 degrees F. For 5- 8 minutes
- Makes 3 dozen

25. Bacon Cheese Dip Recipe

Serving: 10 | Prep: | Cook: 60mins | Ready in:

Ingredients

- 1 two lb. loaf of round bread (preferred pumpernickle or rye)
- Cut off lid and hollow out inside.
- 1 lb. of bacon (fried and crumbled)
- 1 cup of grated sharp cheddar cheese
- 1 cup of monterey jack shredded-sometimes sub jack with jalapeno
- 1 cup of parmesan
- 1 small grated onion
- 1 large glove of garlic minced
- 1 cup of mayonnaise

Direction

- Combine bacon, cheese, onion, garlic and mayonnaise.
- Mix well. (Can add a dash of hot sauce, if desired.)
- Spoon into hollowed out bread.
- Top with reserved lid.
- Double wrap in foil.
- Bake one hour with lid at 350 degrees.
- Serve with breadsticks, bread cubes and sturdy chips for dipping.

26. Baked Brie Pastries With Artichoke And Prosciutto Recipe

Serving: 6 | Prep: | Cook: 15mins | Ready in:

Ingredients

- 1 sheet puff pastry, cut into 9 squares (8 ounces, 1/2 package approx)
- 6 ounces brie cheese (without rind)

- 1 cup finely chopped marinated artichoke hearts
- 2 tablespoons chopped basil
- 1/4 teaspoon balsamic vinegar
- 1/4 teaspoon salt
- 3 dashes fresh ground pepper, to taste
- 1/2 cup chopped prosciutto ends (1/2 cup chopped thick-cut proscuitto)
- 1/4 cup grated parmesan cheese

Direction

- Preheat oven to 350 degrees F.
- If you have frozen puff pastry, allow it to thaw.
- Cut the sheet into 9 squares.
- Push the squares into 9 of the spaces a lightly sprayed muffin tin.
- In the food processor, whir enough artichoke hearts to make 1 cup of them when they are very finely chopped.
- In a bowl, combine the artichoke, basil, vinegar, salt, and pepper.
- Place about 3/4 to 1 teaspoon brie in the bottom of each puff pastry in the muffin tin (note: brie is much easier to cut when it is very cold).
- Add about 1 1/2 teaspoon of the artichoke mixture on top of the brie (use up all of the mixture).
- Top each with the chopped prosciutto and sprinkle with Parmesan.
- Bake at 350 degrees F for about 15 minutes, or until the puff pastry is golden.
- Let sit for about 5 minutes before serving (the brie will be *very* hot).
- Makes 9 appetizers, about 6 servings since some people will have two.

27. Baked Brie Recipe

Serving: 8 | Prep: | Cook: 25mins | Ready in:

Ingredients

- 12 large sheets of phyllo pastry dough.
- 1/2 cup butter
- 1 wedge of brie cheese (about a 1/2 lb)
- raspberry jam, or other favorite jam
- 1/4 cup brown sugar
- 1/4 cup of maple syrup (honey or other flavored syrup)
- 1/4 cup pecans or walnuts (optional)

Direction

- Preheat oven to 350 degrees.
- On a baking sheet layer each phyllo sheet brushed with butter one at a time.
- Spread jam on top of brie.
- Put brie jam side down on top of the phyllo sheets.
- Fold dough over top.
- Flip so that the seam is down and the jam is on top.
- Bake at 350 degrees for 25 minutes.
- Immediately top with brown sugar and syrup. (You want the brown sugar and syrup to melt, so you might place back in the oven for a couple minutes)
- Let cool for 10 minutes before serving.
- Serve with apple slices, crackers, or toast.

28. Baked Brie Two Options Recipe

Serving: 8 | Prep: | Cook: 25mins | Ready in:

Ingredients

- Ingredients:
- sheet of puff pastry
- 4 inch wheel of brie, or suitably sized wedge from a larger piece
- Dijon mustard (option 1)
- ~1 C black berry balsamic (option 2), or 2/3 C balsamic and half a cup of black berries

Direction

- Trim the pastry so it'll fold nicely over the brie and seal, but before combining you have a decision to make.
- Option 1:
- If you want to go with mustard, smear the top of the brie with a nice heavy dose of mustard.
- Option 2:
- If you want to go for the blackberry balsamic, put the blackberry balsamic in a pan and cook down until nice, thick, and syrupy. You might want to add a dash of salt or sugar depending on starting ingredients.
- If you're using regular balsamic and actual blackberries, crush the berries in the balsamic, cook down, then strain to remove seeds and pulp. Again, check salt and sugar.
- Smear whatever option on top of the brie, and possibly add a little on the pastry under the brie.
- Set brie on pastry, wrap, and bake at ~350 F until the pastry is golden brown.
- Serve hot with sliced French bread (it should melt out nicely when cut and spread easily).
- As always, I'm being very approximate here, adjust to taste.

29. Baked Brie With Fig Jam Recipe

Serving: 4 | Prep: | Cook: 40mins | Ready in:

Ingredients

- This is another of those appetizers that is quick to put together, yet makes an impressive presentation and tastes delicious. In place of the fig jam, you could use a jam or chutney of your choice, either sweet or savory
- I like to serve this creamy, warm cheese intact on a platter with slices of crusty bread. I then let guests slice off pieces themselves to spread on their bread.
- One 12 Inch Round Of puff pastry
- One 5 Inch Round Of brie cheese
- 1 egg, Slightly Beaten
- 1/4 Cup fig jam

Direction

- Preheat the oven to 400 degrees.
- Lay the puff pastry open on the counter.
- Spread a 5 inch circle with the fig jam in the centre.
- Lay the Brie in the centre of the puff pastry circle.
- Fold the excess pastry up around the Brie, completely enclosing it. Slightly twist the top into a knot to seal.
- Place it on a parchment lined sheet tray.
- Brush with egg.
- Bake for 20 minutes or until the outside is golden, reduce the oven temperature to 325 degrees and cook for 20 minutes longer.
- Place the finished product on a nice plate and serve with crusty bread for spreading.

30. Baked Brie With Honey And Pecans Recipe

Serving: 4 | Prep: | Cook: 10mins | Ready in:

Ingredients

- 1 small brie (about 300 grams or 10 ounces)
- a drizzle of olive oil
- 2 sprigs tyme, leaves stripped off
- 2 tablespoons honey
- 1/4 cup pecans, toasted and cut into large pieces

Direction

- Heat the oven to 400 degrees.
- Remove the Brie from its wrapping and put in an oven proof dish.
- Make a few cuts in the top, drizzle with the olive oil and sprinkle with thyme leaves.
- Cover with foil and bake for 10 minutes, or until gooey.

- Remove the foil and drizzle with the honey and sprinkle with the chopped pecans.
- Serve with lots of French bread to scoop up the gooey cheese.

31. Baked Brie With Maple Bacon Apples Recipe

Serving: 6 | Prep: | Cook: 30mins | Ready in:

Ingredients

- • 1 apple, unpeeled, cored, and cut into thin wedges
- • 2 slices thick-cut bacon, cut into 1/2-inch pieces
- • 2 tbsp maple syrup, divided
- • 350g wheel of brie
- • Crackers or sliced bread
- • Chopped chives (optional)

Direction

- 1. Cut apple into thin wedges. Heat a medium frying pan on medium-high. Add bacon and cook 3 to 6 minutes or until crispy. Remove from pan using a slotted spoon. Drain on paper towels. Remove and discard half of fat from pan.
- 2. Add apples to bacon fat in pan. Reduce heat to medium-low and cook while stirring often, about 6 to 10 minutes or until apples are very soft. Add reserved bacon and 1 tbsp. maple syrup.
- 3. Preheat oven to 350°F (175°C). Line a pie dish with parchment paper or aluminum foil. Place brie on top of foil and poke holes in it with a skewer. Spoon apple mixture on top. Bake until cheese is very soft, about 10 to 15 minutes. Drizzle with remaining maple syrup and sprinkle with chives. Serve immediately with crackers.
- Tip: You can make the apple topping up to a day in advance, just be sure to keep refrigerated.

32. Baked Brie With Mushrooms And Almonds Recipe

Serving: 8 | Prep: | Cook: 20mins | Ready in:

Ingredients

- 1 tablespoon butter
- 1 teaspoon crushed garlic
- 2 tablespoons slivered almonds
- 8 ounces fresh Baby Bella mushrooms, chopped
- 1 tablespoon brandy
- 1 teaspoon dried tarragon
- 1 (8oz)wedge brie cheese (It is optional as to weather you remove the coating)

Direction

- Preheat oven to 350
- Melt butter in a medium saucepan over medium heat
- Mix in garlic and almonds, heating until almonds are lightly browned
- Stir in mushrooms and cook until tender, about 5 minutes
- Cover with brandy and sprinkle with tarragon
- Place Brie in a small baking dish
- Pour the mushroom and brandy mixture over the Brie
- Bake in the preheated oven 20 minutes, or until bubbly
- This is nice served with baguette slice

33. Baked Brie And Pear Chutney Recipe

Serving: 6 | Prep: | Cook: 20mins | Ready in:

Ingredients

- 3 pears (diced)
- 1/2 onion (diced)
- 2 Tbsp. pickled ginger (chopped)
- 1/2 cup sugar
- 1/2 cup cider vinegar
- 1 cinnamon stick, broken
- 1 oz. limoncella (lemon liqueur)
- 8 cloves
- Pinch of nutmeg
- Pinch of salt
- 1 sheet filo pastry
- 4 tbsp. melted butter
- 2-3 oz. brie cut 2" long x 3/8" thick slices

Direction

- Place all ingredients (except vinegar) in a sauce pot and simmer over medium heat until sugar begins to caramelize.
- Add vinegar and reduce by one half. Season with salt. When finished remove the cinnamon stick and cloves
- Cut filo sheet in half.
- Place one half on top of the other, turning it 90 degrees to form the shape of a cross.
- Place the brie in the centre of the pastry layering it into a tower, approximately 3" circumference.
- Take two opposite corners of the pastry and pull them together over top of the cheese.
- Pinch the pastry together just above the cheese being careful to leave the top open to resemble a flower.
- Drizzle a small amount of butter on a baking sheet. Place cheese on butter.
- Drizzle more butter over pastry and bake at 450 degrees until golden brown. Spoon some chutney onto centre of plate and place cheese on top of chutney.

34. Baked Brie WCaramelized Onions Pecans And Cranberries Recipe

Serving: 8 | Prep: | Cook: 60mins | Ready in:

Ingredients

- ½ lg sweet onion
- 2 Tbs. butter
- 2 Tbs. sugar (or honey)
- ½ c. pecans
- ½ c. fresh cranberries
- 1 8″ to 10″ Brie Wheel (16 oz) (thicker cakes work better)
- 1 french baguette

Direction

- Slice onion thinly.
- Finely chop Pecans and Cranberries in food processor.
- In a 10″ sauce pan:
- Melt butter over medium heat.
- Add onions and sauté until limp and translucent.
- Sprinkle sugar and stir gently until the onions turn brown.
- Add Pecans and cranberries, stir to blend.
- Continue to sauté until the pecans give off a light toasted aroma.
- Preheat oven to 400 degrees.
- Preparing the Brie cake:
- Carefully remove the top rind to within ¼″ of the side rind.
- Place the cake in a close fitting oven-proof casserole dish.
- Top the brie cake with the Onion/Pecan/Cranberry topping.
- Cover loosely with foil.
- Bake 30 minutes.
- Remove Foil and bake for an additional 20 to 30 minutes.
- You know this is done when most of the topping sinks into the almost liquid cheese and the rind forms a toasted crust.

- Serve with croutons made from a French Baguette:
- Cut ¼" slices on the bias; drizzle with EVOO; spread loosely on a baking sheet and place in a 300 degree oven until lightly toasted.

35. Baked Brie With Amaretto Recipe

Serving: 5 | Prep: | Cook: 15mins | Ready in:

Ingredients

- 1/2 cup firmly packed brown sugar
- 1/2 cup butter
- 1/4 teaspoon ground cinnamon
- 1/8 teaspoon ground nutmeg
- 1 ounce Amaretto
- 1 round brie cheese
- 1/4 cup sliced almonds or chopped walnuts
- baguette slices, toast rounds, crackers, or sliced apples

Direction

- Preheat oven to 350 F.
- In a heavy saucepan, heat brown sugar and butter over medium heat until smooth and thickened. Remove from heat. Add cinnamon, nutmeg, and amaretto. Mix well.
- Place brie in an oven-safe casserole dish. Top with sauce and sprinkle with almonds or walnuts. Bake 10 to 15 minutes until brie is soft. (Instead of baking, you may microwave brie at 30-second intervals until soft and warm.)
- Serve with baguette slices, toast rounds, crackers, or sliced apples.
- Yield: 4 to 6 servings, depending on the size of the brie round

36. Baked Brie With Apple Compote Recipe

Serving: 6 | Prep: | Cook: 45mins | Ready in:

Ingredients

- 1 Tbs. unsalted butter
- 2 golden delicious apples, peeled, cored and
- cut into 1/2-inch dice
- 1/4 cup sugar
- 1/8 tsp. ground cardamom
- 1 round brie cheese, 6 to 8 oz. and about 4 1/2
- inches wide, slightly chilled
- 10-inch round of puff pastry dough, rolled out to
- 1/4-inch thickness
- 1 egg, beaten with 1 Tbs. water
- Plain water crackers for serving

Direction

- In a 2-quart sauté pan over medium heat, melt the butter. Add the apples and sauté, stirring occasionally, until the apples are tender and have released most of their liquid, 5 to 7 minutes. Add the sugar and cardamom, stir to dissolve and cook, stirring occasionally, until most of the liquid has evaporated, 12 to 15 minutes more. Remove from the heat and let the apple compote cool to room temperature.
- Preheat an oven to 375°F. Line a baking sheet with parchment paper.
- With a sharp knife, cut the cheese in half horizontally. On a clean work surface, place one half of the cheese, sliced side up, and evenly spread 1/2 cup of the apple compote over it. Set the other half, sliced side down, over the compote and spread 1/2 cup compote over the top.
- Place the dough on a lightly floured surface and set the cheese in the centre of the dough. Fold the dough up over the sides of the cheese, pleating the upper edges to fit snugly around the cheese. Pinch the dough together in the centre to seal. Brush the dough evenly with the

egg wash and place on the prepared baking sheet.
- Bake until the pastry is golden all over and crisp, 40 to 45 minutes. Let it rest for 5 minutes, then transfer to a platter along with a sharp knife and the crackers. Serve any remaining compote alongside. Serves 6 to 8.

37. Baked Brie With Apricot Preserves Recipe

Serving: 20 | Prep: | Cook: 10mins | Ready in:

Ingredients

- loaf of French bread
- 2 bries, i like the kind w/out a wax coating
- 1 c. apricot preserves
- 1 jalapeno, seeded and minced
- olive oil or melted butter

Direction

- Preheat oven to 425
- Slice the French bread into thin, diagonal slices
- Brush lightly with the oil or butter
- Place your unwrapped brie in the centre of a large baking dish (big enough to hold the bread too)
- Mix apricot preserves and jalapeno well
- Spoon on top of the brie
- Arrange the bread slices around brie
- Bake for 8-10 min. or until the bread is golden and the cheese is soft.

38. Baked Brie With Caramelized Onions Recipe

Serving: 8 | Prep: | Cook: 45mins | Ready in:

Ingredients

- 1 head garlic
- 1/4 cup butter
- 1 medium yellow onion, sliced
- 1 Granny Smith apple, peeled, cored and sliced
- 8 ounce wedge brie cheese
- 1 sheet frozen puff pastry, thawed
- 1 tablespoon butter, melted

Direction

- Preheat oven to 400 degrees F.
- Place garlic head on baking sheet.
- Drizzle with olive oil.
- Roast for 15 to 20 minutes OR until soft.
- Set aside.
- Meanwhile, melt 1/4 cup butter in skillet over medium heat.
- Cook and stir onion and apple in butter until tender and browned.
- Set aside.
- Arrange Brie on top of unfolded sheet of puff pastry.
- Top the cheese with the apple and onion mixture.
- Fold pastry over the cheese and pinch closed.
- Brush with melted butter.
- Bake 20 to 25 minutes OR until golden brown.
- Serve warm.
- Garnish with whole cloves of roasted garlic, if desired.

39. Baked Brie With Cherries And Pecans Recipe

Serving: 6 | Prep: | Cook: 60mins | Ready in:

Ingredients

- 6" wheel of brie cheese softened
- 1/4 cup dried cherries chopped
- 1/4 cup toasted pecans chopped
- 3 tablespoons light brown sugar
- 1 puff pastry sheet

- 1 egg beaten with 1 teaspoon water

Direction

- Cut brie in half with knife.
- Sprinkle bottom half with cherries, nuts and sugar the replace top half and apply pressure to secure and seal stuffing.
- Working on well-floured surface roll pastry to full cover brie then place in middle of pastry and fold excess around wheel.
- Brush with egg glaze and bake on parchment lined baking sheet at 40 for 30 minutes.
- Reduce heat to 325 and bake 20 minutes longer.

40. Baked Brie With Cran Raisins Recipe

Serving: 12 | Prep: | Cook: 25mins | Ready in:

Ingredients

- 2 Tbsp. butter
- 1 medium onion, chopped
- 3/4 to 1 cup cran-raisins or cranberries
- 2 Tbsp. brown sugar
- 1 Tbsp. balsamic vinegar
- 1 Wheel of brie cheese
- 1/2 package of puff pastry defrosted and unfolded

Direction

- Preheat oven to 375 Degrees
- Brown onions in butter cooking on low.
- Stir in brown sugar, cran-raisins or cranberries, balsamic vinegar, heat together on low for five minutes.
- Open up puff pastry sheet.
- Cut off top of brie.
- Place cheese in centre of pastry.
- Spread cran-raisin onion jam mixture on top of Brie.
- Gently pull up puff pastry to completely enclose the brie and cranberry onion jam.
- (Brush the outside with some beaten egg white to facilitate browning)
- Bake on 375 degrees for 25 to 30 minutes.
- Serve with apple or pear slices, water crackers or toast rounds.

41. Baked Brie With Cranberries Recipe

Serving: 6 | Prep: | Cook: 20mins | Ready in:

Ingredients

- 1 pkg of puff pastry
- 1/4 c of dried cranberries
- 4 oz round of Brie
- 1 egg, beaten with some water
- 1/3 sliced almonds

Direction

- Roll out puff pastry into 1/4" thickness.
- Place Brie in the middle and top with cranberries.
- Bring up the sides and pleat to cover cranberries/cheese.
- Crimp and seal edges with egg wash.
- Brush pastry top with egg wash and top with almonds.
- Baked at 450 degrees for 15 minutes. Reduce to 350 degrees and bake for another 5 minutes.
- Serve with apple slices, grapes and crackers.

42. Baked Brie With Honey And Walnuts Recipe

Serving: 8 | Prep: | Cook: 20mins | Ready in:

Ingredients

- 1 sheet thawed puff pastry dough
- 1 8-oz wheel brie cheese
- 1 beaten egg
- 3 Tbsp honey
- ¼ c. butter
- 1.5 tsp minced garlic
- 2 Tbsp chopped walnuts
- 1 Tbsp chopped fresh rosemary

Direction

- Preheat oven to 400o. Roll out pastry on lightly floured surface. Place Brie in centre and fold pastry around it, seeing seams by pressing with fork.
- Transfer to baking sheet, seam side up. Brush pastry with beaten egg as glaze. Bake 18-20 minutes until pastry is golden. Cool for 30 minutes before serving.
- Combine butter, honey and garlic in small saucepan and place over low heat to melt butter. Stir occasionally. Pour sauce on plate, sprinkle with walnuts and rosemary, reserving a bit of each for garnish. Place wrapped Brie atop sauce, garnish and serve with apples and sliced French bread. YUM!

43. Baked Brie With Pecans Recipe

Serving: 8 | Prep: | Cook: 35mins | Ready in:

Ingredients

- 1 small wheel of brie or camembert(9oz.)
- 1/2c. pecans
- 3T. lt.brown sugar
- 3T pure maple syrup
- crackers or sliced baguette,for serving

Direction

- Preheat oven to 350 degrees. Place cheese on rimmed baking sheet, bake until softened; 15-20 mins. Transfer to serving plate; cool about 20 mins.
- While cheese cools, place nuts on separate baking sheet; bake until toasted and fragrant, 7-10 minutes. Sprinkle nuts over cheese.
- In a small saucepan, combine sugar and maple syrup. Bring to a boil over medium heat; simmer until foamy, 1-2 mins. Drizzle warm sauce over slightly cooled cheese and nuts; serve with crackers or baguette.

44. Baked Brie With Raspberry And Almonds Recipe

Serving: 10 | Prep: | Cook: 18mins | Ready in:

Ingredients

- 1 11x17" sheet of frozen puff pastry, defrosted
- 1-pound wheel of brie cheese, about 5 inches in diameter
- 2 tablespoons raspberry jam
- 1/4 cup sliced almonds, toasted
- 1 egg, beaten with a splash of water

Direction

- Preheat the oven to 350°F.
- Spread the puff pastry sheet onto a counter and roll it out to 1/8-inch thick.
- Cut the Brie through the centre to make two, equal, round pieces. Place one half on the puff pastry, cut side up.
- Spread the jam on the cheese and sprinkle with the almonds.
- Replace the top half of the Brie.
- Wrap the dough up and over the Brie, and brush with egg wash to secure. Place the Brie package on a non-stick baking sheet, seam side down.
- Brush with the egg wash.
- Bake for 18-20 minutes, or until golden brown.

45. Baked Buffalo Chicken Strips With Blue Cheese Dip Recipe

Serving: 8 | Prep: | Cook: 10mins | Ready in:

Ingredients

- 2 lob boneless,skinless chicken breasts
- 1-1/2 c plus 1/2 c buttermilk
- 2/3 c hot sauce
- 1 c sour cream
- 5 oz blue cheese,crumbled
- 1/2 Tbsa white wine vinegar
- 1-1/2 tsp worcestershire sauce
- salt and pepper
- 8 oz. rRitz crackers (2 sleeves)
- 3 Tbs buffalo wing sauce
- 4 Tbs canola oil
- 6 large celery ribs,cut in quarters lengthwise

Direction

- Cut each chicken breast into 4 strips, lengthwise and place in a large bowl. In a separate bowl, whisk together 1-1/2 c buttermilk and hot sauce till blended. Pour over chicken; mix till chicken is coated. Cover and refrigerate 1 hour.
- Make dip: In med. bowl, combine sour cream, 1/2 c buttermilk, blue cheese, vinegar and Worcestershire sauce. Whisk to mix well. Season to taste with salt and pepper. Cover and refrigerate
- Preheat oven to 350 degrees. Mist 2 large baking sheets with cooking spray. In food processor, pulse crackers till crushed. Add seasoning mix and pulse to combine.
- Spread cracker mixture on a large platter. Remove chicken from marinade and carefully dredge each strip in cracker mixture.
- In large skillet, warm 2 Tbsp. oil over med-high heat until shimmering. Add half of the chicken and cook, turning till brown and crisp on all sides, about 2-3 mins. Place on baking sheet. Repeat with remaining oil and chicken.
- Place baking sheets in oven and bake until chicken is cooked through, 8 to 10 mins. Serve chicken hot with celery sticks and blue cheese dip.

46. Baked Caramelized Onion, Bacon And Cheese Dip Recipe

Serving: 0 | Prep: | Cook: 35mins | Ready in:

Ingredients

- caramelized Onion, Gruyere, and bacon Spread
- Serve this savory caramelized onion, Gruyère, and bacon spread with crackers or bread slices. If you can't find Gruyere, substitute raclette, fontina, or Swiss cheese.
- •Yield: Serves 8 (serving size: 3 tablespoons)
- Cooking spray
- 3 1/2 cups chopped onion
- 2 ounces Gruyère cheese, shredded and divided
- 2 tablespoons chopped fresh chives, divided
- 1/3 cup canola mayonnaise or plain mayo
- 1/3 cup fat-free sour cream
- 1/4 teaspoon salt
- 1/4 teaspoon black pepper
- 3 bacon slices, cooked and crumbled
- .

Direction

- Preparation
- 1. Preheat oven to 425°.
- 2. Heat a large cast-iron skillet over medium-high heat. Coat pan lightly with cooking spray. Add onion to pan; sauté 5 minutes, stirring frequently. Reduce heat to low; cook 20 minutes or until golden brown, stirring occasionally. Cool slightly.
- 3. Reserve 2 tablespoons cheese. Combine remaining cheese, caramelized onion, 1 tablespoon chives, and the remaining ingredients in a medium bowl. Transfer the mixture to a 1-quart glass or ceramic baking dish coated lightly with cooking spray.

Sprinkle with reserved 2 tablespoons cheese. Bake at 425° for 20 minutes or until browned and bubbly. Sprinkle with remaining 1 tablespoon chives.

47. Baked Cheddar Olives Recipe

Serving: 4 | Prep: | Cook: 15mins | Ready in:

Ingredients

- 1 cup coarsely grated sharp cheddar
- ½ cup all-purpose flour
- 1/8 teaspoon cayenne
- 2 tablespoons unsalted butter, softened
- 20 small pimiento-stuffed green olives (from a 3 ounce jar), drained and patted dry

Direction

- Put a rack in middle of oven and preheat oven to 400 degrees.
- Stir together cheese, flour and cayenne in a bowl.
- Blend in butter with your fingertips until a dough forms.
- Drop tablespoons of dough onto a sheet of wax paper and place 1 olive on each piece of dough.
- Lightly flour your hands and wrap dough around olives, enclosing each one completely.
- Transfer olives to a baking sheet with sides and bake until pastry is golden, about 15 minutes. Serve Warm.

48. Baked Cheese Balls Recipe

Serving: 0 | Prep: | Cook: 30mins | Ready in:

Ingredients

- 1 jar old English cheese spread
- 1 cup flour
- 1/2 cup soft butter
- 1/2 teaspoon Worcestershire sauc

Direction

- Make into small balls; bake in 400 degree F oven 10 minutes.

49. Baked Cheese In Ramekins Recipe

Serving: 8 | Prep: | Cook: 20mins | Ready in:

Ingredients

- 8 tbsp butter
- 1/2 cup grated Parmesan cheese
- 1 cup breadcrumbs
- 1 cup milk
- 4 egg whites
- 1 tsp Salt
- 1 tsp white pepper
- 1 tbsp fresh thyme

Direction

- Mix all the ingredients.
- Pour the mixture into the ramekins
- Bake it at 350 for 15 minutes.
- Optional: Torch or broil additional cheese

50. Baked Cheese And Clam Dip Recipe

Serving: 10 | Prep: | Cook: 40mins | Ready in:

Ingredients

- 2 jars Old English Sharp cheese
- One 8oz package cream cheese
- 3 green onions, chopped
- One 4oz can green chilies, chopped
- 1 can clams, minced

Direction

- Mix together all ingredients; put in casserole dish and bake at 350°F for 40 minutes, or until bubbling. Serve with tortilla chips.

51. Baked Feta Appetizer Recipe

Serving: 8 | Prep: | Cook: 17mins | Ready in:

Ingredients

- 8 slices of thick feta
- 8 slices of fully ripened tomatoes
- 8 garlic of minced cloves
- oregano--Mediterranean
- red pepper flakes
- 8 tbsp. of olive oil
- 8 sheets aluminum foil

Direction

- First you need to preheat oven to approx. 380 degrees.
- Then add a slice of feta on each of the 8 sheets of foil.
- Then you can centre a slice of tomato over that.
- Next season this lightly with salt; sprinkle with garlic and oregano and a light sprinkling of red pepper flakes.
- Now drizzle 1 tbsp. of olive oil over each feta parcel and then seal foil.
- Let this bake for approx. 15-18 minutes.
- Finally, you need to put this on one packet per plate.
- Serve with crusty bread.

52. Baked Feta With Lemon And Herbs Recipe

Serving: 6 | Prep: | Cook: 45mins | Ready in:

Ingredients

- 2 (8oz) blocks feta cheese (I like Athenos)
- 1/4 c olive oil
- 1/2 tsp salt
- 1/2 tsp gr. black pepper
- 1 lemon,sliced,divided
- 1 orange,sliced,divided
- fresh rosemary,oregano and parsley
- Garnish:fresh rosemary,oregano,parsley
- Assorted pita chips
- Mini pita bread rounds

Direction

- Preheat oven to 350'. In a small, ovenproof dish, place blocks of feta, and drizzle with olive oil. Sprinkle with salt and pepper.
- Top evenly with half of lemon and orange slices. Arrange rosemary, oregano and parsley around cheese.
- Bake 25 to 30 mins. Top with remaining lemon and orange slices and garnish with additional fresh rosemary, oregano and parsley, if desired. Serve with assorted pita chips and pita bread rounds.

53. Baked Feta With Marinara Recipe

Serving: 16 | Prep: | Cook: 20mins | Ready in:

Ingredients

- 1tsp. fresh lemon juice
- 1/4tsp crushed red pepper
- 2 garlic cloves,minced
- 1(14.5 oz) can diced tomatoes with basil,oregano and garlic,drained
- 1(4oz)pkg crumbled feta cheese
- cooking spray
- 32(1/2" thick)slices diagonally cut French bread baguette(about 1lb.),toasted

Direction

- Preheat oven to 350.
- Combine first four ingredients in a bowl.
- Sprinkle feta evenly into a 6" gratin dish or small shallow baking dish coated with spray. Top with tomato mixture. Bake 350 for 20 mins. Serve as a spread with bread slices

54. Baked Goat Cheese En Croute Recipe

Serving: 0 | Prep: | Cook: 1hours20mins | Ready in:

Ingredients

- 1-11 oz. fresh goat cheese log, Chavrie
- 1 sheet frozen puff pastry dough
- 1 egg (for egg wash)
- 1 cup dried cherries
- 1 fresh rosemary roughly chopped

Direction

- Thaw puff pastry as directed.
- Spread 1 sheet puff pastry on flat work surface; arrange dried cherries in centre in a 6 inch square shape.
- Sprinkle chopped rosemary over cherries.
- Place the goat cheese in the centre of prepared puff pastry round side down.
- Brush egg wash onto uncovered sides of pastry.
- Begin wrapping sides of pastry around the cheese log gently pressing at the overlap to seal well.
- Pinch ends of pastry firmly around the cheese and trim excess pastry.
- Place on a sheet tray and refrigerate a minimum of 1 hour.
- Preheat oven to 375° F 10 minutes before baking.
- Bake 10-15 minutes, until golden brown.
- Cool 10 minutes before serving.

55. Baked Gouda Recipe

Serving: 6 | Prep: | Cook: 20mins | Ready in:

Ingredients

- 2 small rounds of gouda cheese (you may find it in either
- the dairy section or by the deli).
- 1 roll Pillsbury crescent roll dough
- 1 pkg dry Lipton Onion Soup Mix

Direction

- Separate the crescent dough into 4 squares (2 triangles each).
- Remove wax covering from the cheese and sprinkle each with 1/2 pkg. dry Lipton onion soup mix.
- Wrap two squares around each cheese round - one on the top and one on the bottom so that it is entirely covered.
- Put rounds on a baking sheet and follow the crescent roll instruction for baking temp and time.
- When it comes out, let it cool slightly and then cut into pie shape wedges.
- You'll probably want to make this just before the start of the party so that the cheese is still slightly warm. Enjoy!
- Serves 6-8

56. Baked Havarti Appetizer Recipe

Serving: 10 | Prep: | Cook: 20mins | Ready in:

Ingredients

- 1 can crescent roll dough
- Dijon mustard
- dill
- 1 lb. havarti cheese

Direction

- Unroll one can of crescent roll dough.

- Spread with mustard.
- Sprinkle with dill.
- Wrap dough around one pound of Havarti cheese (with or without dill).
- Bake at 350 degrees for about 20 minutes or until pastry is golden brown.

57. Baked Mozza Sticks Recipe

Serving: 8 | Prep: | Cook: 30mins | Ready in:

Ingredients

- 8 oz package reduced-fat mozzarella
- 1 egg, beaten
- 1 tbsp 1% milk
- 1/4 tsp salt
- pinch paprika
- 1/2 cup panko
- 1 tbsp cornmeal
- cooking spray

Direction

- Preheat the oven to 350F, line a cookie sheet with parchment or greased foil.
- Slice the cheese into 8 even "sticks", set aside.
- Beat the egg with the milk, salt and paprika in a bowl. Whisk together panko and cornmeal in a shallow dish.
- Dip cheese in egg, then into toasted bread crumbs, tossing to coat completely.
- Re-dip into the egg and panko mixtures.
- Place coated sticks on baking sheet 1 1/2" apart.
- Mist lightly with cooking spray.
- Bake 6-8 minutes. Let cool slightly before serving.
- Can be frozen after baking - bake from frozen at 350F for 15 minutes.

58. Baked Pimento Cheese Dip Recipe

Serving: 20 | Prep: | Cook: 20mins | Ready in:

Ingredients

- 1 1/2 cups mayonnaise
- 1 (4-ounce) jar diced pimiento, drained
- 1 teaspoon worcestershire sauce
- 1 teaspoon finely grated onion
- 1/4 teaspoon ground red pepper
- 1 (8-ounce) block extra-sharp cheddar cheese, shredded
- 1 (8-ounce) block sharp cheddar cheese, shredded
- Garnish: chopped parsley

Direction

- Stir together first 5 ingredients in a large bowl; stir in cheeses. Spoon mixture into a lightly greased 2-quart or 11- x 7-inch baking dish.
- Bake at 350° for 20 minutes or until dip is golden and bubbly. Garnish, if desired.

59. Baked Provolone With Tomatoes,marjoram And Balsamic Recipe

Serving: 4 | Prep: | Cook: 15mins | Ready in:

Ingredients

- 4 1/4" thick rounds provolone cheese
- 1 small-diced beefsteak tomato
- 1 TB extra virgin olive oil
- 1 tsp chopped fresh marjoram(or oregano)
- 1 tsp balsamic vinegar,divided
- 1/4 tsp kosher salt
- few grinds black pepper

Direction

- Position a rack in centre of oven and heat to 450'. Arrange 4 5 to 6" individual shallow gratin dishes on rimmed baking sheet...Distribute the slices of provolone among the dishes.
- In a small bowl, combine tomato, garlic, oil, marjoram, kosher salt and black pepper. Portion mixture among the dishes, scattering it over and among the cheese.
- Bake till cheese is slightly melted, about 5 mins. Drizzle each serving with balsamic vinegar

60. Baked Ricotta Recipe

Serving: 20 | Prep: | Cook: 50mins | Ready in:

Ingredients

- 2 pounds fresh ricotta cheese, drained
- 1 clove garlic, minced and made into a paste with salt
- 1/2 cup mix of fresh torn herbs, chopped: thyme, basil, parsley, oregano
- 4 tablespoons extra virgin olive oil (EVOO)
- 1 teaspoon kosher salt
- Freshly ground black pepper
- 1 cup panko crumbs

Direction

- Preheat oven to 375 degrees F.
- Place herbs in a bowl, add garlic and salt.
- Add ricotta, EVOO, and blend to combine.
- Spray 9-inch pie plate with cooking spray.
- Pour panko crumbs in pie plate and smooth to an even layer.
- Pour in the ricotta mixture, and level.
- Drizzle with EVOO.
- Cook in oven for 50-60 minutes, or until golden brown, or semi-firm to the touch.
- Remove from oven and allow to cool slightly prior to serving.
- Drizzle with EVOO, season, and garnish with parsley.
- Serve on a plate with crostini or crackers.

61. Baked Scallops With Brie Recipe

Serving: 4 | Prep: | Cook: 12mins | Ready in:

Ingredients

- 1/4 pound small scallops
- some brie
- white wine (I prefer sweet)
- some fresh ground pepper and kosher or grey salt
- 1 Tsp olive oil
- 3 garlic cloves
- some dried leaf thyme

Direction

- Heat the oven to 450. You'll need several small oven proof serving bowls, or some largish ramekins. I use some shallow Pyrex dishes. You want the scallops to be one or two deep.
- Place the scallops in a mixing bowl and press the garlic over it.
- Add a quick grinding of pepper and some salt.
- Add a small (small!!!) pinch of thyme.
- Mix the whole thing together and then add the olive oil.
- Mix again.
- Put the scallops in the baking dishes.
- Pour in just enough wine to come half way up the scallops.
- This isn't very much. Don't put in too much!
- Place 1/4 inch thick slices of brie on top of the scallops so that it is about half covered.
- Don't cover it all the way.
- It is scallops with brie, not brie with scallops.
- Place these in the oven for 12-15 minutes.
- Serve it right in the baking dishes, but make sure everyone knows they're rather hot. Have ice ready for when they touch them anyway.

62. Baked Spinach And Feta Topped Pita Bread Recipe

Serving: 4 | Prep: | Cook: 12mins | Ready in:

Ingredients

- 6 (6 inch) whole wheat pita breads
- 1 (6 ounce) tub sun-dried tomato pesto
- 2 roma (plum) tomatoes, chopped
- 1 bunch spinach, rinsed and chopped
- 4 fresh mushrooms, sliced
- 1/2 cup crumbled feta cheese
- 2 tablespoons grated parmesan cheese
- 3 tablespoons olive oil
- 1 pinch ground black pepper to taste

Direction

- Preheat the oven to 350 degrees F (175 degrees C).
- Spread tomato pesto onto one side of each pita bread, and place them pesto side up on a baking sheet.
- Top with tomatoes, spinach, mushrooms, feta cheese, and Parmesan cheese.
- Drizzle with olive oil and season with pepper.
- Bake for 12 minutes in the preheated oven or until pita breads are crisp.
- Cut into quarters and serve

63. Baked Spinach Feta Dip Recipe

Serving: 8 | Prep: | Cook: 35mins | Ready in:

Ingredients

- 1 cup mayonnaise
- 16 ounces sour cream
- 10 ounces frozen chopped spinach thawed and squeezed dry
- 1 package spring vegetable mix
- 3 green onions sliced
- 4 ounces feta cheese crumbled

Direction

- Preheat oven to 350.
- Combine all ingredients in a 2-quart casserole.
- Bake 35 minutes then serve with pita chips.

64. Baked Tomatoes With Parmesan Recipe

Serving: 2 | Prep: | Cook: 1mins | Ready in:

Ingredients

- 400g tomatoes
- 250g parmesan
- 100g oregano
- 100 ml oil
- salt
- fresh pepper
- garlic powder

Direction

- Heat the oven at the 180 grades.
- In a tray with baked paper, or a silicon foil, lay slices of tomatoes.
- On them, put a topping, made from shredded parmesan, dry oregano, salt, pepper, garlic powder, oil.
- Cook, till the cheese is melt.

65. Baked Truffled Brie En Croute Recipe

Serving: 8 | Prep: | Cook: 20mins | Ready in:

Ingredients

- 4 ounces cream cheese, room temperature
- 1/2 teaspoon salt
- 1 tablespoon truffle oil

- 1 teaspoon fresh shaved truffles or truffle paste (optional)*
- 1 sheet frozen puff pastry, thawed
- 1 small (8-ounce) round (wheel) brie cheese
- 1 egg, lightly beaten
- baguette, crostini, or crackers
- Serve with baked whole garlic.(Check Shirleyoma's recipe)

Direction

- Butter a baking pan and line with aluminum foil.
- In a small bowl, combine cream cheese, salt, truffle oil, and shaved truffles; set aside.
- On a lightly floured surface, roll out sheet of puff pastry 1/8-inch thick (approximately 15 inches in diameter); using the brie as a guide, cut out one round the size of the brie for the top and cut another round 1-inch larger.
- Using a small cutter (any shape will do), cut out some decorative pieces.
- Halve brie cheese horizontally; spread the truffle cream cheese evenly over the bottom half of the brie.
- Place the top half over the truffle cream cheese.
- On prepared baking pan, centre the brie cheese on top of the larger pastry round; wrap pastry up over brie (without stretching).
- Brush border with some egg and top with remaining smaller pastry round; pressing edges of dough together gently but firmly to seal. Brush top with egg.
- Arrange decorative pieces over the top of the pastry dough; lightly brush with egg, being careful not to leg egg drip over edges (this would prevent them from rising).
- With the back of a table knife, gently score side of pastry with vertical marks (being careful not to pierce through dough).
- Chill brie, uncovered, 30 minutes to set egg wash.
- Brie may be made to this point one day ahead and kept chilled, covered loosely.
- Preheat oven to 425 degrees.
- Bake Truffle Brie in middle of oven 20 minutes or until puffed and golden brown.
- Remove from oven and let stand in pan on a rack about 20 minutes for a very runny melted cheese or about 40 minutes for thicker cheese.
- To serve, transfer to serving dish and serve with baguette, crostini,

66. Baked Shrimp Havarti Recipe

Serving: 4 | Prep: | Cook: 14mins | Ready in:

Ingredients

- raw med shrimp 21 to 24 in bag
- 8 oz creamy havarti cheese slice into 1/8" thick pieces
- 1 tbs minced garlic
- 1 tbs minced onion (optional)
- 1 stick unsalted butter

Direction

- Preheat oven to 350
- In small sauce pan melt butter, garlic, onion
- Remove shell and tails from shrimp
- In small muffin tin place one shrimp in each
- If using large muffin pan place two spoon in small amount of melted butter over each
- Place in oven for 9 min
- Take it out and put one slice of cheese on each bake for 5 more Min's
- Serve hot right out of the oven
- Warm bread good for dipping in the butter

67. Balck Bean Nachos Recipe

Serving: 10 | Prep: | Cook: 15mins | Ready in:

Ingredients

- 5 7- or 8-inch corn or flour tortillas or 4 cups tortilla chips (about 4 ounces)

- 1 cup canned black beans, rinsed and drained
- 1/2 cup salsa
- 2 cups shredded Monterey Jack, cheddar, queso quesadilla, Chihuahua, and/or asadero cheese (8 ounces)
- 1/2 cup roasted red sweet peppers, cut into thin strips
- 2 to 4 tablespoons fresh or canned sliced jalapeno peppers, drained
- salsa (optional)

Direction

- For tortilla chips, stack tortillas and cut into wedges with scissors or a sharp knife. Place wedges in a single layer on an ungreased baking sheet. Bake in a 350 degree F oven for 10 to 12 minutes or until light golden brown. Remove the chips from oven. Arrange tortilla chips in one layer, overlapping slightly, on an 11- or 12-inch ovenproof platter.
- In a medium saucepan combine black beans and the 1/2 cup salsa; cook and stir over medium heat just until heated through. Remove from heat; spoon bean mixture over chips.
- Sprinkle cheese, sweet peppers, and jalapeno peppers over bean mixture on chips. Bake in a 425 degree F oven for 3 to 5 minutes or until cheese is melted. Serve immediately with additional salsa, if desired. (Search Group Recipes for my Roasted Tomato Salsa recipe which is what I serve with these)

68. Barbecue Baked White Bean Cheese Dip Recipe

Serving: 12 | Prep: | Cook: 150mins | Ready in:

Ingredients

- 1 1/2 cup ketsup
- 1/2 cup molasses
- 1/3 cup maple syrup
- 1/3 cup packed brown sugar
- 3 strips bacon finely chopped
- 4 slices of deli ham fine diced
- 1 small onion diced
- 1/4 cup Dijon mustard
- 1 cup water
- 3, 15 oz cans cannellini white beans
- 8 oz cream cheese softened
- 8 oz shreeeded cheddar cheese
- 1 lb bag tortilla or nachoe style chips

Direction

- In a saucepan combine ketchup, syrup, brown sugar, molasses, bacon, ham onion, mustard and water
- Bring to a boil, reduce heat to lowest simmer and cover, stirring often, cooking until very thick about 2 hours
- Add beans and cook 10 mins on simmer
- Heat oven to 325F
- In an 8 x 8 casserole dish or similar dish spread cream cheese on bottom evenly
- Spoons the sauce and beans over the cheese
- Top with cheddar cheese
- Bake until cheese is melted about 10 mins
- Serve with the chips, either have people dip in the chips or spoon the mixture over them like nacho style

69. Barefoot Contessas Parmesan And Thyme Crackers Appetizer Recipe

Serving: 24 | Prep: | Cook: 22mins | Ready in:

Ingredients

- 1/4 pound sweet butter at room temperature
- 4 ounces freshly grated Parmesan (one cup)
- 1 tsp. fresh thyme leaves
- 1/2 tsp. salt (I'll skip this next time, the cheese adds plenty of salt for my palate)
- 1/2 tsp. freshly ground pepper
- 1 1/4 cup all-purpose flour

- A few srigs of fresh thyme as garmish for the serving plate

Direction

- Cream the butter for about a minute with the paddle attachment in your mixer.
- On low speed add the Parmesan, thyme, salt, and pepper.
- Next blend in the flour just until blended. If the dough is too dry add about 1 tsp. water.
- Turn the dough onto a floured surface and press it into a ball. Roll the ball with your hands to form a nine-inch log.
- Wrap this log in plastic and chill for at least 1/2 hour or refrigerate up to four days. (I froze the log a few weeks and then defrosted in my refrigerator a day before using.)
- When ready to prepare preheat your oven to 400 degrees with the rack in the middle.
- Line a baking sheet with parchment paper.
- Slice the log into 3/8-inch thick rounds and place them on the parchment paper.
- Bake 22 minutes, turning the baking sheet 1/2 way through the baking for even heat exposure.
- Cool on a rack.
- When cool arrange the crackers on a plate and garnish with a few sprigs of reserved fresh thyme.

70. Basil Brie In Pastry Recipe

Serving: 12 | Prep: | Cook: 25mins | Ready in:

Ingredients

- 2 tbsp grated parmesan
- 2 tbsp finely chopped fresh basil
- 1 14 oz round brie
- 1 pkg croissant dough

Direction

- Heat oven to 400 degrees.
- Grease cookie sheet.
- Mix Parmesan cheese and basil.
- Cut cheese round horizontally into 2 layers.
- Sprinkle basil mixture evenly over cut surface.
- Reassemble cheese round.
- Roll crescent dough, 15 X 9 inches, on lightly floured surface.
- Cut out 2 circles, 8-1/2 and 6 inches.
- Place 8-1/2-inch circle on cookie sheet.
- Place cheese in centre.
- Bring pastry up and over cheese.
- Press to make smooth and even.
- Brush top edge of pastry lightly with water.
- Place 6-inch circle on top and press gently around edge to seal.
- Cut decorations from remaining pastry if desired. I usually make little leaves to put on it.
- Moisten pastry with water to attach.
- Bake about 25 minutes or until golden brown.
- Cool on wire rack 30 minutes before serving.
- Serve with assorted crackers or fruit if desired.

71. Bbq Ranch Chicken And Cheddar Pizza Roll Em' Ups Recipe

Serving: 6 | Prep: | Cook: 30mins | Ready in:

Ingredients

- 1 roll Pillsbury pizza dough in can (or use other pizza dough of choice)
- 1/4 Cup prepared ranch dressing
- 2 Cups prepared shredded BBQ chicken
- 1/4 Cup chopped fresh cilantro leaves
- 1 1/2 Cups shredded smoked cheddar cheese
- ranch dressing for dipping

Direction

- 1. Preheat oven to 350 degrees F. Open can of dough and press into rectangle. Spread or drizzle ranch dressing evenly over dough then top with evenly with chicken, cilantro and cheddar cheese. Starting at long end roll dough into a log shape. Using a sharp knife, cut 1 inch pieces and place onto a greased baking sheet. Bake for 20-22 minutes or until golden brown. Serve with a side of ranch dressing for dipping.

72. Blue Cheese Appetizer Tart Recipe

Serving: 16 | Prep: | Cook: 37mins | Ready in:

Ingredients

- CRUST:
- 1 1/2 cups all-purpose flour
- 1/2 cup cold butter, in chunks
- 4 to 5 tablespoons ice water
- FILLING:
- 8 ounce cream cheese, siftened
- 1/3 cup blue cheese, crumbled
- 1/4 cup whipping cream
- 1 large egg, slightly beaten
- 1/4 teaspoon coarse ground pepper
- 1/3 cup roasted red peppers, chopped
- 3 tablespoons pine nuts OR your favorite nut, toasted and chopped
- 2 tablespoons fresh parsley, chopped

Direction

- Preheat oven to 375 degrees F.
- Place flour in large bowl OR bowl of food processor.
- Cut in butter with pastry blender OR pulse in processor to coarse crumbs.
- Mix in water until flour is just moistened OR pulse until dough pulls away from sides of processor and forms a ball.
- Shape dough into a ball.
- Roll pastry on lightly floured surface to a 12" circle.
- Place pastry into a 9 or 10" tart pan with removable bottom OR a pie pan.
- Press firmly onto bottom and up sides of pan.
- Cut away excess pastry.
- Prick pastry all over with a fork.
- Line pastry with aluminum foil. Pour dry beans on top of foil.
- Bake 17 to 22 minutes OR until lightly browned.
- Meanwhile, combine cream cheese and blue cheese in a large bowl.
- Beat at medium speed, scraping bowl often, until creamy.
- While beating, gradually add the whipping cream, egg and pepper.
- Blend well.
- Spread into baked pastry shell.
- Sprinkle with roasted red pepper, pine nuts and parsley.
- Bake for 20 to 25 minutes OR until filling is set.
- Let stand 20 minutes before serving.
- Cut into wedges.
- Store leftovers covered and refrigerated.

73. Blue Cheese Appetizers Recipe

Serving: 8 | Prep: | Cook: 10mins | Ready in:

Ingredients

- 2 tbsp. butter
- 2 tbsp. crumbled blue cheese
- 1 pkg. refrigerated biscuits

Direction

- Preheat oven to 450 F. Melt butter and add cheese stirring until smooth. Cut uncooked biscuits into quarters and place in pan touching together. Pour cheese mixture over top and bake approximately 10 minutes or until browned.

74. Blue Cheese Apple And Potato Tart Recipe

Serving: 0 | Prep: | Cook: 20mins | Ready in:

Ingredients

- 1 ea. ready to bake pie shell
- 2 ea. russet potatoes
- 2 tbsp. butter
- 1 cup onion (minced)
- 2 ea. granny smith apples
- 2 pkg. (4oz.) Alouette Crumbled blue cheese
- 1 cup baby arugula Salad
- olive oil
- balsamic vinegar

Direction

- Preheat oven to 400° F.
- Place ready to bake pie shell on a flat surface and begin crimping the edges around the whole shell.
- Slide onto sheet tray or pizza stone and bake until slightly brown, then remove from oven.
- Meanwhile bring small sauce pot of water to a boil. Peel and dice the potatoes into 1/4 inch cubes and par cook them in the boiling water leaving them slightly crunchy.
- Drain the potatoes and set aside.
- Heat butter in a sauté pan and sauté the minced onions until translucent.
- Spread cooked onions evenly over the baked pie shell then layer cooked potatoes on top
- Core and dice the apples and layer them into the tart shell.
- Sprinkle tart with the Blue cheese and immediately place back in the oven.
- Bake until bubble 10 - 12 minutes.
- Remove from oven and top with baby Arugula and drizzle with olive oil and balsamic vinegar.

75. Blue Cheese Bacon Dip Recipe

Serving: 12 | Prep: | Cook: 15mins | Ready in:

Ingredients

- 8 bacon Slices - chopped in small pieces
- 2 cloves of garlic, minced
- 2 8 oz packages of cream cheese, softened
- 1/3 cup half and half
- 4 ounces of blue cheese, crumbled
- 2 T Finely chopped fresh chives
- 3 T Chopped toasted walnuts
- grape clusters
- Flatbread, pretzel sticks or assorted crackers

Direction

- Cook chopped bacon in skillet over med high heat for 10 min or until crisp. Remove bacon to paper towels to drain and set aside. Add minced garlic to skillet and sauté 1 minute.
- Beat cream cheese at medium speed with an electric mixer until smooth. Add half and half, beating until combined. Stir in bacon, garlic, blue cheese and chives. Spoon mixture evenly into a small baking dish. (No more than 4 or 5 cup capacity)
- Bake at 350 for 15 min or until golden and bubbly. Sprinkle with chopped walnuts and serve with grape clusters and your chosen cracker or breads

76. Blue Cheese Bites Recipe

Serving: 0 | Prep: | Cook: 27mins | Ready in:

Ingredients

- 1 package (10 count) biscuits in a can
- 1/2 cup margarine (i use the stick margarine)
- 4 oz. blue cheese crumbles (can use more but dont have to)

Direction

- Melt margarine in saucepan.
- Add cheese and heat until cheese is melted.
- Cut each biscuit into fourths and roll each piece in a ball.
- Roll each ball in the margarine/cheese, mixture until coated.
- Place on cookie sheet.
- Bake at 325 degrees until brown, about 20 minutes.
- Take out and enjoy! =)

77. Blue Cheese Bacon Dip Recipe

Serving: 12 | Prep: | Cook: 15mins | Ready in:

Ingredients

- 7 bacon slices, chopped
- 2 cloves garlic, minced
- 2 (8 oz.) packages cream cheese, softened
- 1/3 cup half-and-half
- 4 oz. crumbled blue cheese
- 2 Tbs chopped fresh chives
- 3 Tbs chopped walnuts, toasted
- flatbread/assorted crackers

Direction

- Cook chopped bacon in skillet over med-high heat, 10 minutes or until crisp. Drain bacon, and set aside. Add minced garlic to skillet, and sauté 1 minutes.
- Beat cream cheese at medium speed with electric mixer until smooth. Add half-and - half, beating until combined. Stir to combine bacon, garlic, blue cheese, and chives. Spoon into 4 (1 cup) baking dishes
- Bake 350 degrees for 15 minutes, or until golden and bubbly. Sprinkle top with walnuts. Enjoy!

78. Bologna Nachos Recipe

Serving: 4 | Prep: | Cook: 10mins | Ready in:

Ingredients

- 1/2 cup diced beef bologna
- (great with any variety)
- 1 can refried beans
- Nacho chips
- 2 cups shredded cheese
- sour cream
- Chopped tomato
- Chopped black olives
- Chopped onions

Direction

- Preheat oven to 350°F. Spread nacho chips out on cookie sheet and cover with shredded cheese. In a pot, heat beans and Bologna. Place chips and cheese in oven until cheese is melted. Remove, cover with beans and bologna mixture and top with sour cream, tomato and black olives onions

79. Bone Suckin' Baked Brie Recipe

Serving: 12 | Prep: | Cook: 20mins | Ready in:

Ingredients

- Bone Suckin' Yaki Sauce, 1 tsp.
- Puff pastry dough, 1 sheet
- Brie, 12 oz.
- dried apricots, 1/4 cup, roughly chopped
- apricot preserves, 1/2 cup
- sliced almonds, 1/4 cup
- egg white, 1
- water, 1 tsp.

Direction

- Preheat oven at 350°.
- Place puff pastry dough on a lightly floured surface and roll out with a rolling pin, so that

the dough is at least twice as big as the brie. Trim the edges off of the dough in order to make a circle. Set dough scraps aside.

- In a small bowl stir together Bone Sucking' Yaki Sauce and roughly chopped apricots.
- Line a baking sheet with parchment paper and place brie on parchment paper.
- Place apricot preserves on top of brie, top with chopped apricots and sliced almonds.
- Carefully drape the dough over the brie and tuck edges underneath the brie. (The brie may also be placed on top of the dough and the sides folded on top.) With the dough scraps, cut out shapes, such as leaves, vines, berries etc. to decorate the top of the dome of dough.
- Mix egg white in a small bowl with water. With a brush, paint the top and sides of dough with the egg wash.
- Bake the brie at 350° for 20 minutes or until the dough is a golden brown. Let cool for 20 minutes before serving. Serves 10.

80. Brandy Baked Brie Recipe

Serving: 10 | Prep: | Cook: 15mins | Ready in:

Ingredients

- 1-1/2 cups light brown sugar
- 1/2 cup brandy
- 2 cups chopped walnuts
- 2 pound wheel of brie

Direction

- In small mixing bowl combine brown sugar and brandy then stir in walnuts.
- Place brie on top of oven proof platter and spoon walnut mixture over top covering completely.
- Wrap platter in plastic and refrigerate for at least two hours.
- Preheat oven to 400 then remove brie from refrigerator then unwrap and bake 15 minutes.
- Cool slightly and serve with graham crackers.

81. Brandy Cheese Fondue Recipe

Serving: 6 | Prep: | Cook: 35mins | Ready in:

Ingredients

- 1 tablespoon butter, unsalted
- 1 small onion, chopped
- 1 tablespoon brandy
- 1 cup mayonnaise
- 2 cups shredded swiss cheese
- 1/2 cup grated parmesan cheese
- Dippers: baguette slices, broccoli and cauliflour florettes, carrot and celery sticks.

Direction

- Position your oven rack to the centre of the oven. Preheat oven to 350°.
- In a saucepan over medium-heat, melt butter.
- Add onion and cook, stirring often, until the onions are translucent.
- Remove from heat and stir in the Brandy.
- In a bowl, mix mayonnaise, Swiss cheese, and parmesan cheese.
- Stir in onions and mix well.
- Transfer to a heat-proof 1 quart baking dish.
- At this point, you can cover with plastic wrap and refrigerate if making the day before. You'll just have to adjust the cooking time to accommodate the chilled dish.
- Bake until bubbly, about 30 minutes, and serve hot with dippers.
- **A breath mint after consumption is optional :D) ...thanks Angel gal!

82. Bread Pot Fondue Recipe

Serving: 8 | Prep: | Cook: 70mins | Ready in:

Ingredients

- 1 each Loaf round white or pumpernickel bread
- 2 cups Shredded sharp or mild cheddar cheese
- 2 pkg 3 oz packages cream cheese, softened
- 1 1/2 cups sour cream
- 1 cup cooked ham, diced small or ground
- 1/2 cup green onion, chopped
- 4 oz Can green chilies, drained chopped
- 1 tsp worcestershire sauce

Direction

- Slice off top of bread; hollow out centre, leave half shell. Combine ingredients and spoon filling into hollowed loaf and replace top. Wrap loaf tightly with two or three layers of heavy duty aluminum foil. Set on cookie sheet and bake 1 hour and 10 minutes at 35OF. Remove from oven; place on platter. Stir gently. Serve with raw vegetables and crackers.

83. Brie Crab Stuffed Mushrooms Recipe

Serving: 8 | Prep: | Cook: 20mins | Ready in:

Ingredients

- 24 large cap mushrooms (washed & pat dried)
- 1 tbsp olive oil
- 1tsp garlic paste (or 1 clove minced garlic)
- 2 tbsp parsley
- 1/2 cup minced onion
- 1 cup chopped spinach
- 1/2 cup shredded parmesan cheese
- 1/2 cup crab shredded crab meat (or lump crab or imitation crab)
- 3 tbsp half & half (or heavy whipping cream)
- 2-3 tbsp breadcrumbs (as needed)
- 24 thin cut pieces of brie

Direction

- Preheat oven to 375. Remove stems from mushrooms and arrange caps on a lightly greased cookie sheet (I use Pam). Mince the mushroom stems.
- In a skillet, heat oil. Add garlic, onion, minced mushrooms & parsley. Sauté over medium heat until mushrooms are soft (5-8 min). Add spinach and lightly sauté 2-3 minutes. Remove from heat.
- In medium bowl, add saluted mixture, parmesan, crab and cream. Mix well. Add bread crumbs slowly, just enough to make mixture sticky, but not too much!
- Place heaping tablespoon of mixture on top of mushroom caps. Top with thin piece of brie.
- Bake 10 minutes--until brie is golden melted. Serve immediately.

84. Brie And Cherry Pastry Cups Recipe

Serving: 15 | Prep: | Cook: 25mins | Ready in:

Ingredients

- 1 sheet frozen puff pastry, thawed
- 1/3-1/2 cup red cherry preserves
- 4 oz. brie cheese, cut into 1/2x1/2 -inch pieces (36 pieces)
- ¼ cup chopped pecans
- 2 tbsp. Chopped fresh chives

Direction

- Heat oven to 375 degrees.
- Spray 36 miniature muffin cups with cooking spray (PAM).
- Cut pastry into 36 (1-1/2-in) squares.
- Slightly press each square into muffin cup; press centre with finger or handle of a wooden spoon.
- Bake 10 minutes.
- Press centre with handle of wooden spoon.

- Bake 6 to 8 minutes longer or until golden brown.
- Immediately press again in centre.
- Fill each with about ½ tsp. Of preserves.
- Top each piece with a piece of brie, chopped pecans and chives.
- Bake 3-5 minutes or until cheese is melted.
- Serve warm. Makes 36 appetizers.

85. Brie Dip With Artichokes And Crab Recipe

Serving: 8 | Prep: | Cook: 15mins | Ready in:

Ingredients

- 1/2c diced onion
- 5tsp.olive oil,divided
- 1/4c dry white wine
- 3/4c canned artichoke hearts,chopped
- 1/2c heavy cream
- 1 wheel brie cheese,rind removed,cubed(13.2oz)
- 1tsp Dijon mustard
- 1tsp lemon juice
- minced zest of 1/2 lemon
- 1/2tsp worcestershire sauce
- cayenne to taste
- 2Tbs miced fresh parsley
- 2tsp miced fresh tarragon or 1tsp. dried tarragon
- 1 can lump creabmeat,drained(6.5oz)
- 1/2c panko crumbs
- Tin sliced toasted baguettes or crackers

Direction

- Preheat oven to 400; coat a 1qt. baking dish with non-stick spray.
- Sauté onion in 3tsp. oil in non-stick skillet over med-high heat till soft, about 5 mins
- Deglaze with wine, simmer until nearly evaporated then stir in artichokes and cream. Simmer 1 min., reduce heat to med-low then add brie in batches, stirring till melted and smooth. Off heat, add Dijon, lemon juice and zest, Worcestershire, cayenne, parsley and tarragon.
- Spread crabmeat in the prepared baking dish, then top with brie mixture. Toss panko and remaining 2rsp.oil together in bowl, sprinkle over cheese.
- Bake till dip is bubbly and topping is golden, about 15 mins. Serve with toasted baguettes or crackers.

86. Brie En Croute Recipe

Serving: 12 | Prep: | Cook: 20mins | Ready in:

Ingredients

- Brie en Croute
- ½ package (17 ¼ oz) frozen puff pastry sheets (1 sheet)
- 1 egg
- 1 TBS. water
- ¼ cup toasted sliced almonds
- ¼ cup fresh chopped parsley
- 1 brie cheese round (about 1 pound)
- Variety of your favorite crackers

Direction

- Thaw pastry sheet at room temperature, about 30 minutes)
- Preheat oven to 400. Mix egg and water and set aside.
- Unfold pastry sheet on lightly floured surface, Roll into a 14- inch square. Cut off corners to make a circle. Sprinkle almonds and parsley in centre of circle. Top with cheese. Brush edge of circle with egg mixture. Fold two opposite sides over cheese. Trim remaining two sides to 2- inches from edge of cheese. Fold these two sides onto the round. Press edges to seal. Place seam-side down on baking sheet. Decorate top with parsley scraps if desired. Brush with egg mixture.

- Bake 20 minutes or until golden brown. Let stand 1 hour. Serve with crackers.

87. Brie En Croute With Fig And Thyme Preserve Recipe

Serving: 25 | Prep: | Cook: 30mins | Ready in:

Ingredients

- Simple Puff Pastry:
- 1 cup (2 sticks) unsalted organic butter
- 1 2/3 cup all-purpose flour
- 1/2 teaspoon kosher salt
- For filling:
- 2 rounds of imported french brie
- 2 jars of fig preserve
- fresh thyme leaves
- Egg wash:
- 2 egg yolks
- 2 tablespoon water

Direction

- FOR THE SIMPLE PUFF PASTRY:
- Cut the butter into 1/4 inch pieces. Place 1 1/3 cups of the flour and the 1/2 tsp. salt in a food processor. Add 1 stick of the cut up butter, pulsing until combined. Add the remaining stick of cut up butter and 1/3 cup of flour to the food processor, tossing the butter pieces until the butter is coated with flour. Pulse 3-4 times to just combine (you want to see specks of butter there still). Add about 1/3 cup ice water and pulse until the dough just forms a ball. If you need to add more water, do so.
- Dust a work surface with flour and roll out to form a 10x14 inch rectangle. Fold into thirds, creating a 3x14 inch rectangle. Fold into thirds again, this time forming a 3x4 inch rectangle. Wrap in plastic wrap and refrigerate at least an hour (dough may be refrigerated up to 2 days or frozen for up to 1 month).
- Preheat oven to 400 degrees F. Mix egg and water.
- Unfold pastry sheet on lightly floured surface. Roll out into 14 inch square. Cut off corners to make a circle. Spread preserves to within 1 inch of pastry edge. Sprinkle thyme over preserves. Top with cheese (I remove excess rind from the top so the cheese had direct contact with the preserves). Brush edge of circle with egg mixture. Fold two opposite sides over cheese. Trim remaining two sides to 2 inch from edge of cheese. Fold these two sides onto the round. Press edges to seal. Place seam-side down on baking sheet. Decorate top with pastry scraps if desired. Brush with egg mixture.
- Repeat with second wheel of brie.
- Bake 25 minutes or until golden and puffed. Let stand 30 minutes.
- Serve with artisan flatbreads and colourful seasonal fruits.

88. Brie Leek Tartlets Recipe

Serving: 15 | Prep: | Cook: 8mins | Ready in:

Ingredients

- 1 med. leek(white portion only) fine chopped
- 1 garlic clove,minced
- 3Tbs butter
- 1/2c heavy whipping cream
- dash of salt and white pepper
- dash ground nutmeg
- 1pkg(1.9oz) frozen miniature phylo tart shells
- 2oz. Brie or camembert cheese,rind removed

Direction

- In small skillet, sauté leek and garlic in butter till tender. Add the cream, salt, pepper and nutmeg, cook and stir for 1-2 mins. Or till thickened.
- Place tart shells on baking sheet. Slice cheese into 15 pieces; place one piece in each shell. Top each with 11/2tsp. leek mixture

- Bake at 350 for 6-8 mins. Or till heated through. Refrigerate leftovers, if there are any.

89. Brie Phyllo Cups Recipe

Serving: 15 | Prep: | Cook: 5mins | Ready in:

Ingredients

- 1/2 cup of crushed gingersnaps. (I used some gingerbread cookies I had left over.) I think any crisp little cookie would work. You could even make them without the cookies.
- 6 ounces Brie rind removed and cubed
- 1/4 Cup spreadable fruit (I used strawberry and raspberry to give a choice.)
- 1 package of phyllo cups (These can be found in the frozen food department at the grocery store) They come in packages of 15.

Direction

- Place the tart shells on an ungreased baking sheet. Sprinkle about 1/2 teaspoon gingersnap crumbs into each shell: top with Brie and spreadable fruit. Bake at 325 for 5 minutes or until cheese is melted. Yield 15

90. Brie With Strawberries On Brioche Crostini Recipe

Serving: 12 | Prep: | Cook: 5mins | Ready in:

Ingredients

- 12 slices brioche bread sliced 1/4-inch thick (I make my own, recipe is on my grouprecipes page)
- 6 ounces whipped cream cheese, at room temperature
- 1 teaspoon chopped chives
- 3 large strawberry
- 1 small (about 2 inches diameter) Brie wheel
- fresh edible flowers for garnish

Direction

- Preheat the oven to 325 degrees F.
- Using a 1 1/2-inch diameter biscuit cutter, cut the sliced bread into 24 circles and put on a baking sheet. Toast the brioche circles in the oven for 3 to 5 minutes, until golden brown.
- With a rubber spatula, fold together the cream cheese and chopped chives and place in a small pastry bag with star tip. Pipe out about 1/2-ounce of cream cheese and chive mixture onto each toasted brioche circle. Cut off top of strawberry, slice in half lengthwise, and then cut each half into 3 wedges. Cut the 1/2 wheel of Brie into 6 triangle wedges. Place 1 wedge of strawberry and 1 wedge of Brie standing up on the cream cheese. Garnish with additional chives/edible flowers

91. Brie And Cranberry Pizza Recipe

Serving: 8 | Prep: | Cook: 15mins | Ready in:

Ingredients

- 1 8 oz. can crescent rolls
- 1 8 oz. pkg. brie cheese, rind removed, cut into 1/2" cubes
- 3/4 cup canned whole berry cranberry sauce, stirred
- 1/2 cup chopped pecans

Direction

- Heat oven to 425.
- Lightly spray a 12" pizza pan or a 13 x 9 dish.
- Unroll dough. Place in prepared dish. Press out dough to form a "crust."
- Bake for 5-8 minutes or until lightly browned.
- Remove from oven and sprinkle partially baked crust with brie.
- Spread sauce evenly over cheese.

- Sprinkle with pecans
- Return to oven. Bake an additional 6-10 minutes until cheese is melted.
- Cool for 5 minutes.
- Cut into wedge or small squares.

92. Brie And Cranberry In Puff Pastry Recipe

Serving: 12 | Prep: | Cook: 15mins | Ready in:

Ingredients

- 1 pkg. puff pastry
- 1 can whole berry cranberry sauce
- 1 wedge of brie cheese

Direction

- Place cut-out puff pastry in mini muffin tin cups. Brown slightly according to directions on box. Add whole berry cranberry sauce to each cup and top with brie. Place in oven until brie melts and browns slightly.

93. Brie Bomb Recipe

Serving: 6 | Prep: | Cook: 20mins | Ready in:

Ingredients

- 1 can of pilsbury dough crossant plain
- triple creme brie
- 1 orange
- 1/2 cup of cranberry sauce with cranberries
- 2 tbs maple syrup
- hand full of pecans

Direction

- Flatten all the dough evenly
- Put the medium size wheel of brie in the centre
- Take orange zest set aside
- With the 1/2 of cranberry and juice from the orange and a bit of zest
- Then add maple syrup and mix
- Then pour onto the brie
- Top it off with a few pecan and wrap entirely with the pastry making sure all is covered
- Then add some pecan on top and orange zest
- Add in the oven @ 350 for 20 minutes or until golden

94. Brie With Roasted Pear And Thyme Recipe

Serving: 6 | Prep: | Cook: 15mins | Ready in:

Ingredients

- 1 6" round of Brie (about 17 oz)
- 2 sweet almost ripe pears
- 2 tsp. lavender or clover honey (or any fancy honey)
- 1 to 2 tsp. finely chopped fresh thyme

Direction

- Cut off top rind of Brie and discard. Set Brie aside. Preheat oven to 425ºF.
- Peel and core pears, then slice 1/4" thick. Lay on a baking sheet lined with buttered parchment paper or a silpat in a single layer. Roast in oven for 15 minutes. Turn slices and continue roasting 10 to 15 minutes or until edges are caramelized and brown.
- Arrange pear slices overlapping in a circle overtop Brie. Refrigerate, uncovered, for up to 6 hours.
- When ready to serve, heat in a preheated 350ºF oven 10 to 12 minutes or until cheese is softened. Drizzle with clover honey and sprinkle with thyme. Serve with slices of fresh baguette or water crackers.

95. Broccoli Ricotta Bake With Roasted Pepper Sauce Recipe

Serving: 6 | Prep: | Cook: 2hours | Ready in:

Ingredients

- 2 red peppers, seeded and chopped
- 1 large onion, chopped
- 6 cloves garlic, peeled but left whole
- ½ tbsp olive oil
- ½ tbsp yellow mustard seed
- 3 tbsp boiling water
- ½ tsp crumbled saffron threads or turmeric (optional)
- 2 ¼ cups diced broccoli
- 1 cup low-fat ricotta cheese
- 1 egg
- zest of 1 lemon
- ½ tsp dried basil
- ¼ tsp fresh ground black pepper
- ¼ tsp paprika
- pinch nutmeg
- pinch salt

Direction

- Preheat oven to 350°F.
- Place peppers, onion and garlic cloves into a 9" x 13" baking pan.
- Drizzle with olive oil, add mustard seed, salt and pepper and toss well.
- Put in oven and roast for about 45 minutes, or until very soft and caramelized.
- Meanwhile, stir together boiling water and saffron, if using. Allow to steep while vegetables are roasting.
- When they have finished roasting, add the vegetables to a blender, add the saffron water and puree smooth. Pour into a jug or gravy boat and set aside.
- Reduce oven temperature to 325°F.
- Place broccoli florets in a steamer and steam until just tender.
- Take half the broccoli, break it up with a fork or potato masher, and add to a bowl with the ricotta, egg, lemon zest, basil, pepper, paprika, nutmeg and salt.
- Fold in the larger broccoli pieces.
- Grease an 8" or 9" round casserole dish, and fill with broccoli mixture.
- Bake for 20 minutes.
- Serve alongside warm pepper sauce

96. Broccoli Cheese Bites Recipe

Serving: 1 | Prep: | Cook: 30mins | Ready in:

Ingredients

- 16 oz. package of frozen chopped broccoli, thawed and drained of liquid
- 1 1/2 cup of grated cheddar cheese
- 3 eggs
- 1 cup of seasoned Italian breadcrumbs

Direction

- Mix all the ingredients together in a large bowl.
- With your hands, form small patties and lay on a parchment lined baking sheet.
- Bake at 375F for 25 minutes, turning the patties after the first 15 minutes.

97. Broccoli Cheese Dip Recipe

Serving: 12 | Prep: | Cook: 25mins | Ready in:

Ingredients

- 8 ounces cream cheese softened
- 1 cup sour cream
- 1 envelope ranch salad dressing mix
- 10 once package frozen chopped broccoli thawed and well drained
- 2 cups shredded mild cheddar cheese

Direction

- Beat cream cheese, sour cream and salad dressing mix with electric mixer until well blended.
- Stir in broccoli and 1-1/2 cups of the cheddar cheese.
- Spoon into pie plate then bake at 350 for 20 minutes.
- Top with remaining cheese and bake 5 minutes longer then serve with crackers.

98. Broccoli And Cheddar Tartlets Recipe

Serving: 8 | Prep: | Cook: 30mins | Ready in:

Ingredients

- 3 eggs
- 1 cup half and half
- 1/4 cup chopped green onions
- 1 cup shredded cheddar cheese
- 1 1/2 cups chopped broccoli florets or 1 (10oz) package frozen choped broccoli
- 8 unbaked frozen tartlet shells (1 oz each)

Direction

- Preheat oven to 350'F
- Beat eggs in a medium bowl until frothy for just a few seconds
- Add half and half to bowl, mix well
- Add green onions, cheddar, and broccoli, mix well
- Spoon filling into tartlet shells
- Place shells 3 inches apart on baking sheet
- Bake tartlets until knife inserted in centre comes out clean, about 30 minutes
- Let stand for several minutes before serving

99. Broccoli Cheese Muffins Recipe

Serving: 12 | Prep: | Cook: 35mins | Ready in:

Ingredients

- 1 1/2
- cups Original Bisquick® mix
- 1/2
- cup whole milk
- 3
- tablespoons vegetable oil
- 1
- large egg
- 1/2
- cup Green Giant® Valley Fresh Steamers® frozen broccoli cuts, steamed until crisp tender, drained and finely chopped
- 1
- cup shredded sharp cheddar cheese (4 oz)
- 1/4
- teaspoon onion powder

Direction

- 1 Heat oven to 400°F. Spray 12-cup muffin pan with cooking spray.
- 2 In large bowl, stir together Bisquick mix, milk, oil and egg. Stir in broccoli, cheese and onion powder just until combined. Spoon mixture evenly into prepared muffin cups.
- 3 Bake 8 to 10 minutes or until golden brown. Cool 5 minutes; remove from pans. Serve warm.

100. Bruschetta Polenta

Serving: 0 | Prep: | Cook: | Ready in:

Ingredients

- 1 tube (1 pound) polenta, cut into 1/2-inch slices
- 1 tablespoon olive oil
- 1 cup bruschetta topping
- 3 tablespoons shredded Parmesan cheese

Direction

- In a large skillet, cook polenta slices in oil over medium heat for 2 minutes on each side or until golden.
- Place the bruschetta topping in a microwave-safe bowl; cover and cook on high for 1 minute. Spoon 1 tablespoon onto each slice of polenta; sprinkle with cheese.
- Note: Look for bruschetta topping in the pasta aisle or your grocer's deli case.
- Nutrition Facts
- 2 each: 116 calories, 5g fat (1g saturated fat), 2mg cholesterol, 603mg sodium, 16g carbohydrate (2g sugars, 1g fiber), 2g protein.

101. Bruschetta With Sauteed Sweet Peppers And Creamy Gorgonzola Recipe

Serving: 8 | Prep: | Cook: 8mins | Ready in:

Ingredients

- EVOO
- 1 red bell pepper, seeded and sliced into thin strips
- 1 yellow bell pepper, seeded and sliced into thin strips
- 1/2 tsp sugar
- 1 TBS capers, drained
- 2 TBS julienned fresh basil leaves
- kosher salt
- black pepper
- baguette
- 3 oz creamy gorgonzola or other bleu cheese at room temperature

Direction

- Preheat oven to 375
- Heat 2 Tbsp. EVOO in sauté pan over med-high heat
- Add peppers and cook until soft, about 12 minutes
- Sprinkle with sugar and cook 2 more minutes
- Stir in capers and basil, season to taste with salt and pepper
- Set aside
- Slice baguette crosswise into 18 thin slices
- Brush rounds with EVOO on one side
- Arrange in rows, oil side up on sheet pan lined with parchment or foil
- Toast in oven until lightly browned, about 7 minutes
- Top each toast round with teaspoonful of pepper mixture
- Place 2 small pieces of gorgonzola on top of each
- Return to oven 1-2 minutes and warm through

102. Buffalo Chicken Cheese Dip Recipe

Serving: 12 | Prep: | Cook: 20mins | Ready in:

Ingredients

- 3 boneless skinless chicken breasts
- 1 jar premium blue cheese or ranch dressing (Marzetti's or Marie's)
- 1/4 cup prepared buffalo wing sauce (Franks or Wing it) mild or medium
- 1 8 oz pkg cream cheese softened
- Tabasco sauce

Direction

- Poach chicken in water till tender
- Let cool and shred or chop finely
- Mix dressing and buffalo sauce together.
- Use Tabasco sauce to fire it up if desired
- Spread cream cheese in a 13x9 baking dish
- Mix chicken into dressing
- Pour evenly over cream cheese
- Bake at 350F for 20 minutes
- Serve with tortilla chips

103. Buffalo Chicken Dip Recipe

Serving: 0 | Prep: | Cook: 35mins | Ready in:

Ingredients

- 2 chicken breasts cooked and shredded
- 5 oz. bottle of Frank's hot sauce
- ½ cup bleu cheese dressing
- 8 oz. cream cheese
- ¼ cup shredded cheddar

Direction

- Mix together and bake at 350 degrees until cheese is melted. Serve with Fritos scoops or tortilla chips.

104. Buttery Cheese Straws Recipe

Serving: 30 | Prep: | Cook: 75mins | Ready in:

Ingredients

- 375g/13oz plain Four
- Pinch Salt
- 225g/8oz butter - diced
- 150g/5oz mature cheddar cheese - grated
- 60g/2oz grated Parmesan cheese - grated
- ½tsp English/Dijon mustard
- Small pinch cayenne pepper
- 2 Egg Yolks

Direction

- Preheat oven to 190C/375F/Gas 5;
- Sift the flour and a pinch of salt into a bowl;
- Using your fingertips, rub in the butter until all the lumps are gone and the texture is like fine breadcrumbs;
- Stir in the cheese, mustard powder, cayenne, and egg yolks;
- Add 4 to 5tbsp cold water and mix to a firm dough;
- Wrap in cling film and chill in the fridge for some 30 minutes or so;
- Line a baking sheet with baking parchment;
- Roll out the dough to a square, roughly the thickness of a £2 coin;
- Cut the square in half, then cut each half into 1cm/½in strips;
- Transfer carefully onto the lined baking sheet and bake for some 10 to 15 minutes or so until crisp;
- Leave to cool on the tray.

105. California Walnut Cheese Ball Recipe

Serving: 2 | Prep: | Cook: 45mins | Ready in:

Ingredients

- 3 cups shredded old white cheddar cheese
- 1/2 cup butter, softened
- 1 clove garlic, minced
- 1 teaspoon Dijon mustard
- 1/2 teaspoon onion powder
- 1/2 teaspoon worcestershire sauce
- 2 tablespoons fresh chives, finely chopped
- 1 tablespoon port or sherry, optional
- 1/2 to 3/4 cup toasted* California walnut pieces

Direction

- In food processor, combine all ingredients except walnuts. Pulse until mixture is smooth. Remove to medium bowl; cover and chill until slightly firm.
- Shape into a 5-inch ball or roll into 7 x 2-inch log.
- Roll in toasted walnuts to coat evenly. Wrap in plastic wrap chill until firm.
- Allow to warm at room temperature for 30 minutes before serving. May be kept in refrigerator for up to 5 days.

- Makes one ball or log.
- *Toasted Walnuts:
- Oven Method: Spread chopped walnuts evenly onto a baking sheet or in a shallow pan. Bake at 350°F for 5 to 7 minutes or until lightly browned. Stir several times for even toasting. Be sure to keep an eye on them, they burn easily. Cool before using.
- Microwave Method: In glass pie plate spread 3/4 cup walnuts in a single layer. Microwave on HIGH 5 to 6 minutes, stirring every 2 minutes. Cool before using.
- Skillet Method: In large, dry skillet over medium to high heat, heat walnuts until lightly toasted, about 1 to 2 minutes.

106. Caramel Apple Baked Brie Recipe

Serving: 68 | Prep: | Cook: 15mins | Ready in:

Ingredients

- 1 tablespoon of butter
- 112 cup chopped and peeled gala or granney apples
- 114 cuo sweentened dried cranberries
- 1 tablespoons of chopped pecans
- 2tablespoons of brandy or apple juice
- 1/4 cup of packed brown sugar

Direction

- Oven 350 degrees
- Melt butter and add apples, cranberries, sugar, pecans and brandy
- Cook for 3 minutes, stirring till sugar dissolves
- Cut brie in half
- Place bottom half in ungreased 9 inch pie pan
- Spoon 1/2 topping over cheese.
- Place the other 1/2 cheese on top, secure with toothpicks, and pour remaining sauce on top
- Bake 15 to 20 minutes
- Serve with warm baguettes

107. Carmelized Onion And Brie Bites Recipe

Serving: 24 | Prep: | Cook: 50mins | Ready in:

Ingredients

- 1 can of biscuit dough
- ¼ cup flour
- 1 cup caramelized onion
- ½ cup brie, diced
- cooking spray

Direction

- Preheat oven to 350 degrees. Prepare muffin pan by spraying the inside of each well with cooking spray.
- Open can of biscuit dough and separate into individual biscuits. Cut each biscuit in quarters to form dough pieces. Place a dough piece in each well. Gently push the dough piece inside the well to form a cup. Repeat until all wells are filled with a dough piece. Fill each well with brie. Top each well with caramelized onion.
- Bake in preheated oven for 7-10 minutes or until golden brown
- How to Caramelize Onions:
- Slice onions into 1/4-inch wide rings
- Heat butter or combination of butter and oil in heavy skillet.
- Add onions and a small amount of sugar (optional) and slowly cook over medium heat.
- Cook until onions are caramel colored, stirring often, 30 to 40 minutes.
- For more flavor, add a touch of vinegar at the end of cooking, stirring to deglaze the pan.
- Tips:
- Large, mild-flavored onions work best
- Caramelized onions can be frozen in an airtight container up to three months.

108. Castle Nacho Grande Recipe

Serving: 10 | Prep: | Cook: 10mins | Ready in:

Ingredients

- 10 white castle hamburgers
- 1 large can nacho cheese
- 1 head lettuce chopped
- 2 chopped tomatoes
- 1 medium chopped onion
- 1 large jar salsa
- 1 large bag nacho chips
- 8 ounces sour cream
- 25 chopped black olives
- 1 large bag shredded cheddar cheese

Direction

- Spread 1/3 of the salsa on the bottom of a rectangular pan.
- Sprinkle with 1/2 cup shredded cheese and chopped onion.
- Cut each sandwich into 6 pieces and arrange on top of salsa, cheese and onion.
- Add more salsa, shredded cheese, onion and black olives.
- Pour nacho cheese over all and bake at 350 for 20 minutes then remove and cool 5 minutes.
- Top with lettuce, chopped tomatoes, onions, shredded cheese, black olives and sour cream.
- Serve with nacho chips.

109. Cha Cha Cheese Dip Recipe

Serving: 6 | Prep: | Cook: 25mins | Ready in:

Ingredients

- 8 slices cooked bacon, crumbled
- 8 ounces cream cheese, softened
- 1 cup mayonnaise
- 1 cup swiss cheese, shredded
- 1 tablespoon jalapeños, chopped
- 5 Ritz® crackers, crushed

Direction

- In a bowl, mix cream cheese, mayonnaise, Swiss cheese and jalapeño pepper.
- Transfer mixture to a pie plate.
- Top with crumbled bacon and crushed Ritz crackers.
- Bake at 325° for 25 minutes.
- Serve warm.

110. Cheddar And Green Onion Biscuit Poppers Recipe

Serving: 12 | Prep: | Cook: 9mins | Ready in:

Ingredients

- 2 CUPS Bisquick
- 2/3 CUP milk
- 4 MED GREENS CHOPPED OR LEAVE OUT IF YOU DONT LIKE THEM.
- 2 TABLESPOONS butter OR margarine MELTED
- 1/2 CUP CHEDDAR cheese

Direction

- 1. HEAT OVEN TO 450 DEGREES, SPRAY COOKIE SHEET WITH COOKING SRAY, STIR IN BISQUICK,MILK AND CHEESE AND ONIONS UNTIL SOFT DOUGH FORMS.
- 2. DROP DOUGH BY ROUNDED TEASPOONFULS ONTO COOKIE SHEET.
- 3. BAKE 7 TO 9 MIN OR UNTIL GOLDEN BROWN.
- 4. BRUSH BUTTER OVER POPPERS WITH DONE AND SPRINKLE WITH GARLIC POWDER OR SALT
- SERVE WITH SALSA OR DESIRED DIP RANCH ETC
- MAKES 35 TO 40 BISCUIT POPPERS

111. Cheddar Cheese Puffs Recipe

Serving: 2 | Prep: | Cook: 13mins | Ready in:

Ingredients

- 1 cup cheddar cheese, shredded
- 1/2 cup all-purpose flour
- 1/4 cup butter, softened
- 1/2 teaspoon ground mustard

Direction

- Preheat oven to 400 degrees F.
- Combine all ingredients in a bowl.
- Mix well.
- Roll into 1" diameter balls.
- Place at least 1" apart on ungreased baking sheet.
- Bake for 12 to 15 minutes OR until lightly browned.
- Serve warm.

112. Cheddar Cheesy Puffs Recipe

Serving: 18 | Prep: | Cook: 25mins | Ready in:

Ingredients

- 6 Tbsps. butter, cut into small pieces
- 1 cup water
- 1 tsp. salt
- 1 cup flour
- 1/4 tsp. cayenne pepper (you can always add more or not at all - it depends on your taste)
- 2 Tbsps. chopped chives or parsley
- 5 eggs
- 1 cup cheddar cheese, shredded
- Fresh ground salt and pepper

Direction

- Preheat oven to 450 degrees.
- Combine butter, water and salt in a saucepan and bring to a boil, stirring often.
- Remove from heat, then add flour, cayenne pepper and chives/parsley, stirring until the mixture is smooth.
- Return to heat and continue to stir for about 1 minute to melt remaining lumps of butter.
- Remove from heat and allow to cool somewhat.
- Add eggs, one at a time, gently mixing in each egg completely before adding another egg.
- While dough is still warm, mix in cheese, salt and pepper.
- Spray baking sheet with non-stick spray and spoon out individual dough/cheese poofs onto baking sheet.
- Poofs should be about 1 to 2 inches round.
- You can also spoon mixture into muffin tins that have been sprayed with non-stick cooking spray.
- Bake for approximately 15 – 18 minutes or until lightly golden brown in colour.

113. Cheddar Chili Cheesecake Recipe

Serving: 20 | Prep: | Cook: 45mins | Ready in:

Ingredients

- 1/2 cheddar crackers, crushed to crumbs
- 1 pound Philly cream cheese, softened
- 1 tea. lime juice
- 2 large eggs
- 1/2 tea. chili powder
- 1/2 tea. chipotle chili powder
- 1/4 tea. cayenne powder(or to taste)
- 1/4 tea. black pepper
- 1/2 tea. lime flavored sea salt
- 1 cup extra sharp cheddar cheese, shredded

Direction

- Preheat oven to 325^.
- Spray 6" spring-pan with cooking spray.
- Swirl cracker crumbs to evenly cover bottom and sides.
- Set aside in fridge to set.
- Blend cream cheese and lime juice until smooth.
- Add eggs one at a time.
- Add chili powders and salt.
- Fold in shredded cheese and mix well.
- Pour into prepared pan.
- Bake at 325^ for 45-50 minutes.
- Let cool and serve at room temperature with cracker or bread.

114. Cheddar Chili Tomatoe Pots Recipe

Serving: 6 | Prep: | Cook: 20mins | Ready in:

Ingredients

- 6 medium tomatoes
- 31/2 cups (14ounces) Sargento Dancy Supreme Shredded sharp cheddar cheese
- 2 cans (4ounces each) chopped green chilies, well drained
- 1/2 teaspoon dried oregano leaves, crushed
- 1/2 teaspoon minced garlic
- 6 tablespoons sour cream
- 3 green onions, sliced
- breadsticks for serving

Direction

- Preheat oven to 325 degrees F. Grease 11x7 inch baking dish. Cut 1/2 inch slice from the top of each tomatoes; scoop out pulp and seeds, leaving 1/4 inch shell (save pulp for another use, such as salads or sauces.
- Invert tomatoes on paper towel lined plate; let drain 20 minutes.
- Combine 3 cups cheese, chilies, oregano and garlic in medium bowl
- Using large spoon, stuff tomato shells with cheese mixture.
- Arrange tomato shells in prepared dish. Bake 20 minutes. Top with sour cream, remaining 1/2 cup cheese and green onions. Serve with breadsticks.

115. Cheddar Cornmeal Sticks Recipe

Serving: 24 | Prep: | Cook: 15mins | Ready in:

Ingredients

- The 90 Minutes includes sitting time
- 2 cups finely shredded sharp cheddar cheese
- 1/2 cup butter
- 1 1/4 cups all-purpose flour
- 1/4 cup yellow cornmeal
- 1/4 teaspoon salt
- 1/4 teaspoon cayenne pepper
- 1/4 teaspoon ground nutmeg

Direction

- In a large bowl, combine shredded cheese with butter
- Let stand until room temperature, about one hour
- Beat with electric mixer until well mixed
- Stir in flour, cornmeal, salt, cayenne and nutmeg
- Divide dough in half
- Preheat oven to 350F
- Lightly grease baking sheets, set aside
- On a lightly floured surface, roll each dough half into a 12x4 inch rectangle
- Using a sharp knife, slice dough into 4x1/2 inch pieces
- Place dough pieces 1/2 inch apart on prepared baking sheets
- Bake about 15 minutes or until bottoms are lightly browned

- Transfer to a wire rack to cool
- Makes 48 crackers

116. Cheddar Crisp Appetizers Recipe

Serving: 60 | Prep: | Cook: 12mins | Ready in:

Ingredients

- 2 sticks of butter (1/2 lb) softened (not melted)
- 2 Cups sharp cheddar cheese, shredded
- 2 Cups flour
- 2 Cups Rice Krispies
- 2 pinches of salt
- 2 tsp cayenne pepper
- (it's the tooo tooo recipe)

Direction

- Mix everything together. Form small balls and place them on an aluminum lined cookie sheet. Press them flat a bit. (I recommend a one bite, popper size. If you bite them it's very likely you'll have fine crumbs on your shirt.) It makes about 60 pieces.
- Sprinkle a bit more cayenne on top, just for looks.
- Bake at 375 degrees for 10 to 12 minutes, or until golden brown.
- Let them cool before you remove them from the pan, or you'll bust a few.
- The original recipe says they can be made ahead of time and frozen, but I've never done it.
- Note: The cheese flavour will be subtle if a "gentle cheese" is used. That's why I recommend a very sharp cheddar.

117. Cheddar Ham Cups Recipe

Serving: 20 | Prep: | Cook: 10mins | Ready in:

Ingredients

- 2 cups cheddar cheese shredded
- 2 packs (2.5 oz each) thinly sliced ham chopped
- 3/4 cup mayo
- 1/3 cup real bacon bits
- 2-3 tsp Dijon mustard
- 1 can large flaky biscuts

Direction

- In bowl combine cheese, ham, mayo, mustard and bacon. Mix well
- Split large biscuits into 3rds and press each piece into the bottom of a mini muffin pan and up the sides forming a bowl
- Fill with 1 tablespoon of the mixture
- Bake for 9-11 min
- Serve warm

118. Cheddar Sausage Cheesecake Recipe

Serving: 8 | Prep: | Cook: 75mins | Ready in:

Ingredients

- 1 1/4 cups butter crackers crumbs
- 1/3 cup sharp cheddar cheese (about 3 oz)
- 1/4 cup butter or marg. melted
- 1 lb. mild Italian pork sausage
- 1 medium onion finely chopped
- 2 pkgs cream cheese (8 oz.) softened
- 4 eggs
- 1/4 cup all-purpose flour
- 8 oz. sour cream
- 1/2 tsp ground sage
- 1/4 tsp white pepper

- 2 cup sharp cheddar cheese shredded (about 8 oz)

Direction

- Preheat oven to 350°F.
- Combine first 3 ingredients; mix well. Press evenly onto bottom of a 9-inch springform pan. Set aside.
- Remove sausage from casings; crumble into a heavy. Add onion; cook until sausage is browned and onion is tender, stirring to crumble sausage. Drain and cool.
- Beat cream cheese until fluffy in a large mixing bowl; add eggs, one at a time, beating well after each.
- Add flour, sour cream, sage and pepper; beat at low speed just until smooth and blended.
- Stir in two cups cheese and sausage mixture. Pour into pan.
- Bake for 15 minutes. Reduce heat to 225°F and bake 1 hour and 15 minutes.
- Cool 30 to 45 minutes on rack. Remove side of pan.
- Serve warm.

119. Cheddar Sesame Crackers Recipe

Serving: 8 | Prep: | Cook: 7mins | Ready in:

Ingredients

- 1/2 lb. extra sharp cheddar cheese, grated
- 1 stick (1/2 cup) cold unsalted butter, cut in bits
- 1/2 cup all-purpose flour
- 1/2 cup toasted and cooled sesame seeds
- 1/4 cup minced shallot
- 1/2 teaspoon sea salt
- pepper to taste

Direction

- Pre-heat oven to 400 degrees
- Put all above ingredients in the food processor
- Blend until it forms a ball of dough
- Halve the dough and on sheets of plastic wrap & form each 1/2 into 6" log 1 1/2 " in diameter
- Chill the dough in plastic wrap for 2 hours or until firm enough to slice
- Cut dough into 1/4" slices and place on ungreased cookie sheet 2" apart
- Bake in centre of oven in batches for 7minutes or till edges are browned
- Transfer to cooling rack carefully with metal spatula to cool.
- About 56 crackers

120. Cheddar Shrimp Nachos Scoops Recipe

Serving: 48 | Prep: | Cook: 10mins | Ready in:

Ingredients

- 3/4 pound deveined peeled cooked shrimp, chopped
- 1-1/2 cups (6 ounces) shredded cheddar cheese
- 1 can (4 ounces) chopped green chilies, drained
- 1/3 cup chopped green onions
- 1/4 cup sliced ripe olives, drained
- 1/2 cup mayonnaise
- 1/4 teaspoon ground cumin
- 48 tortilla chip scoops

Direction

- In a large bowl, combine the shrimp, cheese, chilies, onions and olives. Combine the mayonnaise and cumin; add to shrimp mixture and toss to coat.
- Drop by tablespoonfuls into tortilla scoops. Place on ungreased baking sheets. Bake at 350° for 5-10 minutes or until cheese is melted. Serve warm.
- Yield: 4 dozen.

121. Cheddar Spinach Squares Recipe

Serving: 10 | Prep: | Cook: 40mins | Ready in:

Ingredients

- 4 tablespoons butter, cubed
- 3 large eggs
- 1 cup all-purpose flour
- 1 cup milk
- 1 teaspoon salt
- 1 teaspoon baking powder
- 1 pound sharp cheddar, shredded
- 2 10-ounce packages frozen chopped spinach, thawed and drained
- 3 tablespoons onion, chopped

Direction

- Place butter pats in a 9x13x2 pan.
- Place pan in oven.
- Preheat oven to 350 degrees F.
- While butter is melting (keep an eye on it), beat the eggs in a large bowl.
- Add flour, milk, salt and baking powder.
- Mix well.
- Add cheese, spinach and onion.
- Mix well again.
- Spoon into baking dish and level off.
- Bake for 40 minutes.
- Remove from oven.
- Allow to cool for 45 minutes.
- Cut into squares.
- **These can be frozen and baked at 350 for 20 minutes to heat.

122. Cheddar Stuffed Chilies Recipe

Serving: 8 | Prep: | Cook: 20mins | Ready in:

Ingredients

- 2 cans whole green chilies
- 1/2 pound cheddar cheese cut into 1 inch strips
- 1 cup cracker crumbs
- 1 egg beaten with small amount of milk

Direction

- Wash chilies under cold running water and spilt to remove seeds.
- Put cheese strip inside and fasten with toothpicks.
- Dip in egg mixture and roll in cracker crumbs.
- Brown on all sides in a skillet in oil then reduce heat and cook until cheese is melted.

123. Cheddar Triangles From Ireland Recipe

Serving: 32 | Prep: | Cook: 12mins | Ready in:

Ingredients

- 1-3/4 cups flour
- 1/2 cup yellow cornmeal
- 1 teaspoon sugar
- 3/4 teaspoon salt
- 1/2 teaspoon baking soda
- 1 stick butter, cut into small pieces
- 6 ounces shredded sharp cheddar cheese
- 1/2 cup cold water
- 2 tablespoons white vinegar
- coarsely ground black pepper

Direction

- Preheat oven to 375 degrees F
- In a food processor, mix flour, cornmeal, sugar, salt and baking soda.
- Add the butter and process until mixture forms coarse crumbs. Transfer to a large bowl and stir in cheese, water and vinegar until mixture forms a soft dough.

- Form it into a ball, wrap it in cellophane and chill in the refrigerator for 1 hour.
- Divide dough into 4 sections.
- On a floured board, roll each section into a paper thin circle, trimming the edges.
- Sprinkle with pepper and press it firmly into the dough.
- Cut each circle into 8 wedges, place on a greased baking sheet and bake for about 10 to 12 minutes, until crisp.
- Do not over bake.
- Cool on wire rack.
- Store in an airtight container.
- Serve with your favourite dip.
- Makes: 32
- Note: For a dip I use Knorr vegetable soup mix, which I combine with 16 ounces of sour cream and chill for 3 hours before serving.

124. Cheddar Biscuits Recipe

Serving: 810 | Prep: | Cook: 10mins | Ready in:

Ingredients

- 2 cups Bisquick
- 2/3 cup milk
- 1/2 cup shredded cheddar cheese
- 1/2 cup butter or margarine, melted
- garlic powder
- Hidden Valley buttermilk ranch dressing mix (the seasoning pack), to taste (recommend 1/3 to 1/2 pack of ranch dressing mix)

Direction

- Heat oven to 450 degrees.
- Mix Bisquick, milk, cheese, 1/4 tsp. garlic powder, and ranch seasoning mix until a soft dough forms.
- Drop by spoonfuls onto an ungreased cooking sheet.
- Bake 8- 10 min until golden brown.
- Brush melted butter over warm biscuits, then sprinkle with a little bit of garlic powder and ranch seasoning mix before removing from cookie sheet.
- Enjoyed best while still warm. :)

125. Cheddar Jelly Thumbprints Recipe

Serving: 24 | Prep: | Cook: 15mins | Ready in:

Ingredients

- 6 oz. white cheddar cheese or extra-sharp cheddar cheese, shredded
- ½ cup finely shredded parmesan cheese (2 oz.)
- ½ cup butter, softened
- 1 egg yolk
- 1 cup all-purpose flour
- 1 egg white
- 1 Tbsp. water
- 1 ¼ cups finely chopped pecans
- 1/3 to ½ cup green and/or red jalapeno jelly or pomegranate jelly

Direction

- Preheat oven to 350 degrees F.
- Line 2 large cookie sheets with parchment paper or lightly grease and set aside.
- In a food processor combine cheeses and butter.
- Cover; process until well combined.
- Add egg yolk and ¼ teaspoon ground black pepper; cover and process until combined.
- Add flour; pulse several times until a soft dough forms; set aside. (Or in a bowl beat butter with electric mixer 30 seconds; beat in cheeses until well combined.)
- Beat yolk and pepper until combined.
- Add flour; beat until soft dough forms.)
- In a small bowl, combine egg white and water.
- Place pecans in a shallow dish.
- Shape dough into ¾-inch balls.
- Roll balls in egg white mixture, then in pecans.
- Place 1 inch apart on prepared cookie sheets.

- Press your thumb into centre of each ball, reshaping as necessary. Bake about 15 minutes or until edges are firm and cookies are lightly golden.
- Press puffed centres down using the rounded side of a measuring teaspoon.
- Transfer to a wire rack and let cool.
- Just before serving, place a small amount of jelly in the centre of each thumbprint.
- Store unfilled in refrigerator up to 3 days or in the freezer up to 3 months.
- Fill with jelly before serving.
- I made this recipe Christmas 2005 and 2007and everybody raved about it! They are best when made fresh, but if you have to make ahead, just be sure to bring these "cookies" to room temperature before serving for full flavour.
- Makes a nice presentation!

126. Cheese Bite Appetizer Recipe

Serving: 35 | Prep: | Cook: 10mins | Ready in:

Ingredients

- 1/2 - cup warm butter or margaine
- 1 - cup plain flour
- 2 - cups grated medium or sharp flavor cheddar cheese
- 1/4 - tsp ground cayenne pepper
- 1 - tsp paprika/red pepper
- ....
- optional....
- add some crumbled bacon, sausage or ham into the batter. Also, try some chopped green onion for a stronger taste.

Direction

- Preheat oven to 400°F
- Mix the butter, pepper and flour together.
- Add the cheese and mix in well.
- Shape into small bite-size balls
- Arrange on a baking sheet and bake in a preheated oven (400°F) for about 10 minutes

127. Cheese Cracker Recipe

Serving: 0 | Prep: | Cook: 17mins | Ready in:

Ingredients

- 1 Stick of butter – at room temperature
- 1 Cup sharp cheddar cheese
- 1 Cup parmesan cheese
- 1 1/2 Cups All Purpose flour
- 1 teaspoon salt
- 1/4 teaspoon cayenne pepper

Direction

- 1. Preheat your oven to 325°
- 2. Mix flour, salt, cayenne pepper.
- 3. Rub in the butter till it resembles cornmeal. Add cheese.
- 4. Dump the mixture out onto a lightly floured surface, add little water if necessary and use your hands to bring it together forming a ball of stiff dough.
- 5. If the consistency allows, roll the dough out into a very thin layer. Maybe 1/8 inch. If the dough is too loose to roll, toss it into the fridge for 15 minutes.
- 6. Once rolled out, cut the crackers. You can use cookie cutters here if you would like fancy shapes.
- 7. Place the crackers onto a cookie sheet covered with foil.
- 8. Bake for 15 minutes or until the crackers start to get just golden on the edges.
- 9. Place on a cooling rack until the crackers are no longer warm.

128. Cheese Olive Balls Recipe

Serving: 12 | Prep: | Cook: 20mins | Ready in:

Ingredients

- 1 lb sharp cheese, grated
- 1/8 lb margarine, soft
- 1 cup flour (or slightly more)
- red pepper to taste
- 1/4 tbs garlic salt
- 2 tbs worcestershire sauce
- 1 or 2 tbs water
- Large jar medium-sized stuffed olives, drained

Direction

- Grate cheese, let soften. Mix cheese, margarine, flour, seasonings and water. Work into a smooth dough. Use a piece of dough about the size of a walnut and flatten with fingers. Press dough smoothly around each olive. Bake on a greased baking sheet at 350F for 15-20 minutes, or until light brown. Freeze before baking if desired.
- Yield: About 6 doz.

129. Cheese Puffs Recipe

Serving: 0 | Prep: | Cook: 1hours | Ready in:

Ingredients

- 1pound butter sticks
- 4mini jars of Kraft Old English cheese
- 15 Shakes oh Tabasco
- 1\2 tsp. Worcestershire sauce to taste
- 1Tbls. Beau Monde Seasoning
- 3 loaves Pepperidge Farms white thin bread (trim crusts)

Direction

- Combine all ingredients. Spread bread with cheese mixture. Stack 3slices bread with cheese mixture on all slices (cheese side up)
- Keep preparing 3slice groups. Use all the bread and cheese.
- Refrigerate until chilled.
- Cut each stack into four pieces.
- Sprinkle with a little bit of Cayenne Pepper if desired or else Paprika.
- Freeze for later baking
- Take out and bake at 400 degrees for 8 minutes. Bake frozen.
- Store puffs in airtight containers in the freezers.

130. Cheese Straws Recipe

Serving: 16 | Prep: | Cook: 50mins | Ready in:

Ingredients

- 16 Rhodes™ dinner rolls, thawed but still cold
- 1/4 to 1/2 cup melted butter
- 1/2 pound sharp cheddar cheese, grated
- 1/4 cup parmesan cheese
- 1/2 teaspoon garlic salt
- fresh cracked black pepper, if desired

Direction

- Cut each roll in half and roll into a 15-inch rope.
- Combine cheeses together and place on the counter.
- Brush each rope with butter and roll in the cheese mixture.
- Place on large sprayed baking sheet.
- Sprinkle with garlic salt and pepper, if desired.
- Let rise for 15 minutes.
- Bake at 375°F 12 to 15 minutes or until golden brown and crispy.
- Serve with your favorite soup or salad.

131. Cheese Tidbits Recipe

Serving: 0 | Prep: | Cook: 20mins | Ready in:

Ingredients

- 1/2 c. butter or margarine
- 2 c. shredded cheddar cheese
- 1/4 t. salt
- 1 c. flour
- Sesame seeds

Direction

- 1. Preheat oven to 450 degrees.
- 2. Cream the butter and cheddar cheese.
- 3. Mix the salt and flour together.
- 4. Rub the flour mixture into the butter/cheddar mixture with your hands until you can roll it into small balls.
- 5. Roll the balls into sesame seeds.
- 6. Bake for 10 minutes.
- Makes 2 dozen.

132. Cheese Olive Dip Recipe

Serving: 24 | Prep: | Cook: 25mins | Ready in:

Ingredients

- 1 1/2 cups pimiento-stuffed olives, finely chopped
- 1 cup shredded mozzarell cheese
- 1 cup shredded cheddar cheese
- 1 cup mayonnaise
- 3/4 cup pitted ripe olives finely chopped
- 2 small green onion, finely chopped
- corn chips
- Assorted crackers

Direction

- Combine all ingredients in a medium bowl
- Stir well
- Spoon into an ungreased shallow 1 quart baking dish
- Bake uncovered at 350 degrees for 25 minutes or until thoroughly heated
- Serve with corn chips or assorted crackers
- Yield: 3 1/2 cups

133. Cheesy Biscuits Recipe

Serving: 0 | Prep: | Cook: 20mins | Ready in:

Ingredients

- 200g parmesan cheese
- 200g all purpose flour
- 200g butter

Direction

- Preheat oven to 200C/390F.
- Grate cheese and weigh (I say 200g because that's how much a block of parmesan usually comes in here but however much you have just match the same weight of flour and butter).
- Weigh and add sifted flour and butter and mix.
- Roll out and cut out with cookie cutter (I like to use a fairly small one as these are best served bite sized.)
- Transfer to baking sheet and cook for 10-15 minutes, they should be golden brown.
- Put onto cooling rack until fully cool then serve or store.

134. Cheesy Chicken Broccoli Bake [recipes + Video] Recipe

Serving: 4 | Prep: | Cook: 20mins | Ready in:

Ingredients

- 1 cup long grain rice
- ¼ teaspoon black pepper
- ½ teaspoon onion powder

- 1 can cream of chicken
- 1 cup cheddar cheese, shredded
- 2 cups broccoli, diced
- 1 ½ cups chicken broth
- Extra cheddar cheese for topping

Direction

- Heat oven to 375°F/190°C.
- In a casserole dish, combine rice, pepper, onion powder, cream of chicken, cheese, broccoli, and chicken stock. Mix until everything is combined.
- Lay chicken on top of the rice mixture. Space evenly.
- Cover with foil and bake for 50 minutes.
- Take off cover and top the chicken with more cheese. Bake uncovered for another 5 minutes or until cheese is melted.
- Enjoy!

135. Cheesy Crescent Nachos Recipe

Serving: 6 | Prep: | Cook: 25mins | Ready in:

Ingredients

- 1 can crescent rolls
- 3 T cornmeal
- 1 small can green cilies, draned
- 1 c shredded cheddar
- 1 c shredded monterrey jack (or mozzerella, or pepper jack)
- salsa or other dip

Direction

- Heat oven to 350
- Separate dough into 4 rectangles
- Coat both sides of each rectangle with cornmeal
- Place in ungreased 9" non-stick pie pan
- Press over bottom and up sides to form crust
- Press edges and seal perforations
- Sprinkle with any remaining cornmeal
- Top evenly with chiles and cheeses
- Bake 24-28 minutes until golden brown
- Cool 5 minutes
- Cut into triangles (I use pizza cutter) and serve with salsa or other dips

136. Chicken And Feta Stuffed Peppers Recipe

Serving: 12 | Prep: | Cook: 10mins | Ready in:

Ingredients

- 12 Lg banana peppers
- 6- 6oz Boneless chicken breasts
- 12oz feta cheese
- 12oz Shredded Mozzarela cheese
- 2 dozen cherry tomatoes
- 1Tb Fresh minced garlic
- 3 Lg eggs
- 1 Tb kosher salt
- 1 tsp fresh ground black pepper
- olive oil
- romano cheese

Direction

- Preheat oven to 380 degrees
- Grill chicken breasts being careful not to overcook
- Clean banana peppers removing seeds and casing
- Slice cherry tomatoes in half
- Mix feta, mozzarella, garlic, eggs, tomato, salt, and pepper
- Cut cooled chicken breasts into thin strips
- Stuff equal portions of chicken strips into peppers
- Stuff equal portions of cheese mixture into peppers on top of chicken
- Place peppers onto baking sheet
- Drizzle peppers with olive oil

- Sprinkle Romano cheese over peppers (to your taste)
- Bake in oven 8-10 min (look for peppers to just begin browning)
- Note (you may have extra cheese mixture depending on pepper size)

137. Chicken Nacho Dip Recipe

Serving: 20 | Prep: | Cook: 10mins | Ready in:

Ingredients

- 4 large cans white chunk chicken breast, drained
- 1 package cream cheese
- 3/4 of a large container of sour cream
- 1/2 cup salsa
- 1 small bottle of Ortega taco sauce
- 1 8 oz bag shredded taco or colby cheese
- pinch of hot cayenne pepper and garlic powder (optional)
- nacho chips

Direction

- Combine first three ingredients
- Spread in an 8x12 inch baking dish
- Sprinkle with hot pepper and garlic
- Pour salsa and taco sauce over chicken mixture and top with cheese
- Bake in a 375 oven until cheese is melted
- Serve warm or cold with nacho chips

138. Chicken Pear And Gorgonzola Tarts Recipe

Serving: 30 | Prep: | Cook: 5mins | Ready in:

Ingredients

- 8 bacon strips
- 11/2tsp brown sugar
- 1/4tsp cinnamon
- 3/4c finely chopped cooked chicken breast
- 1/3c pear nectar
- 1/4c finely chopped dried pears
- 3Tbs apricot preserves
- 2tsp butter
- 1/4tsp salt
- 1/4tsp pepper
- 2 pkgs(1.9oz ea) frozen miniature phyllo tart shells
- 1/3c crumbled gorgonzola cheese

Direction

- Place bacon in a jelly roll pan; broil 4 " from the heat for 4-6 mins on each side or till crisp. Combine brown sugar and cinnamon; sprinkle over bacon. Broil 1 min. longer or till bacon is glazed and bubbly. Drain on paper towels. Cool slightly and crumble.
- In small skillet, combine chicken, pear nectar, pears, preserves, butter, salt and pepper. Bring to a boil; cook, stirring occasionally, for 3-4 mins or till thickened. Spoon about 1 teaspoonful of filling into each tart shell; place tarts on baking sheet. Sprinkle with bacon and cheese.
- Bake at 350 for 5 to 7 mins. Or till heated through.

139. Chicken Wing Dip WBlue Cheese Recipe

Serving: 12 | Prep: | Cook: 55mins | Ready in:

Ingredients

- 3 skinless, boneless chicken breast halves
- 3/4 of a (12 ounce) bottle hot chicken wing sauce
- 3 T. butter
- 1 (8 ounce) package of cream cheese
- 1/3 c. quality blue cheese dressing

Direction

- Preheat oven to 350 degrees F.
- Place chicken in a pot with enough water to cover. Bring to a boil and cook for 25 minutes, or until chicken juices run clear. Drain liquid from pot and shred chicken. Mix wing sauce and butter in pot with shredded chicken. Bring to a boil, reduce heat to low and simmer 10 minutes.
- Spread cream cheese over the bottom of an 8 x 8 inch baking dish. Pour chicken mixture over cream cheese. Top with dressing.
- Bake 15 minutes in the preheated oven, until hot and bubbly. I serve with Frito chips for scooping. VERY tasty! =D

140. Chile Cheese Appetizers Recipe

Serving: 28 | Prep: | Cook: 40mins | Ready in:

Ingredients

- 1/2 cup butter melted
- 10 eggs
- 1/2 cup flour
- 1 teaspoon baking powder
- 1 8 oz can chopped green chiles
- 1 pint cottage cheese (small curd)
- 1 lb monterey jack cheese shreeded
- salsa warmed optional

Direction

- In a 13 x 9 inch pan melt butter
- Beat eggs lightly in a large bowl
- Add flour and baking powder, combine
- In another bowl, combine remaining ingredients, except salsa
- Combine cheese mixture to the flour; blend well
- Pour batter into pan and bake at 400 F for 14 minutes
- Reduce heat to 350 F and bake 35-40 minutes longer. Cut into appetizer size squares and serve warm with salsa.

141. Chile Cheese Dip Recipe

Serving: 6 | Prep: | Cook: 30mins | Ready in:

Ingredients

- 2 8 oz packages cream cheese
- 2 beaten eggs
- 2 1/2 cups monterey jack cheese
- 1 4oz can chopped green chiles

Direction

- Mix ingredients and Bake at 325 degrees for 30 min.

142. Chili Brie Cheese Dip In Sourdough Round Recipe

Serving: 8 | Prep: | Cook: 30mins | Ready in:

Ingredients

- 1 round loaf sourdough bread
- 8 ounce wheel brie cheese
- 1 tablespoon butter softened
- 1 teaspoon chili powder
- 1/2 teaspoon dry ground mustard
- 1/2 teaspoon garlic powder
- 1/2 teaspoon granulated sugar

Direction

- Preheat oven to 350.
- Combine spices and sugar then set aside.
- Cut circle in top of bread and remove bread centre to make room for brie.
- Spread butter in bread then sprinkle with 2 teaspoons spice mixture.

- With knife make 2" cuts around edge of bread at 1" intervals.
- Remove rind from brie and place in bread then sprinkle brie with remaining spice.
- Replace top of bread then bake on baking sheet for 25 minutes.
- To serve remove bread top and break into bite size pieces then dip bread pieces in hot brie.

143. Chokes And Cheese Dip Recipe

Serving: 8 | Prep: | Cook: 15mins | Ready in:

Ingredients

- 1 Cup mayonnaise
- 1 can diced green chiles
- 1 can artichoke hearts (5-7 count, drained) cut into bite sized pieces
- 1 Cup Kraft three cheese blend (in shaker) can use parm (reserve 4 tbsp)
- 1/4-1/2 Cup sour cream
- 1/4 tsp chopped/minced garlic (more if you like)
- 1/2 tsp horseradish
- salt and pepper to taste

Direction

- Mix together in an oven/microwave safe container (can use a round loaf of bread that has been cored with room for the filling).
- Microwave for 5 minutes.
- Top with remaining cheese.
- Bake in a 300oF oven until top is brown.

144. Crab Cheese Dip Recipe

Serving: 4 | Prep: | Cook: 30mins | Ready in:

Ingredients

- 1/2 cup light mayoniae
- 1 pkg 8 oz. light cream cheese softened
- 2 tablespoons skim milk
- 4 scallions sliced
- 1 tbs lemon juice
- 1 tsp. red hot sauce
- 1 tsp. Woorcherstershire sauce
- 1/2 tsp garlic salt
- 1/2 cup grated parmeasan cheese
- 1 lb. lump crab meat picked over to remove cartilage
- 1/4 cup parsely chopped
- {May omit crab and use Shrimp}

Direction

- Heat oven to 350 degrees spray a 6 oz. cup shallow baking dish with non-stick cooking spray and set aside
- In a large bowl stir together mayonnaise, cream cheese, Milk scallions ,lemon juice, red pepper sauce Worcestershire sauce, Garlic salt and 1/4 cup parmesan cheese until smooth
- Gently stir in crab meat to keep from breaking up to finely spoon mixture evenly into baking dish
- Sprinkle remaining parmesan cheese over top crab mixture
- Bake 350 for 30 minutes until lightly brown let stand 5 minutes
- Sprinkle chopped Parsley over top serve warm with your favourite dip chip.
- Was given to me by a friend who clipped it out of a magazine

145. Crab Cheese Melts Recipe

Serving: 0 | Prep: | Cook: 30mins | Ready in:

Ingredients

- 6 English muffins
- 1/2 c. cheese Whiz
- 1 T. mayo

- 1 tin crab meat, drained
- Dash garlic salt
- Pepper

Direction

- Mix Cheese Whiz, mayo and spices together. Fold in crab meat. Butter muffin halves. Spread with crab mixture. Bake in a 375 degree oven until toasty and cheese is bubbly.
- Cut into quarters so you have 48. Place on a tray and serve hot.

146. Crab N Brie Strudel Slices Recipe

Serving: 24 | Prep: | Cook: 20mins | Ready in:

Ingredients

- 1/2 pound fresh crabmeat
- 6 ounces Brie or camembert cheese rind removed and cut into 1/4-inch cubes
- 2-1/2 cups finely chopped peeled ripe pears
- 1/2 cup thinly sliced green onions
- 1/2 cup diced fully cooked ham
- 2 teaspoons lemon juice
- 1 garlic clove, minced
- Dash pepper
- 14 sheets phyllo dough inches x 9 inches)
- 3/4 cup butter, melted

Direction

- In a large bowl, combine the first eight ingredients; set aside.
- Place a piece of plastic wrap larger than a sheet of phyllo on a work surface. Place one phyllo sheet on plastic wrap; brush with butter. (Keep remaining phyllo covered until ready to use.) Repeat six times. Spread half of crab filling to within 1 in. of edges. Fold the two short sides over filling. Using the plastic wrap to lift one long side, roll up jelly-roll style.
- Transfer to a greased 15-in. x 10-in. x 1-in. baking pan; discard plastic wrap. Brush top with butter; score top lightly at 1-in. intervals. Repeat with remaining phyllo, butter and filling.
- Bake at 375° for 20-25 minutes or until golden brown. Let stand for 5 minutes. Cut into slices along scored lines. Yield: 2 dozen.

147. Cranberry Camembert Pizza Recipe

Serving: 12 | Prep: | Cook: 22mins | Ready in:

Ingredients

- 1 tube (13.8 ounces) refrigerated pizza crust
- 8 ounces Camembert or brie cheese rind removed and cut into 1/2 inch cubes
- 3/4 cup whole berry cranberry sauce
- 1/2 cup chopped pecans

Direction

- Unroll crust onto a lightly greased 12-inch pizza pan; flatten dough and build up edges slightly. Bake at 435 degrees for 10-12 minutes or until light golden brown.
- Sprinkle cheese over crust. Spoon cranberry sauce evenly over crust; sprinkle with pecans. Bake 8-10 minutes longer or until cheese is melted and crust is golden brown. Cool for 5 minutes before cutting.

148. Cranberry Crab Meat And Cream Cheese Appetizers Recipe

Serving: 15 | Prep: | Cook: 15mins | Ready in:

Ingredients

- 1/2 cup Ocean Spray® whole berry cranberry sauce
- 1/3 cup cream cheese, softened
- 1/4 cup minced crab meat
- 2 tablespoons green onion, white and green parts, sliced
- 15 individual mini-phyllo shells, thawed

Direction

- Preheat oven to 375°F (190°C).
- Place cranberry sauce in a small mixing bowl; beat with a fork or wire whisk until smooth.
- Combine cream cheese, crab meat and green onion in a small mixing bowl. Fill each shell with about 1 teaspoon of the cream cheese mixture. Top with 1/2 teaspoon cranberry sauce.
- Bake for 10 minutes or until heated through

149. Cranberry Rum Brie Recipe

Serving: 8 | Prep: | Cook: 5mins | Ready in:

Ingredients

- 1 round (8 ounces) brie cheese
- 1/3 cup crushed cranberry sauce
- 2 tablespoons packed brown sugar
- 1/4 teaspoon rum extract or Pure orange extract
- 1/8 teaspoon ground nutmeg
- 2 tablespoons chopped pecans
- Assorted crackers

Direction

- 1. Remove top rind of Brie to within 1/4 inch of edge all the way around.
- 2. Lightly coat cookie sheet with non-stick cooking spray and place Brie on cookie sheet. Set aside.
- 3. Combine cranberry sauce, brown sugar, rum or orange extract, and nutmeg in small bowl. Spread mixture over top of Brie to edge of rind and sprinkle with pecans.
- 5. Bake in 500 degree F oven 4 to 5 minutes.
- 6. Remove to serving dish with spatula, surround with assorted crackers and serve immediately.
- Makes 8 servings

150. Cranberry Almond Brie Recipe

Serving: 8 | Prep: | Cook: 20mins | Ready in:

Ingredients

- Pastry Ingredients:
- 3/4 cup all-purpose flour
- 1/4 cup butter, softened
- 1 (3-ounce) package cream cheese, softened
- Filling Ingredients:
- 1 (8-ounce) 4 1/4-inch diameter round brie cheese
- 3 tablespoons cranberry orange sauce
- 3 tablespoons chopped almonds, toasted
- Topping Ingredients:
- 1 egg
- 1 teaspoon water
- Dippers Ingredients:
- apple or pear slices
- crackers
- Added To Shopping List!

Direction

- Combine flour, butter and cream cheese in large bowl.
- Beat at low speed, scraping bowl often, until mixture leaves sides of bowl and forms a dough.
- Divide dough in half; wrap in plastic food wrap.
- Refrigerate until firm (1 hour).
- Heat oven to 400F.

- Roll each half of dough on lightly floured surface to 1/8-inch thickness.
- Cut 8-inch circle from each half (save dough scraps for decoration). Place 1 circle onto ungreased baking sheet.
- Place Brie on centre of pastry circle.
- Spread cranberry sauce over top of cheese; sprinkle with toasted almonds.
- Top with other pastry circle.
- Pinch edges of pastry to seal.
- Flute edges as desired
- . Decorate top with small pastry cut-outs.
- Beat egg with water in small bowl; brush top and sides of pastry. Bake for 15 to 20 minutes or until golden brown.
- Remove from baking sheet immediately.
- Let stand 30 minutes to allow cheese to set.
- Cut into small wedges. Serve with apple slices and crackers.
- TIP: Do not remove outer rind of the Brie cheese. It is acceptable to eat and keeps the cheese contained inside pastry.

151. Cream Cheese Puff Balls Recipe

Serving: 48 | Prep: | Cook: 31mins | Ready in:

Ingredients

- 2 packages of Pillsbury Refrigerated Crescent Dinner Rolls
- 1 package of cream cheese
- 1 package of hormel sliced pepperoni

Direction

- First you want to take out the crescent rolls, and then you will separate into the individual triangles.
- Then flatten each triangle and slice it.
- Now chop the pepperoni into small pieces.
- Then mix the pepperoni with the cream cheese, making sure the cream cheese is mixed well.
- Now take a little bit of your cream cheese/pepperoni mixture and place in the middle of one of your crescent rolls triangles.
- Now use your fingers and pinch up all of the sides around the filling.
- Then repeat and place them all on a baking sheet.
- Next bake around 11 min at 350 degrees.
- Note: You want them golden.
- Serve warm!

152. Crescent Wrapped Cranberry And Brie Recipe

Serving: 12 | Prep: | Cook: 30mins | Ready in:

Ingredients

- 1 (8 ounce 0 can Pillsbury Refrigerated Crescent Dinner Rolls
- 1 (8 ounce) round brie cheese
- 4 to 5 tablespoons whole - berry cranberry sauce
- 1 tablespoon chopped pecans
- 1 egg beaten
- 8 small seedless red and green grapes clusters
- 2 pears unpeeled and sliced
- 2 apples unpeeled and sliced

Direction

- Heat oven to 350 degrees f.; spray cookie sheet with non-stick cooking spray. Unroll crescent roll dough, separate dough crosswise into 2 sections, press dough to form 2 squares; firmly pressing perforations to seal.
- Cut corners off both dough squares and reserve to use for cut outs.
- Place 1 dough round on sprayed cookie sheet.
- Cut cheese crosswise into 2 equal layers. Place bottom half of cheese on centre of dough circle on cookie sheet; spread cranberry sauce over the cheese, sprinkle with chopped pecans.
- Top with remaining half of cheese.

- Bring dough up around side of cheese, pressing and pinching dough.
- With small cookie cutter or canapé cutter, cut shapes from reserved corners of dough; set aside place remaining dough on top of cheese round, press dough evenly around side of cheese;
- Brush dough with beaten egg. Top with cut-outs; and brush with additional beaten egg.
- Bake at 350 degrees for 20 to 30 minutes or until deep golden brown, cool 15 minutes before serving.
- To serve place warm pastry - wrapped cheese on platter, and surround it with the fruit. Use any fruit you like......

153. Crescent Dogs Recipe

Serving: 0 | Prep: | Cook: 13mins | Ready in:

Ingredients

- 8 hot dogs
- 4 slices American cheese, each cut into 6 strips
- 1 (8 ounce) can Pillsbury® refrigerated crescent dinner rolls

Direction

- Heat oven to 375 degrees F. Slit hot dogs to within 1/2 inch of ends; insert 3 strips of cheese into each slit.
- Separate dough into triangles. Wrap dough triangle around each hot dog. Place on ungreased cookie sheet, cheese side up.
- Bake 12-15 min or until golden brown.

154. Crescent Wrapped Brie Recipe

Serving: 12 | Prep: | Cook: 24mins | Ready in:

Ingredients

- 1 (8 ounce) can Pillsbury® refrigerated crescent dinner rolls
- 1 (8 ounce) round natural brie cheese
- 1 egg, beaten
- 48 water crackers or baguette French bread slices

Direction

- Heat oven to 350 degrees F.
- Unroll dough and separate crosswise into 2 sections; press dough into 2 squares, firmly pressing perforations to seal.
- Place cheese round on centre of 1 dough square.
- With small cookie or canapé cutter, cut 1 shape from each corner of remaining dough square; set cut-outs aside.
- Place remaining dough square on top of cheese round.
- Press dough evenly around cheese, folding bottom edges over top edges; press to seal completely.
- Place on ungreased cookie sheet. Brush dough with egg.
- Top with cut-outs; brush with egg.
- Bake 20 to 24 minutes or until golden brown.
- Remove from cookie sheet; place on serving plate.
- Cool 15 minutes.
- Serve warm with crackers

155. Crispy Parmesan Potato Wedges With Lemon Basil Dip Recipe

Serving: 12 | Prep: | Cook: 60mins | Ready in:

Ingredients

- potato WEDGES:
- 2 - 3 lbs potatoes
- EVOO

- coarse salt
- cracked black pepper
- Grated Parmesan
- DIP:
- 1.5 c Kraft Mayo
- 4 garlic cloves
- 1 T lemon juice
- handful fresh green basil
- handful fresh opal basil
- salt and pepper

Direction

- POTATO WEDGES:
- Preheat oven to 450
- Cut potatoes into thick wedges, (slice into bowl of ice water)
- Remove potatoes from water and place in large Ziploc baggie
- Drizzle with EVOO and seasonings
- Shake
- Pour onto baking sheet and bake 1 hour, or until done and edges are crispy
- DIP:
- Peel, crush, and chop garlic
- Tear both types of basil into small pieces
- Stir garlic, basil, and lemon into mayo
- Salt & Pepper to taste
- Transfer to serving bowl
- Cover with plastic wrap and chill until serving. (I make the dip, and let it chill while potatoes are baking, pull it out of the fried as soon as the potatoes are done).

156. Crispy Parmesan Wedges With Creamy Dipping Sauce Recipe

Serving: 4 | Prep: | Cook: 40mins | Ready in:

Ingredients

- 300g sweet potatoes cut into wedges (i don't peel- just scrub)
- 300g sebago potatoes cut into wedges (scrubbed but not peeled)
- 1 tbsp olive oil
- sea salt, cracked black pepper, chili flakes
- 2 tsp thyme leaves
- 1/3 cup parmesan, finely grated
- Sauce:
- 1/4 cup sour cream or natural yoghurt
- 1/4 cup whole egg mayonnaise
- 1 clove gralic- peeled and crushed
- 2 tsp lemon juice

Direction

- Preheat oven to 200degC
- Sauce: combine sauce ingredients and set aside
- Place wedges on baking tray and sprinkle with oil. Toss to coat and roast 30mins.
- Sprinkle seasoning and parmesan over the potato wedges and roast a further 10 mins or until the parmesan is crispy and golden brown.

157. Crunchy Nacho Dogs Recipe

Serving: 4 | Prep: | Cook: 22mins | Ready in:

Ingredients

- 1 can refrigerated crescent dinner rolls
- 4 slices of American cheese.or your choice
- 4 hot dogs
- 1 tablespoon milk
- 1/2 cup crushed Doritos nacho -cheese-flavored tortilla chips

Direction

- Preheat oven to 375 degrees F; lightly grease a cookie sheet. Separate dough into 4 rectangles; press perforations to seal.
- Place cheese slices on rectangles; place hot dog in centre of each; fold short sides of dough over hot dogs; roll up each. Press edges

together to seal. Brush rolls with milk; then roll in crushed chips. Place rolls, seam side down, on greased cookie sheet.

- Bake at 375 degrees F for 15 to 22 minutes or until deep golden brown. , remove to plates and cut in half or leave whole.
- Serve with ketchup, mustard or salsa or sour cream

158. Crème De Brie Stuffed Mushrooms Recipe

Serving: 24 | Prep: | Cook: 30mins | Ready in:

Ingredients

- 24 large mushrooms
- 2 tbsp. extra virgin olive oil
- 1 stalk celery, diced
- ½ red pepper, diced
- 2 tbsp. drained non pareil capers
- 1/8 tsp. dried thyme or 1/4 tsp. of fresh thyme
- 1/8 tsp. dried oregano leaves or 1/4 tsp. or fresh thyme
- salt and pepper to taste
- 2 pkgs. (5 oz.) Alouette Crème de Brie, Original

Direction

- Preheat oven to 350° F.
- Wash mushrooms thoroughly. Remove stems and set aside.
- Place cap (hollow) side down into a shallow baking dish. Brush the bottom and sides of the mushroom caps lightly with oil and bake for 15 minutes in the preheated oven.
- Chop the mushroom stems finely and sauté in olive oil with diced celery and peppers for 5 minutes.
- Stir in the capers and season to taste with the thyme, oregano, salt and pepper.
- Remove mushrooms from oven, and fill with mixture and top with 1 tbsp. of the Brie. Broil on the top rack of the oven for 3-4 minutes until cheese is browned and bubbly.

159. Curry Cheese Dip Recipe

Serving: 1 | Prep: | Cook: 30mins | Ready in:

Ingredients

- 1 cup sharp cheddar cheese, shredded
- 1 cup mayonnaise
- 1 cup onions, chopped
- 1/4 cup green bell peppers, chopped
- 1/2 tsp fresh dill weed
- 1/4 - 1/2 tsp curry powder

Direction

- Mix ingredients and put in oven proof bowl.
- Bake at 325 degrees for 30-40 minutes.
- Serve with corn chips and crackers

160. Diabetic EGGPLANT PARMESAN Recipe

Serving: 6 | Prep: | Cook: 68mins | Ready in:

Ingredients

- olive oil spray
- 1 eggplant (about 1-1/2 pounds)
- 1 teaspoon olive oil
- 8 ounces fresh mushrooms, sliced (2 to 2-1/2 cups)
- 1 cup chopped onions (2 medium)
- 3 or 4 medium cloves garlic, minced, or 1-1/2 to 2
- teaspoons bottled minced garlic
- 1/2 teaspoon salt-free dried Italian herb seasoning,
- crumbled
- 1/4 teaspoon salt

- pepper to taste
- 8-ounce can no-salt-added tomato sauce
- 4 ounces fat-free or park-skim mozzarella cheese,
- shredded (1 cup)
- 1 ounce (1/4 cup) grated or shredded parmesan cheese

Direction

- 1. Preheat broiler. Spray a baking sheet, 13x9x2-inch baking pan, and 11x15-inch piece of aluminum foil with olive oil spray.
- 2. Peel eggplant and cut crosswise into 1/4-inch slices.
- Put on baking sheet and broil 6 inches from heat for 2 to 3 minutes on each side. Remove from broiler and set oven to 375 degrees F.
- 3. Heat oil in a large non-stick skillet over medium heat, swirling to coat bottom. Add mushrooms, onions, garlic, herb seasoning, and salt. Cook, covered, for 7 to 9 minutes, stirring occasionally. Increase heat to high and cook, uncovered, for 2 to 3 minutes, or until pan juices have evaporated, stirring frequently.
- 4. Spread 1 cup mushroom mixture in baking pan. Cover with half of eggplant slices. Sprinkle with pepper.
- Top with 1/2 cup tomato sauce and half the mozzarella. Repeat layers except cheese. Cover with prepared foil.
- 5. Bake for 1 hour. Top with remaining mozzarella and all the Parmesan. Bake, uncovered, for 5 to 8 minutes, or until cheese is melted. Cool for at least 10 minutes before cutting.
- Nutritional Information per Serving:
- Calories: 118; Fat: 3 grams; Carbohydrates: 15 grams;
- Protein: 10 grams; Sodium: 372 mg; Cholesterol: 5 mg
- Exchanges: 2 Vegetable; 1 Bread/Starch; 1 Low-Fat Meat

161. Dried Cherries Pecans And Rosemary Brie En Croute Recipe

Serving: 12 | Prep: | Cook: 20mins | Ready in:

Ingredients

- 1/2 (17.3 ounce) package puff pastry sheets
- 1 large egg
- 1 tablespoon water
- 1/3 cup dried cherries, softened by soaking in water to cover
- 1/4 cup toasted pecans
- 1/4 cup honey
- 1/2 teaspoon fresh rosemary leaves, finely chopped
- 1 (13.2 ounce) round brie cheese
- 16 ounce box of crackers

Direction

- Thaw the pastry sheet at room temperature for40 minutes OR until it is easy to handle.
- Heat oven to 400 degrees F.
- Beat and water together in a small bowl.
- Unfold pastry sheet on a lightly floured surface.
- Roll the sheet into a 14" square.
- Drain the cherries.
- Stir the cherries, pecans, honey and rosemary in a small bowl.
- Spread the mixture in the centre of the pastry square.
- Top with the round of Brie cheese.
- Brush the edges of the pastry with the egg mixture.
- Fold two opposite sides of the pastry over the cheese.
- Trim the remaining two sides of the pastry square to 2" from the edge of the cheese.
- Fold the sides up onto the cheese and press the edges to seal.
- Place the pastry-wrapped cheese seam-side down onto a baking sheet.
- Brush the pastry with the egg mixture.

- Decorate the top with pastry scraps or additional rosemary, if desired.
- Brush the pastry with the egg mixture.
- Bake for 20 to 25 minutes OR until pastry is deep golden brown.
- Remove from oven.
- Allow to stand for 45 minutes to an hour.
- Serve with fancy entertaining crackers.
- **OMG, I can't wait!

162. Easy Baked Mozzarella Sticks Recipe

Serving: 8 | Prep: | Cook: 15mins | Ready in:

Ingredients

- 1 pkg. mozzarella cheese strings (8 sticks)
- 2 tbsp flour
- 2 large egg whites, lightly beaten
- 1 cup dry bread crumbs, cracker crumbs, cornflake crumbs, or panko (Japanese bread crumbs)
- salt and pepper to taste
- marinara sauce for dipping

Direction

- Place the cheese strings in the freezer at least 1 hour before you plan to make these. These will lessen the oozing of the cheese. Preheat oven to 400ºF.
- Place the flour, egg whites and crumbs in 3 separate dishes. Season the flour with salt and pepper. Cut the cheese strings in 1/2 width wise. Dip one cheese stick at a time into the flour to coat, then into the egg whites and then the crumbs. Dip it into the egg again and then the crumbs again, squeezing to help them adhere. It'll be messy, but try to cover the cheese completely. Place on a cookie sheet lined with parchment or sprayed with cooking spray. Repeat with all of the cheese.
- Bake for 10 to 15 minutes, until golden. Serve immediately with warmed marinara sauce.

163. Easy Cheese Stuffed Jalapenos

Serving: 10 | Prep: | Cook: 15mins | Ready in:

Ingredients

- 24 medium fresh jalapeno peppers
- 1 package (8 ounces) cream cheese, softened
- 3 cups finely shredded cheddar cheese
- 1-1/2 teaspoons Worcestershire sauce
- 4 bacon strips, cooked and crumbled

Direction

- Preheat oven to 400°. Cut jalapenos in half lengthwise; remove seeds and membranes. In a large saucepan, boil peppers in water for 5-10 minutes (the longer you boil the peppers, the milder they become). Drain and rinse in cold water; set aside.
- In a small bowl, beat the cream cheese, cheddar cheese and Worcestershire sauce until smooth. Spoon 2 teaspoonfuls into each jalapeno; sprinkle with bacon. Arrange on greased baking sheets. Bake until filling is warmed, 3-5 minutes.
- Note: Wear disposable gloves when cutting hot peppers; the oils can burn skin. Avoid touching your face.
- Nutrition Facts
- 1 piece: 141 calories, 12g fat (8g saturated fat), 39mg cholesterol, 200mg sodium, 3g carbohydrate (0 sugars, 1g fiber), 6g protein.

164. Easy Chili Cheese Frito Nachos Recipe

Serving: 8 | Prep: | Cook: 5mins | Ready in:

Ingredients

- Your Favorite chili (Mo Meaty chili, posted)
- Fritos Scoops
- 2 c Mexican Blend shredded cheese
- Garnishes: sour cream, green onion, black olives, chopped tomatoes, jalepenos

Direction

- Preheat oven to 400
- Place Fritos on oven safe pan
- Cover with chili and cheese
- Bake about 4 minutes
- Serve with garnishes

165. Easy Frito Taco Nachos Recipe

Serving: 6 | Prep: | Cook: 4mins | Ready in:

Ingredients

- 25 Frito Lays Scoops or more
- 1 lb. 93% lean ground beef or chicken
- 1 Package of taco seasoning
- 1 t cumin
- seasoned salt
- garlic pepper
- 1 T worcestershire
- 2 T dry ranch seasoning (optional)
- 1/2 onion, chopped
- 1/2 red bell bepper, chopped (or yellow, green, or all 3)
- 1small can green chiles, drained
- 1/4 c water or beef stock
- 1-2 cup Mexican fine shredded cheese
- 1/2 cup salsa, hot, or mild which ever you prefer.
- Chopped fresh tomatoes
- Chopped black olives
- Sliced jalepenos
- 3 green onions
- small carton sourcream

Direction

- Slice the green onions and stir into the sour cream
- Preheat oven to 400 degrees.
- Brown ground beef with seasonings, onion, pepper(s), and chiles.
- Add stock once all pink colour disappears and veggies are soft
- Arrange Fritos on oven safe pan
- Add ground beef first then salsa then cheese.
- Bake in oven for 3-4 mins.
- Serve with a dollop of sour cream/green onion topping, tomatoes, olives and jalapeños as desired.

166. Easy Hot Artichoke & Jalapeno Cheese Dip With Or Without Spinach Recipe

Serving: 25 | Prep: | Cook: 45mins | Ready in:

Ingredients

- 1 can of artichoke hearts, in water, drained quartered and diced into bite size pieces
- 1/2 - 1 can of roasted, diced jalapenos
- 1 8 oz. pkg. cream cheese, softened
- 4 oz. grated Parmesan cheese, extra for top
- 1 cup mayonnaise
- 1 box of chopped, well drained chopped spinach, if desired

Direction

- Preheat oven to 350 degrees. Mix cream cheese with mayonnaise. Stir in Parmesan cheese, artichoke hearts and 1/2 - 1 can of jalapeno peppers (add spinach at this point, if desired). Spread into a 10 X 8 glass dish, greased or sprayed with baking spray. Sprinkle a little extra Parmesan on top. Bake until lightly brown around edges and middle, approximately 25 minutes. Serve with fresh cubed French bread, crackers, or tortilla chips.

167. Easy Pesto Brie Recipe

Serving: 8 | Prep: | Cook: 4mins | Ready in:

Ingredients

- 1 8 oz. Brie wheel
- 2 tablespoons pesto sauce
- 2 tablespoons Dijon mustard
- 1/2 cup chopped tomatoes
- 1/4 cup chopped walnuts
- fresh basil for garnish

Direction

- Oven 350.
- Blend together pesto and mustard and set aside.
- Cut Brie in half and place 1 half on a greased baking sheet.
- Spread Brie with half of the pesto mixture, top with other half of Brie and top with rest of mixture. Sprinkle nuts over top and bake 4 minutes. Garnish top with tomatoes and fresh basil. Fast, easy and pretty!

168. Eggplant Parmesan Recipe

Serving: 6 | Prep: | Cook: 45mins | Ready in:

Ingredients

- Ingredients:
- 5 eggplants, cut into 1/4 inch slices
- salt
- 1/4 vegetable oil
- 250 grams ricotta cheese
- 6 ounces shredded mozzarella cheese
- 1/4 cup grated parmesan cheese
- 1 egg, beaten
- 1/4 cup chopped fresh basil
- 1 liter pasta sauce

Direction

- Directions
- 1 Fry eggplant slices to a light brown using vegetable oil.
- 2 Preheat oven to 350 degrees F (175 degrees C). In a medium bowl, mix the ricotta, mozzarella cheese and 1/4 cup Parmesan cheese. Mix in egg and basil.
- 3 In a lasagna baking dish, evenly spread spaghetti sauce. Arrange a single layer of eggplant slices on top of the sauce. Top the eggplant with 1/2 of the cheese mixture. Repeat layering process until all the eggplant and cheese mixture is used. Pour remaining sauce on top of layers, and sprinkle with remaining Parmesan cheese.
- 5 Bake 30 to 45 minutes in the preheated oven, until sauce is bubbly.

169. Elaines Bacon Cheese Pastry Appetizers Recipe

Serving: 4 | Prep: | Cook: 25mins | Ready in:

Ingredients

- 8 slices partly cooked lean bacon
- 8 pieces puff pastry, about 3 oz in size each
- 16 thin slices old cheddar cheese

Direction

- Roll dough between the palms of your hands to form a 'cigar' shape
- Place one piece of cheddar at either end, pressing down to hug the pastry
- Leave the middle space of the pastry open
- Place one piece of bacon on top of the cheese
- Fold the package in half, sandwich style
- Bake @ 350*F 20-25 minutes, or until golden brown.

170. Emily's Pizza Fries Recipe

Serving: 8 | Prep: | Cook: 30mins | Ready in:

Ingredients

- 1 bag of french fries
- 1 cup pizza sauce
- 2 cups mozzarella cheese
- sliced pepperoni

Direction

- Bake fries according to bag
- Drizzle pizza sauce and mozzarella cheese and pepperoni, if adding
- Bake another 5-10 minutes or till cheese melts
- Watch kid chow down!

171. Fab Brie Phyllo Dough Wrap Recipe

Serving: 68 | Prep: | Cook: 20mins | Ready in:

Ingredients

- Brie triangle
- 4-5 sheets phyllo dough
- 1/2 stick butter
- 2 cups mushrooms diced (I use baby bellas)
- little bit of flour to make mushroom pate

Direction

- Place diced mushrooms in sauté pan with 1/2 stick of butter melted and sauté, add a little flour to make a pate - like paste consistency
- Place brie on 2 sheets of phyllo dough and spread mushroom pate over and wrap with rest of sheets.
- Place in a shallow baking dish (as it can get a little oozy) and bake for 20 minutes at 325-350. Check at 15 min to see how it is doing!
- Enjoy! Please let me know how you LOVE this!!

172. Fabulous Party Hors D Oeuvre Warm Fruited Brie Recipe

Serving: 24 | Prep: | Cook: 30mins | Ready in:

Ingredients

- Ingredients:
- 1 Pkg. (15-oz) refrigerated all-ready piecrust
- 2 Lb. Wheel brie cheese, about 8 inches in diameter
- 2 apples, cored and sliced
- 1 cup seedless green grapes
- ½ pint raspberries
- 1 cup apple juice
- 1 Tbs. cornstarch
- all-purpose flour as needed

Direction

- 1) Preheat oven to 400F. On a large baking sheet, unfold one piecrust. Place Brie in centre of piecrust. Turn under edge of piecrust to within ½ -inch of cheese and decoratively flute edge. Remove Brie and set aside.
- 2) Prick piecrust with fork to prevent pastry from puffing while it is baking. Place baking sheet on centre rack of oven and bake piecrust for 10 minutes; remove from oven. Lightly flour a wooden board, marble slab or other working surface.
- 3) Unfold the second piecrust and place on floured board. With tip of a paring knife, cut four 2-inch-long oval-shaped leaves; mark veins on leaves with back of the knife. Place leaves on a baking sheet; bake 5 minutes or until golden brown. Transfer to a wire rack to cool.
- 4) Lower oven temperature to 350F. Place Brie on fluted piecrust. Arrange apple slices around the top edge of cheese; place grapes

and raspberries in the centre. Return fruit-topped Brie to oven and bake 10 minutes.

- 5) Meanwhile, in a small saucepan, blend apple juice and cornstarch. Bring to boiling over moderately high heat and cook, stirring constantly, for 1 minute or until mixture is clear and thick. Remove saucepan from heat.
- 6) Remove Brie from oven and arrange pastry leaves on top. Brush leaves and fruit with apple juice glaze. Allow to stand 15 minutes, until cheese softens. Carefully transfer to a serving board. Cut into wedges to serve. Makes 24 wedges.
- Nutritional Values per Serving: Calories: 208, Protein: 9g, Carbohydrate: 11g, Fat: 15g, Cholesterol: 38mg, Sodium: 346mg.
- Note: This is a Diabetic Friendly and a low carbohydrate for the dieter.

173. Family Size Italian Club Calzone Recipe

Serving: 0 | Prep: | Cook: 52mins | Ready in:

Ingredients

- 12 Rhodes™ dinner rolls, thawed to room temperature
- 1 tablespoon dry Italian salad dressing mix
- 3 tablespoons olive oil, divided
- 2-3 cloves fresh garlic, minced
- ½ red onion, thinly sliced
- 1 ½ cups sliced fresh mushrooms
- ½ of a 6 ounce jar marinated artichoke hearts
- ¼ pound deli turkey breast
- ¼ pound deli ham
- 10 slices cooked bacon
- 1 cup grated swiss cheese
- 1 tablespoon chopped fresh basil

Direction

- Spray counter lightly with non-stick cooking spray.
- Combine rolls together and roll into a 10X16-inch rectangle.
- Cover with plastic wrap and let rest.
- Combine 1 tablespoon salad dressing mix with 1 tablespoon of the olive oil and set aside.
- Heat ½ tablespoon oil in the same skillet and add mushrooms and garlic.
- Sauté until mushrooms are full cooked.
- Drain on paper towel and set aside.
- Slice artichoke hearts and drain on paper towel.
- Remove plastic wrap from dough and brush with salad dressing and oil mixture avoiding the edges of the dough.
- If the ham and turkey are moist, pat dry with a paper towel.
- Layer half of the lengthwise dough with turkey, ham, bacon, onions, mushrooms, artichoke hearts, cheese and basil. Wet the edge of the dough with the fillings on it.
- Fold the other half of the dough over the filled half and pinch the edges to seal.
- Cut some vent holes on the top and brush with the remaining olive oil.
- Cover with sprayed plastic wrap and let right 20-30 minutes. Bake at 375°F 20-25 minutes.

174. Feta Artichoke Dip Recipe

Serving: 46 | Prep: | Cook: 30mins | Ready in:

Ingredients

- 1 minced clove of garlic
- 1 14 oz can of drained artichoke hearts, chopped
- 1 2 oz jar of diced pimentos, drained
- 8 oz of crumbled feta cheese
- 1 c of mayonnaise
- 1/2 c of shredded parmesan cheese
- 3 chopped green onions (optional)
- 1 chopped tomatoe (optional)

Direction

- Let's start by preheating your oven at 350 F
- Grab you large mixing bowl and stir in all the ingredients.
- Take the mixture and pour it into a pie pan.
- You want to bake it for about 20-25 minutes or until it's slightly brown.
- If you want a little colour you could add some tomatoes or even onions on top.
- Goes great with tortilla chips, pita bread, crackers and a bagel.

175. Feta Baked In Eggplant Recipe

Serving: 12 | Prep: | Cook: 10mins | Ready in:

Ingredients

- 3 large eggplants (eggplants get smaller after baking)
- some parsley
- 3 garlic cloves
- olive oil
- 3 teaspoon vinegar
- 10 oz feta
- 5 tablespoon breadcrumbs
- salt and pepper

Direction

- Poke eggplant skins slightly with a fork. Grill for 15 minutes.
- Mince the garlic. Roughly chop the parsley.
- Crumble your feta cheese if it needs crumbling. Put bread crumbs, feta and garlic into bowl. Use your hands to toss everything together, mixing it well.
- When eggplants are finished, cut each of them in half. Break its flesh slightly with your knife. There should be a total of 6 long eggplant logs. Add just a pinch of salt and a bit more pepper on each half. Drizzle olive oil over each half generously.
- Put halves on baking sheet. Layer chopped parsley (evenly distributed) across each half. Layer feta onto each half evenly. Bake at 390°F for 10 minutes. When they are browned, pour some vinegar and olive oil over each half. SERVING SUGGESTION: Serve each side by side on a long serving platter. Sprinkle some chopped parsley across the eggplants.

176. Feta Cheese Appetizers Recipe

Serving: 50 | Prep: | Cook: 10mins | Ready in:

Ingredients

- 1/2 pound cream cheese
- 1/2 pound feta cheese
- 2 to 2-1/2 tablespoons cream or milk
- 1 package Greek phyllo pastry
- 1 stick butter, melted

Direction

- Blend the cheeses and cream until smooth.
- Using 4 leaves of phyllo, brush melted butter onto first leaf, place second on top of it and brush that; continue until all 4 leaves are buttered.
- Cut leaves into 3-inch squares with scissors.
- Place 1 tablespoon cheese mixture in the centre of each square and fold up like an envelope.
- Continue until mixture is used up.
- Brush with melted butter to seal.
- Cover carefully with foil and freeze until ready to use.
- Place uncovered on a cookie sheet straight from freezer and bake at 350 degrees F until phyllo is brown and crisp -- about 10 or more minutes.

177. Feta Cheese Foldovers Recipe

Serving: 12 | Prep: | Cook: 20mins | Ready in:

Ingredients

- 1/2 pound feta cheese, crumbled
- 3 T green onion, finely chopped
- 1 egg, beaten
- 1 (17.5 oz). pkg. frozen puffed pastry, thawed
- 1 egg yolk, beaten
- 1 tsp water

Direction

- Preheat oven to 375 degrees
- In a small bowl, mix feta, green onions & egg
- Cut pastry into twelve 3 inch squares
- Place a mounded tablespoon of feta mixture in the centre of each square. Moisten edges with water and fold pastry over forming a triangle.
- Press edges together firmly with a fork to seal
- In a small bowl, mix egg yolk and water. Lightly brush pastries with the egg mixture.
- Bake in the preheated oven for 20 minutes or until golden brown
- Serve warm or at room temperature

178. Feta Cheese Stuffed Pastry Bundles Recipe

Serving: 4 | Prep: | Cook: 20mins | Ready in:

Ingredients

- feta cheese Stuffed Pastry Bundles
- 2 square sheets puff pastry
- 1 egg yolk
- 2 teaspoons poppy seeds
- 1/2 cup feta cheese
- 1 tablespoon flat leaf parsley chopped finely
- 1 tablespoon dill chopped finely
- 1 teaspoon pepper flakes

Direction

- Smash feta with the back of a fork.
- Mix with parsley, dill and pepper flakes.
- Divide each puff pastry into 9 equal squares.
- Place some feta cheese filling into each pastry and fold into bundles.
- Brush with beaten egg yolk and put black seeds on top.
- Bake at 400 until golden brown.

179. Feta Cheese Tomato Amp Onion Torte Recipe

Serving: 8 | Prep: | Cook: 30mins | Ready in:

Ingredients

- 1 pasty crust (9 inch not in shell - Pillsbury ready made pie crust works very well)
- 1 lb Italian plum tomatoes - thinly sliced
- 1/2 lb swiss cheese - shredded
- 1/8 cup spicy mustard
- 1 medium onion - sliced
- 6 - 8 oz feta cheese (I use herbed feta)
- Marinade:
- 1/2 cup fresh parsley
- 3 cloves garlic
- 1 cup vegetable oil
- 2 tsp dried basil
- 2 tsp salt
- 1 tsp dried oregano
- 1 tsp dried thyme
- Freshly ground pepper

Direction

- Marinade:
- In food processor, chop parsley and garlic until minced.
- Add remaining marinade ingredients and pulse to make marinade. Place sliced tomatoes and onions in plastic container with lid. Refrigerate for at least six hours.
- Be sure to turn container a few times.

- Preheat oven to 350 degrees.
- Place pastry in 9 inch spring form pan (torte or cheesecake pan). Use pie weights or poke pastry with fork so it does not bubble.
- Bake pasty for 5 - 8 minutes.
- Do not let pastry brown.
- Remove pastry from oven.
- Let cool.
- Spread spicy mustard evenly on pastry.
- Sprinkle shredded cheese evenly over mustard.
- Arrange marinated onions over cheese.
- Arrange marinated tomatoes over onions.
- Sprinkle Feta cheese over tomatoes.
- Bake for 25 - 35 minutes.
- Remove and place on wire rack.
- Let stand for 10 minutes.
- Use pizza cutter to slice.

180. Feta Cheesecake Recipe

Serving: 32 | Prep: | Cook: 35mins | Ready in:

Ingredients

- CRUST:
- 1 1/3 cups sesame cracker crumbs
- 1/4 cup parmesan cheese, shredded
- 1/3 cup butter, melted
- FILLING:
- 16 ounces cream cheese, softened
- 8 ounces feta cheese with basil and tomato
- 3 large eggs
- 1/2 cup pitted ripe olives, drained and chopped
- 1/3 cup green onions, chopped
- 1 teaspoon dried oregano leaves
- 1/2 teaspoon coarse ground black pepper
- 1/4 teaspoon garlic salt
- TOPPING:
- 2 medium roma tomatoes, finely chopped
- 1/3 cup green onions, chopped

Direction

- Preheat oven to 325 degrees F.
- Combine crust ingredients and press on bottom and up sides of an Ungreased 9" springform pan OR a 9" foil-lined round pan with 1" foil overhang to aid in cake removal.
- Combine cream cheese and feta in a large bowl.
- Beat at medium speed, scraping bowl often, until creamy.
- Add eggs, beating until just combined.
- Stir in all remaining filling ingredients.
- Pour into crust.
- Bake for 35 to 40 minutes OR until just set at 3" distance from pan edge.
- Remove from oven.
- Cool for 15 minutes.
- Loosen sides of springform.
- Cool on wire rack for 2 hours.
- Loosely cover.
- Refrigerate at least 2 hours.
- To serve, cut into wedges.
- Top each wedge with tomato and green onion.
- Serve with cracker, if desired.
- Refrigerate leftovers.
- **Check cheesecakes at minimum bake time for doneness by gently shaking (I tap side with knife) the pan. If the centre still jiggles and the edges appear firm, the cheesecake is done. Cheesecakes continue to set as they cool.

181. Feta Stuffed Baby Portabella Mushrooms Recipe

Serving: 6 | Prep: | Cook: 20mins | Ready in:

Ingredients

- 24 oz baby portabella mushrooms
- 2 cups crumbled feta cheese
- 1/4 cup finely chopped Italian parsley
- 1/2 cup crushed walnuts
- shredded parmesan cheese (the fresh shredded kind, not the powdered kind)

Direction

- Clean mushrooms and remove stems
- Hollow out the center of the mushrooms (allowing the mushrooms to fully dry will make this much easier!)
- Preheat oven to 350 degrees.
- Combine walnuts, Feta and parsley in a bowl, squeezing mixture together.
- Lightly spray a glass baking dish with oil or baking spray.
- Use a small spoon to fill the mushroom cap with the cheese mixture and place, flat side down, in the baking dish.
- Sprinkle a pinch of grated parmesan on top of each mushroom cap.
- Bake for 20 minute or until cheese is melted.
- Can be served hot or cold.

182. Feta Stuffed Portabello Caps Recipe

Serving: 4 | Prep: | Cook: 10mins | Ready in:

Ingredients

- 4 portabello mushrooms
- 1/2 - 1 cup feta cheese, crumbled
- 2 tbsp oregano
- balsamic vinegar
- olive oil

Direction

- Remove stems from mushroom and place bottom up on cookie sheet covered with foil.
- Fill the center of each cap with feta cheese.
- Add a sprinkle of oregano.
- Drizzle with olive oil and balsamic vinegar to taste.
- Bake in 400 degree oven until feta is softened (about 10 mins).

183. Feta Turnovers Recipe

Serving: 36 | Prep: | Cook: 15mins | Ready in:

Ingredients

- Dough:
- 1 cup butter
- 1 pkg. cream cheese
- 2 cups flour
- 1 egg yolk
- 1 Tbsp heavy cream
- Filling:
- 8 oz feta
- 1 to 2 Tbsp cream
- 1/8 tsp nutmeg
- 1/4 cup chopped parsley
- 1/4 tsp pepper
- 1/8 tsp dried mint leaves

Direction

- Dough:
- Blend butter and cream cheese.
- Cut in flour and mix well.
- Divide pastry in half and roll into balls.
- Wrap in wax paper and chill for four hours.
- Roll pastry between two sheets of wax paper to 1/4" thickness.
- Remove top layer of wax paper and cut into 2 1/2" rounds.
- Filling:
- Soften feta with cream.
- Add remaining ingredients and mix well.
- Place 1 tsp. filling at one side of the round and fold over; seal edges.
- Continue with remaining rounds.
- Brush each turnover with egg yolk that is lightly beaten with 1 Tbsp. heavy cream.
- Prick tops of turnovers with fork.
- Place on lightly greased baking sheet.
- Bake at 425 degrees for 12 to 15 minutes.
- Serve warm.

184. Fig & Stilton Savory Thumbprint Cookies Recipe

Serving: 0 | Prep: | Cook: 30mins | Ready in:

Ingredients

- 1 cup all-purpose flour
- 1/2 cup unsalted butter, room temperature
- 4 ounces stilton blue cheese, crumbled
- freshly ground rainbow peppercorns
- fig preserves (or quince)

Direction

- Preheat the oven to 350 degrees. Line a baking sheet with parchment paper.
- Place the flour, butter, blue cheese and a few grinds of black pepper in the bowl of a food processor. Process until the dough just comes together and starts to form a ball.
- Dump the dough onto a lightly floured surface and knead a few times to pull the dough together. Roll out to 1/8 inch thick with a floured rolling pin. Cut rounds out of the dough with a floured 1-inch cutter and transfer the rounds to the parchment-lined baking sheet.
- Using the back or a round half-teaspoon measure or your thumb, make an indentation in the top of each dough round. Spoon about ¼ teaspoon of fig preserves into each indentation, using your spoon/finger to push the preserves as best as possible into the indentations.
- Bake the savouries for 14-16 minutes, until the preserves are bubbling and the pastry is light golden on the bottom. Let cool on the baking sheet for at least 10 minutes, the remove to a wire rack to cool.
- You can make these a day ahead and keep them in two layers separated by waxed paper in an airtight container.

185. Fig And Toasted Almond Brie Recipe

Serving: 12 | Prep: | Cook: 25mins | Ready in:

Ingredients

- 1/2 cup brown sugar
- 2 tablespoons water
- 6 fresh figs, stemmed and quartered
- 1 (14 ounce) round 4 1/4" diameter brie cheese
- 1/2 cup toasted almonds
- 1/2 teaspoon vanilla extract

Direction

- Preheat oven to 325 degrees F (165 degrees C).
- Heat brown sugar and water in a small saucepan over medium heat until sugar is completely dissolved.
- Add figs and cook until softened, about 10 minutes.
- Stir in almonds and vanilla extract.
- Place Brie wheel in a baking dish.
- Pour fig mixture over top.
- Bake for 10 to 15 minutes OR until softened but not melted.
- Serve with crackers.

186. Fontina And Asparagus Tart Recipe

Serving: 24 | Prep: | Cook: 20mins | Ready in:

Ingredients

- 1 lb. fresh asparagus, trimmed
- 1 sheet frozen puff pastry, thawed
- 1/2 lb. Fontina cheese, shredded, divided
- 2 tbls. lemon juice
- 1 tbls. olive oil
- 1 tsp. grated lemon peel
- 1/4 tsp. salt
- 1/4 tsp. pepper

Direction

- Preheat oven to 400
- In a large skillet, bring 1 in. of water to a boil, then add asparagus Cover and cook 3 minutes or so, until crisp tender, then drain
- On floured surface, roll out pastry to 12 x 16 rectangle
- Transfer to parchment paper lined baking sheet
- Bake 10 minutes and remove from oven
- Sprinkle 1 1/2 cups cheese over pastry
- Arrange asparagus on top of cheese
- Sprinkle with remaining cheese
- Combine lemon juice, olive oil, lemon peel, salt and pepper
- Sprinkle over top
- Bake 10-15 minutes or until asparagus is tender and cheese is melted
- Slice and serve warm

187. Fresh Mozzarella And Tomato Crostini Recipe

Serving: 8 | Prep: | Cook: 18mins |Ready in:

Ingredients

- Ingredients:
- extra-virgin olive oil for brushing, plus 1/4 cup
- 1 baguette, cut crosswise into 1/4-inch-thick
- slices
- salt and coarsely ground pepper, to taste
- 8 vine-ripened tomatoes, about 1 1/2 lb. total
- 1/2 cup slivered fresh basil leaves
- 2 Tbs. finely minced red onion
- 1/4 tsp. minced garlic
- 1 Tbs. aged balsamic vinegar
- 1 1/2 lb. fresh mozzarella cheese

Direction

- Preheat oven to 350.
- Brush a baking sheet with olive oil and arrange the baguette slices on the sheet in a single layer. Brush the tops with oil, and season with salt and pepper. Bake until crisp and golden, 15 to 18 minutes. If not using immediately, let the crostini cool, then store in an airtight container at room temperature until ready to use.
- Core, seed and dice the tomatoes. In a bowl, stir together the tomatoes, half of the basil, the onion, garlic, vinegar, the 1/4 cup olive oil, salt and pepper.
- Slice the mozzarella into 1/4-inch-thick pieces or into smaller pieces so they fit on the crostini. To assemble, lay a piece of mozzarella on each crostini and spoon 1 to 2 Tbs. of the tomato salad on top. Garnish each with a pinch of the remaining basil. Serve immediately.

188. Fun Do Fondue Recipe

Serving: 6 | Prep: | Cook: 30mins |Ready in:

Ingredients

- --Bread--
- 1 pkg. active dry yeast
- 1 cup warm water, 110*
- 1 cup mashed potato flakes
- 1 Tbsp. sugar
- 2 Tbsp. cooking oil
- 1 tsp. salt
- 1 egg
- 1 3/4 to 2 cups flour
- 3 Tbsp. sesame seeds
- milk
- -----------------------
- --Fondue--
- 4 cups (1 lb.) shredded swiss cheese
- 1/4 cup flour
- 1/4 tsp. salt
- 1/4 tsp. nutmeg
- Dash of pepper

- 1 clove garlic
- 2 cups white wine
- 2 Tbsp. kirch, if desired

Direction

- --Bread--
- Soften yeast in warm water. Blend in potato flakes, sugar, oil, salt and egg. Add flour gradually to form a stiff dough. Knead on floured surface until smooth, about 1 minute. Place in a greased bowl. Cover; let rise in a warm place until light and doubled, about 1 hour. Sprinkle 1 Tbsp. sesame seeds on greased cookie sheet. Place dough on cookie sheet and press out with your fingers to a 14x10" rectangle. Brush with milk; sprinkle with 2 Tbsp. sesame seed. Cover and let rise, about 45 minutes.
- Preheat oven to 400* and bake for 15-18 minutes until golden brown. Remove to cooling rack. Cool. Cut into 1" squares

189. Garlic Cheddar Biscuits Recipe

Serving: 8 | Prep: | Cook: 10mins | Ready in:

Ingredients

- 2 cups Bisquick
- 2/3 cup milk
- 2/3 cup cheddar cheese
- 1 tsp garlic powder, divided
- ¼ cup butter, melted

Direction

- Preheat oven to 450, or 475 for high altitude
- In a medium bowl, mix together the Bisquick, milk, cheese, and ½ tsp. garlic powder; beat for 30 seconds
- Fill lightly-greased muffin tins with the mixture, filling up 2/3 of the way
- Bake for 8-10 minutes or till the tops are nice and golden
- Combine the melted butter and the remaining ½ tsp. garlic powder; brush this over the warm biscuits.
- Add sesame and poppy seeds into the dough mixture
- Omit the garlic and use your favourite nut
- The add-in options are endless

190. Garlic Mozzarella Rolls Recipe

Serving: 20 | Prep: | Cook: 20mins | Ready in:

Ingredients

- 16 Rhodes™ dinner rolls, thawed but still cold
- 16 ounce block of mozzarella cheese, cut into 16 equal cubes
- butter, olive oil or beaten egg
- 2 teaspoons garlic salt
- 2 teaspoons italian seasoning
- 2 teaspoons oregano flakes
- marinara sauce

Direction

- Flatten each dinner roll into a 4-inch circle and place a cheese cube in the middle.
- Bring the edges together and pinch firmly to seal completely.
- Place seam side down on a sprayed baking sheet.
- Cover with sprayed plastic wrap and let rise until double in size.
- In a bowl, combine garlic salt, Italian seasoning and oregano until well combined.
- Remove plastic wrap from rolls and brush each one with butter, olive oil, or beaten egg.
- Sprinkle with seasoning mixture.
- Bake at 350°F 15-20 minutes or until golden brown.
- Remove from oven and serve hot with warm marinara sauce.

191. Glazed Brie Recipe

Serving: 1 | Prep: | Cook: 7mins | Ready in:

Ingredients

- 1/4 cup packed brown sugar
- 1/4 cup chopped nuts (your favorite kinds)
- 1 tablespoon brandy
- 1 (14-ounce) round brie or camembert
- apple wedges, pear wedges, celery sticks
- 2 to 3 tablespoons lemon juice
- Crackers, for serving

Direction

- Stir together the sugar, nuts, and brandy.
- Preheat oven to 500 degrees F.
- Bake the brie for 4 or 5 minutes or until the cheese is slightly softened. Spread the sugar mixture in an even layer on top of the cheese and bake for 2 to 3 minutes longer, or until the sugar melts. Serve with the fruit, celery, and crackers. (The lemon juice is to brush on the fruit so that it doesn't brown.)

192. Goat's Cheese And Onion Marmalade Parcels Recipe

Serving: 2 | Prep: | Cook: 45mins | Ready in:

Ingredients

- Goat's cheese and Onion Parcels
- 6 Large Sheets Filo Pastry - Pack Suitable
- Extra Virgin Olive Oil - for brushing
- 3 x 100g/3½oz - rind-on Goat's cheese rounds - each cut in half to make semi - circles
- 2tbsp Red Onion Marmalade
- 6tbsp Walnuts - chopped
- 6 Sprigs Thyme - leaves only
- 1 to 2 Lemons - Zest only - to taste
- Salt and freshly ground Black

Direction

- Preheat oven to 200c/fan 180c/400f/fan 360f/gas 6
- Lay filo sheet on clean work surface and cut into 4 equal slices;
- Brush the top of each with oil and stack, oil side down, rotating the slices so they don't completely overlap one another;
- Repeat with remaining filo sheets and oil to create 6 stacks;
- On each parcel, now spoon on 1tsp marmalade in the centre, top with a goat's cheese semi - circle, 1tbsp walnuts, thyme leaves and lemon zest - to taste;
- Season with salt and pepper and pinch the pastry together to cover the filling and make a parcel;
- Repeat with 5 other parcels;
- Place the parcels on a lightly oiled baking tray and cook in the oven for some 12 to 16 minutes or so until golden all over;
- Serve immediately.

193. Gorgonzola And Wild Mushroom Tart Recipe

Serving: 8 | Prep: | Cook: 30mins | Ready in:

Ingredients

- 1 recipe simple puff pastry - recipe follows
- 2 C wild mushrooms (MYCopia chef sampler: Trumpet Royale, Alba Clamshell, Brown Clamshell mushrooms)
- 1 large shallot, thinly sliced
- 2 Tbsp. balsamic vinegar
- 2 Tbsp. sugar
- 1 tsp. fresh thyme leaves
- 1 tsp. fresh sage, chopped
- 1 Tbsp. fresh Italian parsley, minced

- 1 cup gorgonzola cheese (my fav is Mountain gorgonzola from Italy, domestic Amish Blue is awesome too)
- parchment paper
- 2 eggs, beaten with 1 Tbsp. water
- kosher salt and white pepper to taste
- extra virgin olive oil, for sauteing
- Simple Puff Pastry:
- 1 cup (2 sticks) unsalted organic butter
- 1 2/3 cup all-purpose flour
- 1/2 teaspoon kosher salt

Direction

- FOR THE SIMPLE PUFF PASTRY:
- Cut the butter into 1/4 inch pieces. Place 1 1/3 cups of the flour and the 1/2 tsp. salt in a food processor. Add 1 stick of the cut up butter, pulsing until combined. Add the remaining stick of cut up butter and 1/3 cup of flour to the food processor, tossing the butter pieces until the butter is coated with flour. Pulse 3-4 times to just combine (you want to see specks of butter there still). Add about 1/3 cup ice water and pulse until the dough just forms a ball. If you need to add more water, do so.
- Dust a work surface with flour and roll out to form a 10x14 inch rectangle. Fold into thirds, creating a 3x14 inch rectangle. Fold into thirds again, this time forming a 3x4 inch rectangle. Wrap in plastic wrap and refrigerate at least an hour (dough may be refrigerated up to 2 days or frozen for up to 1 month).
- FOR THE TART:
- Preheat oven to 400 degrees. Line a sheet pan with parchment paper. Cut mushrooms into small pieces and sauté in olive oil until tender. Put aside and hold. Sauté onions with sugar in oil and vinegar until caramelized. Add the thyme, sage and parsley.
- In a large mixing bowl, combine the mushrooms, onions, garlic and cheese. Mix until well blended. Salt and pepper to taste.
- Cut the puff pastry in half (save other half for another use). Roll the dough out to a 10 inch circle. Divide the mixture into the middle of the pastry round and fold the pastry around the mixture in a pleated fashion. Egg wash the edge with a pastry brush.
- Bake in preheated oven for 15-20 minutes or until done. Cut in wedges and serve with baby arugula mix and balsamic vinaigrette.

194. Gorgonzola Bread Appetizers Recipe

Serving: 10 | Prep: | Cook: 15mins | Ready in:

Ingredients

- 1 french baguette, sliced into 1/4 inch rounds
- 1/4 cup olive oil or melted butter
- 2 pears - peeled, cored and sliced
- 8 ounces crumbled gorgonzola cheese
- 1 cup chopped walnuts

Direction

- Preheat the oven to 350 degrees F (175 degrees C).
- Arrange the baguette slices in a single layer on a baking sheet.
- Brush the top of each one with olive oil or melted butter.
- Place a slice of pear onto each onto each piece of bread, then crumble some of the cheese over the top. Sprinkle with walnuts.
- Bake for 12 to 15 minutes in the preheated oven, or until the pears are browned and the cheese has started to melt.

195. Gorgonzola Cheesecake With Toasted Walnuts Recipe

Serving: 32 | Prep: | Cook: 45mins | Ready in:

Ingredients

- 1/4 cup chopped walnuts

- 2 packages (8 oz) cream cheese
- 2 eggs
- 1/2 cup sour cream
- 1 cup crumbled gorgonzola
- 3/4 tsp coarsely ground pepper
- 1/2 cup chopped toasted walnuts

Direction

- Heat oven to 325 degrees. Line outside of springform pan, 9x3inches with heavy aluminum foil. Spray inside of pan with cooking spray, sprinkle ground walnuts over bottom.
- Beat cream cheese until smooth. Add eggs, beat until smooth. Stir in sour cream, cheese and pepper until blended. Spoon evenly over walnuts in pan.
- Place springform in large roasting pan: Pour hot water into pan until 1/4 full. Bake uncovered 40-45 minutes or until centre is almost set. Remove cheesecake from roasting pan. Run knife around edge of cheesecake to loosen. Cool completely at room temperature, about 2 hours. Remove side of pan. Garnish with toasted walnuts.
- Serve with crackers

196. Gorgonzola Hazelnut Stuffed Mushrooms Recipe

Serving: 35 | Prep: | Cook: 20mins | Ready in:

Ingredients

- 1 lb. fresh whole mushrooms
- 1/3 c crumbled gorgonzola cheese or blue cheese
- 1/4 c Italian bread crumbs
- 1/4 c chopped hazelnuts
- 1/4 c fine chopped red pepper
- 4 med. green onions,chopped (1/4c)
- 1/2 tsp salt

Direction

- Heat oven to 350. Remove stems from mushroom caps; reserve caps. Finely chop enough stems to measure out about 1/2 c. Discard remaining stems.
- In small bowl, mix chopped mushroom stems and remaining ingredients till well blended. Spoon into mushroom caps, mounding slightly. Place in ungreased 15x10" pan.
- Bake 15 to 20 mins or till hot. Serve warm.

197. Gorgonzola Phyllo Cups Recipe

Serving: 30 | Prep: | Cook: 8mins | Ready in:

Ingredients

- 2 pkgs. (1.9 oz. ea.) frozen mini phyllo tart shells
- 1-1/3 c crumbled gorgonzola cheese
- 1/2 c chopped tart apple
- 1/3 c dried cranberries
- 1/3 c chopped walnuts

Direction

- Place tart shells on a baking pan. In a small bowl, combine the remaining ingredients; spoon into tart shells.
- Bake at 350 for 6-8 mins or till lightly browned. Serve warm or at room temperature. Refrigerate leftovers.

198. Gorgonzola Stuffed Dates Tapas Recipe

Serving: 10 | Prep: | Cook: 10mins | Ready in:

Ingredients

- 8 oz package dried pitted dates
- 1/2 cup almonds

- 1 tbsp. confectioner's(powdered) sugar
- 1 tsp. water
- 2 tbsp. crumbled gorgonzola cheese
- 6 oz. proscioutto, or Canadian bacon
- salt for seasoning (to taste)
- olive oil for drizzling
- For sugar syrup:
- 2/3 cup water
- 1/3 cup granulated sugar
- 2 tbsp. rose water (can be purchased in Middle Eastern markets)

Direction

- In a food processor combine almonds, confectioner's sugar, 1 tsp. water, and Gorgonzola cheese. Process until nuts are finely minced and the mixture looks like a paste. Set aside.
- With a knife, cut the dates opened lengthwise (don't cut all the way through).
- Using a teaspoon, stuff the dates with the nut and cheese mixture. Set aside.
- Make sugar syrup:
- Combine 2/3 cup sugar with 1/3 cup water in a small saucepan. Stir over the medium heat until sugar dissolves. Cook and stir for another 7 minutes. Turn off the heat and stir in rose water. Let cool slightly.
- Cut prosciutto in thin strips lengthwise, then cut each strip in half.
- Dip stuffed dates, one at a time, in a sugar syrup, then wrap a strip of prosciutto around them.
- Place dates on a lightly greased cookie sheet. Sprinkle lightly with salt and drizzle with olive oil.
- Bake at 350F oven for 8 min, or until prosciutto is LIGHTLY browned.
- Serve warm or cold as appetizer, or finger food.

199. Gouda Cheese Biscotti Recipe

Serving: 12 | Prep: | Cook: 120mins | Ready in:

Ingredients

- 1 envelope active dry yeast (2 1/4 teaspoons)
- 3/4 cup plus 2 tablespoons warm water
- 1 tablespoon sugar
- 2 3/4 cups all-purpose flour, plus more for dusting
- 8 ounces aged Gouda (preferably 4 years), shredded (2 cups)
- 1/2 cup walnuts, finely chopped
- 1 teaspoon kosher salt
- 6 tablespoons unsalted butter, softened

Direction

- In a medium bowl, combine the yeast with 1/2 cup of the warm water and let stand until foamy, about 5 minutes.
- Stir in the sugar and 3/4 cup of the flour to form a sponge; cover and let stand until billowy, about 30 minutes.
- In a large bowl, combine the remaining 2 cups of flour with the Gouda, walnuts and salt.
- Make a well in the centre and add the yeast mixture and the remaining 1/4 cup plus 2 tablespoons water; add the butter and stir until a dough is formed.
- Line a baking sheet with parchment paper.
- Scrape the dough onto a lightly floured work surface and knead until smooth, about 5 minutes; divide into thirds.
- Roll each piece of dough into a 12-inch log about 1 1/2 inches thick.
- Arrange the logs on the prepared baking sheet 2 inches apart.
- Loosely cover with lightly moistened paper towels and plastic wrap. Let stand for about 45 minutes, until risen.
- Preheat the oven to 350°.
- Remove the plastic wrap and paper towels and bake the logs for about 35 minutes, until they are golden and puffed and an instant-

read thermometer inserted in the centre registers 205°.

- Let the logs cool on the baking sheet for 20 minutes.
- Reduce the oven temperature to 300° and position 2 racks in the lower and upper thirds of the oven.
- Transfer the logs to a work surface.
- Using a serrated knife, slice the logs crosswise 1/3; inch thick.
- Arrange the slices cut side up on 2 baking sheets and bake for 45 minutes to 1 hour, until golden and crisp; flip the biscotti halfway through and shift the baking sheets from top to bottom and front to back.
- Transfer the biscotti to a rack and let cool completely

200. HOT FETA ARTICHOKE DIP Recipe

Serving: 10 | Prep: | Cook: 40mins | Ready in:

Ingredients

- 14 OZ. artichoke hearts-CHOPPED
- 1 C. MAYO
- 1 garlic clove, LARGE, MINCED
- 2 OZ. pimentos-CHOPPED
- 8 OZ. feta cheese-CRUMBLED

Direction

- COMBINE ALL INGREDIENTS
- PUT IN 1 QUART CASSEROLE
- BAKE AT 350 FOR 30-40 MINUTES, OR UNTIL GOLDEN BROWN
- EAT WITH CHIPS, CRACKERS OR CRUSTY BREAD

201. Happy Tizers Recipe

Serving: 0 | Prep: | Cook: 1hours | Ready in:

Ingredients

- 1 recipe for plain pastry
- 36 1" square slices of cheddar cheese
- 36 large pimento stuffed olives
- 36 small slices jalapeno chilis

Direction

- Roll out pastry on a lightly floured board or pastry cloth to 1/8" thickness and cut into 2 1/2" squares.
- Place cheese in centre of square and top with a slice of jalapeno and an olive. Bring two opposite corners of pastry over olive and pinch together. Repeat with other corners.
- Place on ungreased baking sheet and bake in preheated 450 degree oven for 10 to 15 minutes or until lightly browned.

202. Havarti App Recipe

Serving: 8 | Prep: | Cook: 20mins | Ready in:

Ingredients

- Minimun 4 pack croissants - Kind in a can that rolls out
- Small block of havarti
- 2/ 3 fuji apples
- very small loaf pan

Direction

- Roll out the dough smear the perforations together so that it becomes one long piece of dough. Wrap Havarti block completely - like a gift and smear edges together. Place seam down in baking pan and put in preheated oven (350) for 20 minutes. Slice apples.
- Serve!

203. Healthier Hot Nacho Dip Recipe

Serving: 12 | Prep: | Cook: 30mins | Ready in:

Ingredients

- Bean Layer:
- 1 can black beans
- 1 t. minced garlic
- salt and pepper to taste
- 1-2 T. olive oil
- 1-2 T water
- Meat Layer:
- 2 T olive oil
- 1 lb. ground turkey
- 2 poblano peppers, chopped
- 1 medium onion, chopped
- 4 T. taco seasoning of choice
- 2/3 C water
- Guacamole:
- 2 Haas avacados
- 2 T. lime juice
- salt and pepper to taste
- Remaining ingredients:
- 1 1/2 C reduced fat cheese (cheddar or pepper jack)
- 1 small jar (10 ounces) favorite smooth taco sauce
- 1 C light sour cream
- 2 medium chopped tomatoes (about 1 C)
- 3/4 C chopped black olives
- 3/4 C chopped green onions

Direction

- Puree all ingredients for the bean layer in a food processor to good spreading consistency. Spread this mixture in a 9 X 13 baking dish.
- Sauté ground turkey, peppers, and onion in olive oil over medium-high heat in a large sauté pan until turkey is white. Add taco seasoning and water and cook until sauce thickens. Layer this mixture on top of the black beans.
- Next, layer the shredded cheese first and then the taco sauce on top of the beans and meat.
- Bake at 350 for about 20-30 minutes, until hot and bubbly. Let rest for 5 -10 minutes after baking before layering remaining ingredients.
- While hot ingredients are baking, assemble the cold.
- Mash the avocados with the other ingredients to create guacamole.
- Chop tomatoes, olives, and green onions, and mix in a bowl with a pinch of salt.
- After dip is done baking and has cooled slightly, top with remaining ingredients, beginning with the guacamole.
- Layer the sour cream over guacamole, and then top with chopped tomato/olive/scallion mixture.

204. Holiday Cheese Ball Recipe

Serving: 24 | Prep: | Cook: 8mins | Ready in:

Ingredients

- 3 tablespoon finely chopped pecans
- 1 package (8 ounces) Neufchatel cream cheese (at room temperature)
- 3 green onions (finely chopped with tops, 1/3 cup)
- 1 teaspoon Dijon mustard
- 1/4 teaspoon hot red pepper sauce
- 1/4 teaspoon minced garlic
- 1 cup shredded sharp cheddar cheese (4 ounces)
- 1/4 cup minced parsley

Direction

- Step 1:
- Preheat the oven to 350 and spread out the pecans in a small pan. Bake, tossing once, for 8 minutes or until toasted. Meanwhile, in a small bowl, place the cream cheese, onions, mustard, red pepper sauce, and garlic. With an

electric mixer at moderate speed, beat for 3 minutes or until well blended. Stir in the cheddar cheese. Wrap the mixture in plastic wrap, shape into a 4-inch ball, and chill for 15 minutes.

- Step 2:
- On wax paper, toss the toasted pecans with the parsley. Unwrap the cheese ball and carefully roll it in the parsley mixture, coating it completely. Rewrap in plastic wrap and refrigerate until time to serve. Place the ball on a serving platter and surround with an assortment of crackers.

205. Honey Brie Spread Recipe

Serving: 8 | Prep: | Cook: 30mins | Ready in:

Ingredients

- 1 (14 oz)round brie cheese
- 1 (10 oz) can refrigerated crescent roll dough
- 1-1/2 c honey
- 1-1/2 c pecan halves

Direction

- Preheat oven to 375 degrees. Unwrap the brie and crescent rolls.
- Unroll the crescent dough and wrap around the brie. Press seams together to seal the cheese. Place in 9x9" baking dish. Sprinkle pecan halves over the top, and drizzle honey over the whole thing.
- Bake 30 mins until golden brown and cheese is soft.
- Serve with apple slices or crackers.

206. Hot Cheddar Mushroom Spread Recipe

Serving: 12 | Prep: | Cook: 25mins | Ready in:

Ingredients

- 2 c mayonnaise
- 2 c (8oz) shredded cheddar cheese
- 2/3 c grated parmesan cheese
- 4 cans (4-1/2 oz. ea)sliced mushrooms,drained
- 1 envelope ranch salad dressing mix
- minced fresh parsley
- assorted crackers

Direction

- In a large bowl, combine all except parsley and crackers. Spread in greased 9" pie plate.
- Bake, uncovered at 350 degrees for 20-25 mins or till cheese is melted. Sprinkle with parsley. Serve warm spread with crackers.

207. Hot Chicken Blue Cheese Dip Recipe

Serving: 12 | Prep: | Cook: 15mins | Ready in:

Ingredients

- 2 10 oz. cans of chicken (or 3 breasts cooked and chopped)
- 16 oz cream cheese
- 8 oz blue cheese salad dressing
- 5 oz of hot sauce or more (I use Franks)
- 5 oz crumbled blue cheese
- handful of cheddar cheese , for sprinkeling on top

Direction

- Melt cream cheese
- Add blue cheese dressing, and rest of ingredients, except cheddar cheese
- Stir till blended, Place in 9x13 oven proof pan

- Sprinkle handful of cheddar cheese on top
- Bake 350 till bubbles, about 20 min
- Serve with Tostitos, celery, green peppers, or just crackers

208. Hot Crab And Cheese Dip Recipe

Serving: 12 | Prep: | Cook: 30mins | Ready in:

Ingredients

- 16 oz claw crab meat
- 8 oz cream cheese room temp
- 1 cup shredded cheese (I like a sharp cheese but use what you like)
- 3 - 6 drops of your favorite hot sauce (you want some heat but not to take over the flavor)
- 1/2 cup chopped raw peeled and devined shrimp
- 1 clove of garlic minced
- 1 tsp Old Bay Seasoning
- 1 tsp onion powder
- 2 tbsp. fresh chopped parsley or 1 tsp dry
- salt and pepper

Direction

- Mix all ingredients in no special order - except to make sure you whip the cream cheese slightly.
- Pour into a well-greased oven safe bowl and bake for 30 mins or until the cheese bubbles up.
- Serve with crostini or warm bread.
- Crostinis are simple slices of your favourite Italian bread (1/4" or less cut on an angle) rubbed with a raw clove of garlic (cut the clove in half and simply rub over each slice of bread) a drizzle of olive oil and a dash of parmesan on each slice. Bake at 325 till golden brown.

209. Hot Crab Fondue Recipe

Serving: 4 | Prep: | Cook: 20mins | Ready in:

Ingredients

- 3 packages of cream cheese
- 1/2 cup mayonaise
- 1 teaspoon prepared mustard
- 1/2 teaspoon garlic powder
- 2 teaspoons Old Bay Seasoning
- 1/2 cup dry white wine like Chardonnay or 1/4 cup of sherry but I prefer the white wine
- juice of half a lemon
- 1 teaspoon lemon zest
- 1 pound lump crabmeat, canned
- 1/4 cup green onions, sliced
- baguette, cut into cubes
- toothpicks for stabbing bread and dipping in fondue

Direction

- Over a double boiler, heat cream cheese, mayonnaise, mustard, garlic powder, Old Bay, and lemon zest until cheese has melted.
- Then stir in wine and lemon juice.
- Add crabmeat carefully so that you have big chunks.
- To serve, transfer to a fondue pot with the bread and toothpicks.

210. Hot Crab Cheddar Spread Recipe

Serving: 8 | Prep: | Cook: 30mins | Ready in:

Ingredients

- 1- (8 ounces) container of crabmeat, drained and shredded
- 8-10 ounces of mild or sharp cheddar cheese grated
- 1/2- cup mayonnaise
- 1/4- teaspoon worcestershire sauce

- pepper to taste ....or add a liitle zip and put some spicy hot peppers, and spice ....

Direction

- Preheat oven to 350 degrees F.
- In a medium bowl, mix together all ingredients thoroughly
- Transfer to a small 1 quart baking dish
- Bake for 25 - 35 minutes or until lightly browned on top and bubbling at edges
- Serve with crackers or small French bread toasts
- Makes 8- 10 servings

211. Italian Beer Cheese Dip From Mancinos Recipe

Serving: 15 | Prep: | Cook: 35mins | Ready in:

Ingredients

- mayonnaise 1 cup
- beer 1 cup
- ricotta cheese 1 cup
- mozzarella cheese 1 lb.
- cream cheese 8 oz. softened
- pepperoni 12 oz. Cut into strips
- black olives 1 cup sliced
- garlic 1 Tblsp
- **Mancino's seasoning 1 Tblsp
- Italian bread Crumbs
- tortilla chips or toasted Italian bread
- ** Mancino's seasoning Mix : (salt, pepper, garlic, oregano, basil, red pepper flakes) equal parts of each (this is a great seasoning mix, I mix it up by 2 Tablespoons of each, and use until time to mix more!).

Direction

- Combine all ingredients thoroughly place in baking dish
- Sprinkle Italian bread crumbs on top and bake @ 350 for 35-40 minutes
- Serve with Tortilla chips or toasted Italian bread

212. Italian Nachoes Recipe

Serving: 6 | Prep: | Cook: 15mins | Ready in:

Ingredients

- 4 pita bread rounds
- 1/2 cup marinara sauce
- 1/4 cup grated parmesan cheese
- 1 (3.25 ounce) can sliced black olives
- 1/4 cup shredded mozzarella cheese
- 1 clove garlic, minced
- 1 cup fresh basil leaves

Direction

- Preheat the oven to 350 degrees F (175 degrees C).
- Use scissors or kitchen shears to cut the pita breads in half, then into triangles.
- Peel apart the bread halves to make as many triangles as possible.
- Spread the triangles out on a large baking sheet, and sprinkle with Parmesan cheese.
- Toast triangles for 10 to 15 minutes in the preheated oven, until lightly browned and crispy.
- While toasting, combine the marinara sauce and garlic in a small saucepan.
- Cook over medium heat until hot.
- Transfer pita chips to a serving platter, sprinkle with olives, and pour sauce over them.
- Quickly cover with shredded mozzarella cheese, and whole basil leaves.
- Serve immediately.

213. Italian Nachos Recipe

Serving: 8 | Prep: | Cook: 5mins | Ready in:

Ingredients

- 1 (10-ounce) container refrigerated four cheese or alfredo sauce, warmed
- 1/4 teaspoon red pepper flakes
- 8 ounces white corn tortilla chips
- 4 ounces hot italian sausage, cooked
- 8 ounces (2 cups) mozzarella cheese, shredded
- 1/2 cup chopped tomato
- 1/4 cup sliced green onions
- 1 (2 1/4-ounce) can pitted ripe olive slices, drained

Direction

- Heat oven to 450°F. Combine cheese sauce and red pepper flakes in small bowl.
- Spread half of tortilla chips on ovenproof platter; top with half cheese sauce, half Italian sausage and half Mozzarella cheese. Repeat with remaining chips, cheese sauce, sausage and cheese.
- Bake for 5 to 7 minutes or until cheese is melted. Top with remaining ingredients. Serve immediately.

214. Jalapeno Cheese Squares Recipe

Serving: 0 | Prep: | Cook: 45mins | Ready in:

Ingredients

- 4 c. cheddar cheese, shredded
- 4 eggs beatn
- 1 t. onion, minced
- 4 canned jalapeno peppers, seeded and chopped

Direction

- Combine all ingredients and blend thoroughly. Spread mixture in an 8" pan. Bake at 350 degrees for 30 minutes. Cut into 1" squares and serve hot.

215. Jalapeno Cheesecake Recipe

Serving: 0 | Prep: | Cook: 70mins | Ready in:

Ingredients

- 1-1/2 cups crushed tortilla chips
- 6 tablespoons melted butter
- 2 8-ounce packages cream cheese, at room temperature
- 3 eggs
- 1/4 cup all-purpose flour
- 1-1/2 cups sour cream, divided (1 cup and 1/2 cup)
- 1 clove garlic, minced or put through a garlic press
- 4.5-ounce can chopped green chiles
- 1 fresh jalapeño, stemmed, seeded and minced
- 2 cups grated colby/Monterrey Jack-blend or cheddar cheese
- chopped plum tomatoes
- chopped green onions
- diced black olives
- chopped cilantro

Direction

- Preheat oven to 300°F. Lightly grease the sides of a 9-inch springform pan.
- Pour the melted butter over the crushed tortilla chips and toss to combine. Press on bottom and one-half inch up the sides of the pan. Bake for 10 minutes. Remove from oven and set aside.
- With an electric mixer at high speed, beat the cream cheese until light and fluffy. Add the eggs, one at a time, and beat to incorporate. Reduce mixer speed to low, and blend in the flour, 1 cup of the sour cream. Beat until

smooth. Add the garlic, green chiles and minced jalapeño. Turn off the mixer, and stir in the cheese.

- Pour filling into crust, and bake for 1 hour. Turn oven off, and leave cheesecake in the oven for 1 hour with the door closed. Remove from oven and cool. When cool, loosen the cheesecake from the sides of the pan by running a knife around the inside edge. Do not remove cheesecake from pan. Cover and refrigerate for 1 hour.
- When ready to serve, spring the pan and remove the cheesecake. Spread the remaining 1/2 cup sour cream evenly over the top and sprinkle with chopped tomatoes, green onions, olives and cilantro.

216. Jalapeño Cheese Corn "dogs" With Fire Roasted Tomato Sauce Recipe

Serving: 24 | Prep: | Cook: 1hours | Ready in:

Ingredients

- Fire-roasted Tomato Sauce:
- 1 tablespoon olive oil
- 1 small onion, peeled, diced fine
- 1 teaspoon chili powder- mild or hot
- 1 teaspoon cumin
- 3-4 garlic cloves, minced
- 1 28-oz. can crushed organic fire roasted tomatoes
- organic sugar/raw organic agave nectar/honey, to taste
- splash of balsamic vinegar
- 2 tablespoon fresh minced cilantro
- ~
- honey cornbread batter:
- 1 cup all-purpose flour, sifted
- 1 cup yellow cornmeal
- 1 Tbsp baking powder
- 1/2 tsp kosher salt
- 2 free range eggs, beaten
- 1 cup half and half
- 1/4 cup melted unsalted butter
- 1/4 cup honey
- 1/4 cup granulated sugar
- ~
- 2 small blocks organic jalapeno jack cheese, cut into 1/2 inch pieces

Direction

- For sauce:
- Heat the olive oil in a medium saucepan over medium heat and gently sauté the onion and spices for 5 minutes. Add the garlic, tomatoes, sugar, vinegar, and cilantro, stir and bring to a simmer. Cover and cook 15 to 20 minutes. Keep warm until ready to serve or rewarm later.
- For cornbread:
- Sift together the flour, cornmeal, baking powder and salt. Combine the buttermilk, eggs, butter, honey and sugar.
- Add the liquid ingredients to the dry ones and mix just until the flour is moistened, no more than ten seconds. The batter should be visibly lumpy — leave it that way! It's extremely important not to over mix the batter.
- To bake:
- Lightly grease cake pop maker with canola oil. Pour batter in each hole, 3/4 of the way up. Gently place 1 piece of cheese in centre of each then close lid. Bake for 3 minutes, then flip over using 2 bamboo skewers, and bake another 2 minutes (this is what worked best with my machine). Once golden brown on both sides, remove gently with skewers to a plate. Continue until all cheese pieces are used (you might have a little batter left.
- Insert a short bamboo skewer into each pop and enjoy warm with sauce.

217. Jalapeño Popper Dip Recipe

Serving: 0 | Prep: | Cook: 45mins | Ready in:

Ingredients

- To make this milder deseed and devein the jalapenos, most of the heat is in the white pith inside the jalapeno.....tw
- Jalapeño Popper Dip
- Ingredients
- 1 4 oz can diced jalapenos, well drained OR 4-6 fresh... jalapenos, roasted and diced (include seeds if you like it really spicy)
- 1 8 oz package cream cheese, softened
- 1 cup sour cream
- 2 cups shredded cheddar cheese
- 3/4 cup + 1/4 cup shredded parmesan cheese
- 1 cup Italian seasoned bread crumbs
- 4 tablespoons butter or margarine, melted
- 1 tablespoon dried parsley
- Thx to :
- http://www.facebook.com/groups/shreddingwithtammy

Direction

- Instructions
- In a mixer or by hand, combine cream cheese and sour cream. Add cheddar cheese, 3/4 cup parmesan cheese, and diced jalapenos, mix well. Spoon into 8x8 baking dish, spreading evenly. Blend bread crumbs, melted butter, 1/4 cup shredded parmesan cheese, and dried parsley, using a fork or your fingers, until crumbly. Sprinkle the buttery crumb topping evenly over the cream cheese mixture. Bake at 350 degrees for 15 minutes, or until hot and breadcrumbs are golden brown. Do not overcook. Serve with bread or crackers...a friend

218. Jarlsberg Onion And Apple Canapes Recipe

Serving: 16 | Prep: | Cook: 25mins | Ready in:

Ingredients

- 1 tablespoon butter
- 1 medium onion, cut into fourths and sliced
- 4 ounces thinly sliced Jarlsberg or swiss cheese
- 16 slices pumpernickel cocktail bread***
- 1 tablespoon Dijon-mayonnaise blend or Dijon mustard
- 1 to 2 tablespoons chopped fresh chives
- 1 medium unpeeled apple, thinly sliced
- *****I would use a good bakery pumpernickle bread cut into cocktail size instead... if it is too soft, lightly toast it first

Direction

- Sauté onion until soft and caramelized
- Cut cheese to fit bread. Spread each bread slice with Dijon-mayonnaise blend. Top each with onion, apple and cheese. Sprinkle with chives.
- Place in ungreased jelly roll pan, 15 1/2x10 1/2x1 inch.
- Bake about 5 minutes or until cheese is melted. Serve warm.

219. Jumbo Shrimp Parmesan Recipe

Serving: 3 | Prep: | Cook: 10mins | Ready in:

Ingredients

- 12 jumbo shrimp (10 to 12 per lb.)
- 2 tablespoons olive oil
- 1 clove minced garlic
- salt and pepper
- 1/2 cup unseasoned breadcrumbs
- 1/4 cup grated parmesan cheese
- 2 tablespoons melted butter
- 1 medium lemon, cut in wedges

Direction

- Preheat oven to 475F.
- Peel and devein shrimp, leaving tails intact.
- Mix together olive oil, garlic and salt and pepper in a bowl.
- Add shrimp and toss lightly to coat.
- Refrigerate 30 minutes to an hour.
- In shallow bowl, combine bread crumbs and Parmesan cheese.
- Place each shrimp in bread crumb mixture and turn them to lightly coat both sides.
- Arrange shrimp so that they aren't touching each other in an ungreased 9 x 13 pan.
- Drizzle with melted butter.
- Place pan on the centre rack of oven and bake for 10 minutes or until done.
- Serve immediately with lemon wedges.

220. Kaylees Hot Cheese Dip Recipe

Serving: 10 | Prep: | Cook: 90mins | Ready in:

Ingredients

- 8 ounces softened cream cheese, cut into cubes
- 1 cup sour cream
- 1 pound bacon, cooked crispy and crumbled
- 6 green onions (scallions), sliced
- 1 shallot, minced
- 2 cups shredded medium or sharp cheddar cheese
- 1 large sourdough loaf, made into a bowl (reserve pieces taken from middle)

Direction

- Preheat oven to 350 degrees.
- In a large bowl, mix together the softened cream cheese and sour cream.
- Add the crumbled cooked bacon, green onions, shallot, and cheddar cheese, and stir well.
- Pour mixture into the sourdough bowl and cover entirely with tin foil.
- Bake at 350 degrees for 90 minutes.
- Serve with sourdough pieces and other dippers.
- Substitutions: 1/4 cup minced onion plus one clove garlic for shallot.
- Makes 8-10 servings.

221. Kyrrah's Seeded Cheese Recipe

Serving: 5 | Prep: | Cook: 50mins | Ready in:

Ingredients

- 2 tbsp sesame seeds
- 6 oz of your favorite cheese, cut into 10 sticks roughly 1/2 inch thick adn 1/2 inch wide and maybe 3 inches long or so

Direction

- Place the oven rack in the upper position (second from the top).
- Turn the oven on to broil
- Place the sesame seeds in the ungreased pie plate
- Broil the seeds in the oven for about 3 mins, shaking the pie plate occasionally, using the oven mitts, until the seeds are golden brown.
- Use the oven mitts to remove the pie plate to the wire rack, cool slightly
- Place the cheese on the microwave-safe plate
- Microwave, uncovered, on high for about 6 seconds until warm.
- Lightly press and roll the warmed cheese sticks in the seeds.
- Chill for about 30 min.
- Makes 10 cheese sticks

222. La Nacho Potato Skins Recipe

Serving: 24 | Prep: | Cook: 30mins | Ready in:

Ingredients

- 6 medium potatoes, such as russet (2 pounds)
- cooking oil, shortening, butter, or margarine
- 1/4 cup butter or margarine, melted
- 1/4 teaspoon seasoned salt
- ground red pepper
- 4 ounces co-jack cheese, cheddar cheese, or monterey jack cheese with peppers, shredded (1 cup)
- Toppers, such as dairy sour cream, salsa, guacamole, chopped tomato, chopped sweet pepper, sliced green onion, sliced pitted ripe olives, or snipped fresh cilantro

Direction

- Heat oven to 425 degree F. Thoroughly scrub potatoes; pat dry. Rub with cooking oil, shortening, butter, or margarine; prick potatoes with a fork. Bake for 40 to 60 minutes or till tender. (Or, microwave on high for 15 to 20 minutes or till tender.) Cut potatoes lengthwise into quarters. Scoop out the pulp, leaving 1/4-inch-thick shells. Reserve the pulp for mashed potatoes or another use.
- Brush both sides of the potato pieces with the 1/4 cup butter or margarine. Sprinkle the insides with seasoned salt and ground red pepper. Place potato pieces, skin sides up, on the unheated rack of a broiler pan. Broil 3 to 4 inches from heat for 3 minutes.
- Turn potato pieces skin sides down. Sprinkle with shredded cheese. Broil 2 minutes more. Arrange the potato pieces on a heated serving platter. Serve with desired toppers. Makes 24 servings.
- To Make Ahead: Bake, scoop, and season the potatoes. Place in a covered container and refrigerate up to 2 days.

223. Laughing Cow Stuffed Peppers Recipe

Serving: 3 | Prep: | Cook: 25mins | Ready in:

Ingredients

- One bag of mini peppers
- One wheel of your favorite Laughing Cow cheese. Or mix them

Direction

- Wash peppers
- Cut tops off peppers and remove any seeds
- Divide one wedge between three or four peppers and stuff inside
- Place on cookie sheet
- Bake on 400 for 15-20 minutes

224. Lime Jalapeno Cheesecake Recipe

Serving: 8 | Prep: | Cook: 65mins | Ready in:

Ingredients

- 1/2 cup bread crumbs
- 1 pound Philly cream cheese, softened
- 1 Tbsp lime juice
- 2 large eggs
- 1 Tbsp lime infused sugar
- 1 tea. lime infused salt
- 1 1/2 tea. jalapeno powder
- 1 cup Cojack cheese, shredded

Direction

- Preheat oven to 325^.
- Spray 6" spring pan with cooking spray.
- Swirl bread crumbs around sides and bottom to cover.
- Blend cream cheese and lime juice until smooth.

- Add eggs one at a time.
- Add lime sugar, salt and jalapeno powder, mixing thoroughly.
- Fold in cheese, blending well.
- Pour into prepared pan.
- Bake at 325^ for 40 minutes.
- Let cool and serve warm with bread and/or crackers.

225. Little Gouda Bites Recipe

Serving: 12 | Prep: | Cook: 13mins | Ready in:

Ingredients

- 1 8 oz tube of refrigerated crescent rolls
- 1/2 teaspoon garlic powder
- 5 ounces gouda cheese, cut into 24 pieces

Direction

- Unroll crescent dough into one long rectangle; seal seams and perforations.
- Sprinkle with garlic powder.
- Cut into 24 pieces; light press into bottom and up the sides of ungreased miniature muffin cups.
- Bake at 375 degrees for 3 minutes.
- Place a piece of cheese in each cup and bake 8 to 10 minutes longer or until golden brown and cheese is melted.
- Serve warm.

226. Lobster Mascarpone Cheesecake With Herbed Cornmeal Crust Recipe

Serving: 20 | Prep: | Cook: 40mins | Ready in:

Ingredients

- Crust
- 4 Tablespoons butter
- 1 cup cornmeal, sifted
- 1 cup fresh bread crumbs
- 1 teaspoon each fresh basil, fresh oregano, fresh thyme, fresh parsley, minced
- 1 pinch salt and ground black pepper, to taste
- cheesecake
- 9 each large eggs, beaten
- 3 pounds mascarpone cheese
- 2 Tablespoons grated romano cheese
- 1½ pounds lobster meat
- 3 Tablespoons each heavy cream, sour cream, minced corn
- 1 Tablespoon each minced fresh basil, lemon juice
- ½ Tablespoon each minced fresh garlic, minced fresh chive, worcestershire sauce
- 1 pinch salt and ground black pepper, to taste

Direction

- For crust, melt butter. Add remaining crust ingredients. Spray 20 4 oz. ramekins with non-stick cooking spray and form crust in bottoms.
- For cheesecake, mix eggs and cheese. Add remaining ingredients. Divide cheesecake mixture among ramekins. Bake approximately 40 minutes at 325F in water bath until firm in centre. Unmould warm cheesecake onto centre of plate. Surround with fresh herbs, a sprinkling of diced tomatoes and basil oil if desired.

227. Lobster Nachos Recipe

Serving: 10 | Prep: | Cook: 15mins | Ready in:

Ingredients

- 1 13.5-ounce bag of corn tortilla chips
- 4 Tbsp butter
- 2 cloves garlic, minced
- 1 cup red onion, chopped
- 2 4-ounce cans baby shrimp, drained

- 8-14 ounces of cooked lobster meat, cut up (it'll take 2 lobsters)
- 8 ounces shredded monterey jack cheese
- 8 ounces shredded cheddar cheese
- 2 medium tomatoes, chopped
- 2-3 scallions, chopped
- 1 cup sour cream
- 1 16-ounce jar of salsa

Direction

- Preheat oven to 350 degrees.
- Layer tortilla chips in a 13"x9"x2" baking dish.
- Blend cheeses. Sprinkle half of the cheese mixture and tomatoes over tortilla chips.
- Melt butter in large frying pan over medium heat.
- Add garlic and onion to pan and sauté until onions are tender, approximately two minutes.
- Add shrimp and lobster meat and heat until warm, about three minutes.
- Drain and layer warm seafood mixture on top of nachos.
- Top with the remaining cheese and bake at 350 degrees for about 15 minutes until cheese is melted.
- Top with scallions and dollops of sour cream. Serve hot with salsa on the side.

228. Mexican Cheese Fondue Recipe

Serving: 6 | Prep: | Cook: 40mins | Ready in:

Ingredients

- For the sauce:
- 1 1/2 cups heavy whipping cream
- 1/2 teaspoon ground allspice
- kosher salt, to taste
- For the filling:
- 2 poblano chilies, toasted, peeled, stemmed and seeded
- 3 tablespoons canola oil
- 1 white onion, cut into 1/2-inch slices
- 3/4 pound shredded cooked chicken
- salt, to taste
- 1/2 pound queso Oaxaca (mexican cheese), shredded
- 1/4 bunch cilantro, stemmed and chopped for garnish
- 8 fresh corn tortillas, warmed, or tortilla chips (preferably homemade)

Direction

- For the sauce: In a small saucepan, over high heat, combine the cream, allspice and salt.
- Bring to a simmer."
- Reduce heat to medium, and cook for 10 to 15 minutes, until reduced by one-third.
- Pass through a fine mesh strainer to remove any film, and set aside to cool.
- For the filling:
- Cut the chilies into 1/2-by-2-inch strips.
- In a large sauté pan, heat the oil over high heat.
- Add the onion and sauté for 3 to 5 minutes, until translucent, lowering the heat if necessary.
- Add the chili strips and the chicken, and gently stir until evenly mixed.
- Season with salt and remove from heat.
- To finish:
- Preheat the broiler. In an 8-by-10 inch casserole, spread the chicken mixture in an even layer.
- Spread the cream sauce on top.
- Cover with cheese.
- Place the casserole under the broiler for 10 to 15 minutes, until all ingredients have melted together and top is lightly browned.
- Remove from the broiler and sprinkle with cilantro.
- Serve immediately with warm tortillas.
- Cheats: Pre-cooked store-bought chicken and good quality tortilla chips will make quick work of this dish.
- Do-ahead: The sauce and the filling can be made in advance and kept covered and refrigerated overnight.

- Let them sit out at room temperature about an hour before broiling.

229. Mini Brie Cups Recipe

Serving: 45 | Prep: | Cook: 12mins | Ready in:

Ingredients

- 3 pkgs mini fillo cups(45 pieces)
- 1 whole round brie cheese,about 13 ozs.,5" diameter
- 1/3c red pepper jell(or as much as you need)
- 1/4tsp dried sweetened cranberries,chopped(or as much as needed)
- chopped rosemary

Direction

- Preheat oven to 350. Place phyllo shells in mini cupcake pans. Trim entire rind from cheese; cut cheese in 45 pieces. Place 1 piece cheese in each shell. Combine cranberries with jelly and rosemary.
- Divide evenly among cups. Bake 10 to 12 mins or till cheese is melted.

230. Mini Ricotta Spinach Prosciutto Pies Recipe

Serving: 12 | Prep: | Cook: 40mins | Ready in:

Ingredients

- 1 lb baby spinach leaves
- 2 oz. pine nuts
- 2-3 cups ricotta
- 1 1/2 cups freshly grated parmesan
- ½ cup sour cream
- 2 eggs
- 1/2 lb.prosciutto, sliced into thin strips
- freshly cracked blacked pepper to taste

Direction

- Preheat oven to 325°C.
- Blanch spinach in boiling water for a few seconds to wilt.
- Drain, cool, squeeze out excess water and roughly chop.
- Toast pine nuts in the oven for 10 minutes until they are slightly browned and smell nutty.
- Combine all ingredients and mix thoroughly.
- Spoon into muffin tins and bake for 25-30 minutes.

231. Modak Recipe

Serving: 4 | Prep: | Cook: 5mins | Ready in:

Ingredients

- 2 plantains
- ¼ pav maida
- 1 pinch salt
- 2 cardamom pods
- 2 tsp sugar
- ghee for frying

Direction

- Peel plantains. Mash and put sugar, salt, powdered cardamom and Maida.
- Stir properly to make a dough.
- Heat ghee in frying pan, drop small pellets of dough gently into ghee and deep fry till it turns reddish brown in colour.
- Instead of ¼ pav Maida, fine soji and rice flour mixed with Maida (totally ¼ pav) can be used.

232. Moroccan Cheese Pastries Recipe

Serving: 0 | Prep: | Cook: 40mins | Ready in:

Ingredients

- 1 box, 2 sheets of puff pastry dough, chilled, you may or may not use the second sheet, depends how large you cut the squares.
- Filling :
- 1 large egg
- 1 cup ricotta or farmer's cheese
- 2 Tbs cream
- 1 cup shredded mozzarella cheese
- 1 large roasted red bell pepper, skinned and chopped
- 5 or 6 pitted black olives, finely chopped
- 5 or 6 pitted green olives, finely chopped
- 2 tablespoons fresh parsley, chopped
- 1 tsp za'atar or oregano
- pepper, to taste

Direction

- Preheat your oven to 400° F
- Grease a large baking sheet
- In a small bowl, beat the egg with the cream and set aside.
- In another bowl, combine the remaining ingredients for the filling.
- Stir in a little more than half of the egg and cream mixture.
- Reserve the rest to use as an egg wash
- Roll out the puff pastry dough into a very thin square or rectangle.
- With a sharp knife or pastry wheel, cut the dough into 16 to 20 squares. Divide the filling into an equal number of portions, spooning each portion onto the middle of a square of dough.
- Dab a little egg wash on the edges of one square of dough.
- Fold the dough over the filling to make either a triangular or rectangular pastry, and press the edges together.
- Further seal the pastries by pressing around the edges with the tines of a fork.
- Transfer the pastry to the baking sheet, and repeat with the remaining squares of dough.
- Note: the pastries may be covered with plastic and placed in the freezer. Once frozen, they can be transferred to a plastic freezer bag or box.
- Thaw for 30 minutes at room temperature before baking.
- Brush the tops of the pastries with the egg wash and prick each pastry once or twice with a fork to create steam vents.
- Bake the pastries for 15 to 20 minutes, or until golden brown.
- Cool on a rack for at least several minutes before serving.

233. Moroccan Lamb And Feta Phyllo Triangles Recipe

Serving: 10 | Prep: | Cook: 15mins | Ready in:

Ingredients

- 1 lb ground lamb
- 500 grams feta cheese, crumbled
- Half a red onion, very finely diced
- MOROCCAN seasoning [makes 1 tbs] (1/2 tsp ground cumin, 1/2 tsp ground ginger, 1/2 tsp salt, 1/2 tsp pepper, 1/4 tsp cinnamon, 1/4 tsp ground corriander, 1/4 tsp cayenne, 1/4 tsp allspice, 1/4 tsp ground cloves) I use almost 2 tbs of the seasoning, just depends on your personal taste.
- 1 package store bought Pyllo pastry

Direction

- Brown lamb.
- Add feta cheese, Moroccan seasoning and red onion. Mix well.
- Prepare phyllo triangles according to directions on package (use two layers of pastry, brush melted butter between the layers, cut into four strips. Place a healthy teaspoon of filling at the bottom, then fold one side over and then the other and repeat until you run out of pastry!)
- Brush with melted butter and bake about 10 minutes at 350 or until nicely browned.

234. Mozzarella Pepperoni Bread Recipe

Serving: 24 | Prep: | Cook: 15mins | Ready in:

Ingredients

- 1 loaf (1 pound) French bread
- 3 tablespoons butter, melted
- 3 ounces sliced turkey pepperoni
- 1-1/2 cups (6 ounces) shredded part-skim mozzarella cheese
- 3 tablespoons minced fresh parsley

Direction

- Cut loaf of bread in half width wise; cut into 1-in. slices, leaving slices attached at bottom. Brush butter on both sides of each slice. Arrange pepperoni between slices; sprinkle with cheese and parsley.
- Place on an ungreased baking sheet. Bake at 350° for 12-15 minutes or until cheese is melted.
- Yield: 24 slices.
- We just use plain pepperoni.

235. Mozzarella Sticks Recipe

Serving: 6 | Prep: | Cook: 10mins | Ready in:

Ingredients

- 3 tablespoons all-purpose flour
- 2 eggs
- 1 tablespoon water
- 1 cup dry bread crumbs
- 2-1/2 teaspoons italian seasoning
- 1/2 teaspoon garlic powder
- 1/8 teaspoon pepper
- 12 sticks string cheese
- 1 tablespoon butter, melted
- 1 cup marinara or spaghetti sauce, heated

Direction

- Place flour in a shallow bowl. In another shallow bowl, beat eggs and water. In a third shallow bowl, combine the bread crumbs, Italian seasoning, garlic powder and pepper. Coat cheese sticks with flour, then dip in egg mixture and coat with bread crumb mixture. Repeat egg and bread crumb coatings. Cover and chill for at least 4 hours or overnight.
- Place on an ungreased baking sheet; drizzle with butter. Bake, uncovered, at 400° for 6-8 minutes or until heated through. Allow to stand for 3-5 minutes before serving. Serve with marinara or spaghetti sauce for dipping.
- Yield: 4-6 servings.
- Note: Regular mozzarella cheese, cut into 4-in. x 1/2-in. sticks, can be substituted for the string cheese.

236. Mozzarella Tomato Amp Chilli Loaf Recipe

Serving: 2 | Prep: | Cook: 10mins | Ready in:

Ingredients

- 1 can chopped tomatoes
- 500ml mozzarella, grated
- 1 chilli, finely chopped
- 1 french baguette, cut in half
- olive oil

Direction

- Spread each baguette half with olive oil.
- Put in oven for 5 min at 180C.
- In the meantime mix the tomatoes & chilli.
- Take baguette out and top with tomato mixture, then Mozzarella.
- Put in oven for another 5 min or until cheese has melted.
- Enjoy!!

237. Mozzarella And Tomato Crostini Recipe

Serving: 8 | Prep: | Cook: 18mins | Ready in:

Ingredients

- 1/4c. + more for baking extra virgin olive oil
- 1 baguette, cut into 1/4" slices
- salt and coarse ground black pepper
- 8 vine ripened tomatoes
- 1/2c. slivered fresh basil leaves
- 1/4T. minced garlic
- 1T. aged balsamic vinegar
- 1-1/2 lbs. fresh mozzarella cheese

Direction

- Preheat an oven to 350°F.
- Brush a baking sheet with olive oil and arrange the baguette slices on the sheet in a single layer.
- Brush the tops with oil, and season with salt and pepper.
- Bake until crisp and golden, 15 to 18 minutes.
- Let cool, then store the crostini in an airtight container at room temperature until ready to use.
- Core and seed the tomatoes and slice lengthwise into 1/4-inch-thick slices.
- In a mixing bowl, combine the tomatoes, half of the basil, garlic, vinegar, the remaining 1/4 cup olive oil, salt and pepper and mix well.
- Slice the mozzarella into 1/4-inch-thick pieces or into smaller pieces so they fit on the crostini.
- To assemble, lay a piece of mozzarella on each crostini and spoon 1 to 2 Tbs. of the tomato salad on top.
- Garnish each with a pinch of the remaining basil.
- Serve immediately.

238. Mozzarella Cheese Puff Balls Recipe

Serving: 6 | Prep: | Cook: 15mins | Ready in:

Ingredients

- 2 Cups flour
- 1/2 tsp. salt
- 1/2 tsp/ paprika
- 1 Cup butter, softened
- 1 pound mozzarella cheese, shredded

Direction

- Preheat oven to 350 degrees.
- Sift together dry ingredients.
- Cream butter and mix in mozzarella; add flour mixture and mix well.
- Shape into small balls and place on an ungreased baking sheet.
- Bake 15 to 20 minutes, until puffed and golden.

239. Nacho Cheese Bites Recipe

Serving: 20 | Prep: | Cook: 15mins | Ready in:

Ingredients

- 1 sheet puff pastry
- 1 egg
- 1Tbs water
- 1c shredded cheese
- 1/4c salsa
- 5 pitted ripe olives,quartered
- chili powder

Direction

- Thaw pastry at room temperature for 40 mins or till easy to handle. Heat oven to 400. Beat egg and water in small bowl with a fork. Stir the cheese and salsa in a small bowl.

- Unfold pastry sheet on lightly floured surface. Roll the pastry sheet into a 15x12" rectangle. Cut into 20 squares (3"). Place about 1 Tbsp. cheese mixture in centre of each pastry square. Top each with olive piece, if desired. Brush the edges of the pastry squares with the egg mixture. Fold the pastry over filling to form triangles. Crimp the edges with a fork to seal. Place filled pastries onto baking sheet. Brush pastries with egg mixture and sprinkle with chili powder.
- Bake 15 mins or till pastries are golden. Serve warm or at room temperature.

240. Nacho Cheese Dip

Serving: 8 | Prep: | Cook: 20mins | Ready in:

Ingredients

- 1/4 pound bulk spicy pork or Mexican-style sausage
- 2 tablespoons chopped green pepper
- 2 tablespoons chopped onion
- 1 pound American cheese, cubed
- 3/4 cup salsa
- Tortilla chips or raw vegetables

Direction

- In a 1-1/2-qt. microwave-safe container, cook sausage, green pepper and onion on high for 1-2 minutes or until sausage is fully cooked; drain. Add the cheese and salsa. Cover and microwave on high for 1-2 minutes, stirring frequently until cheese is melted and mixture is smooth. Serve with tortilla chips or vegetables.
- Nutrition Facts
- 2 tablespoons: 75 calories, 6g fat (3g saturated fat), 14mg cholesterol, 279mg sodium, 2g carbohydrate (2g sugars, 0 fiber), 4g protein.

241. Nacho Pinwheels Recipe

Serving: 24 | Prep: | Cook: 30mins | Ready in:

Ingredients

- 1
- can (8 oz) Pillsbury® refrigerated crescent dinner rolls or 1 can (8 oz) Pillsbury® Crescent Recipe Creations® refrigerated seamless dough sheet
- 1
- package (3 oz) cream cheese, softened
- 1 1/2
- teaspoons Old El Paso® taco seasoning mix (from 1-oz package)
- 1/3
- cup finely shredded cheddar cheese
- 1/4
- cup Green Giant® SteamCrisp® Mexicorn® whole kernel corn with red and green peppers (from 11-oz can), drained
- 2
- tablespoons finely chopped green onions (2 medium)
- Old El Paso® Thick 'n chunky salsa, if desired

Direction

- 1 Heat oven to 350°F. Spray cookie sheet with cooking spray.
- 2 If using crescent rolls: Unroll dough; separate dough into 4 rectangles. Firmly press perforations to seal. If using dough sheet: Unroll dough and cut into 4 rectangles.
- 3 In small bowl, mix cream cheese and taco seasoning mix. Stir in Cheddar cheese, corn and onions. Spread 2 tablespoons cream cheese mixture over each rectangle to within 1/4 inch of edges.
- 4 Starting with one short side, roll up each rectangle; press edge to seal. With serrated knife, cut each roll into 6 slices; place cut side down on cookie sheet.
- 5 Bake 13 to 17 minutes or until edges are golden brown. Serve warm with salsa.

242. Nachos And Cheese Recipe

Serving: 4 | Prep: | Cook: 15mins | Ready in:

Ingredients

- 1 (12 oz.) pkg. plain nachos
- 1 (8 oz.) pkg. Velveeta
- mexican cheese
- 3 Tbsp. milk
- 4 Tbsp. stewed tomatoes

Direction

- Melt cheese in milk; add tomatoes and stir real well.
- Remove from heat right away. Dip or pour cheese over nachos.
- Nachos can also be warmed up.

243. Nachos Recipe

Serving: 4 | Prep: | Cook: 20mins | Ready in:

Ingredients

- 1 Bag of tortilla chips
- 1 tomato
- 1 small onion
- 1 green pepper
- Shredded monterey jack cheese - 4 Cups
- 1 small can sliced black olives
- 1 Breast of chicken
- guacamole - as much as you want
- sour cream - as much as you want
- salsa - as much as you want

Direction

- One layer of chips to bottom of baking dish
- Chop all veggies
- Shred cheese
- Pan Fry chicken
- Cut up chicken into small pieces
- Put 1/2 of all ingredients on top of chips
- Add another layer of chips
- Add second 1/2 of ingredients onto chips
- Bake 20 minutes at 400 degrees
- Top with Sour cream, salsa, and guacamole

244. New Year Baked Bacon Cheese Dip Recipe

Serving: 25 | Prep: | Cook: 30mins | Ready in:

Ingredients

- 2-8 ounce packages cream cheese, softened
- 2 cups sour cream
- 1 medium onion, chopped
- 2 tablespoons mayonnaise
- 1 pound sliced bacon*, +cooked and crumbled+
- 4 cups shredded cheddar cheese, divided
- crackers or chips, your favorite
- *I prefer to bake the bacon. Line an iron skillet with heavy duty foil, place strips of bacon on foil and bake at 400 degrees until brown. Remove bacon, drain on paper towel, then crumble)
- CAN HALF THIS RECIPE

Direction

- In large mixing bowl, beat cream cheese
- Add sour cream, onion, mayonnaise
- Beat again until combined and smooth
- Fold in cooked crumbled bacon
- Fold in 3 cups of the cheddar cheese
- Place in baking dish (I think a bowl type casserole is best)
- Sprinkle with remaining cheese
- Bake uncovered at 375 degrees for about 30 minutes or until lightly browned

- If using a bowl type casserole, may place on a large platter, or basket tray, and surround with crackers and chips

245. Nutty Caramel Baked Brie Recipe

Serving: 10 | Prep: | Cook: 25mins | Ready in:

Ingredients

- 15 oz round brie, place in the freezer for 15 minutes before using
- 1/4 cup chopped pecans or walnuts
- 1/4 cup packed brown sugar
- 1/2 tsp cinnamon
- package frozen puff pastry, thawed
- 1 egg
- 1 tbsp heavy cream

Direction

- Carefully cut the brie horizontally through the centre, splitting the cheese into two rounds. Set aside
- In a medium bowl, mix together the pecans, brown sugar and cinnamon.
- Unfold one sheet of puff pastry flat on the counter. Set one of the brie rounds, cut side up, in the centre of the pastry. Spread the nut mixture over the brie, then set the second half of the cheese, cut side down on top
- Cut 1 inch off the corners of the pastry to form a rough circle, and then fold the pastry up the sides of the brie
- Place a second sheet of pastry over the top, then cut away any excess, leaving just enough pastry for the two sheets to meet. Using your fingers, crimp the pastry sheets together making sure it is completely sealed.
- At this point, the cheese can be refrigerated for several hours until ready to bake, or wrapped tightly in plastic and frozen. If frozen, place the cheese in the refrigerator to that about 12 hours before baking.
- When ready to bake, preheat oven to 425. Line a baking sheet with parchment paper
- In a small bowl, whisk together the egg and cream. Use a pastry brush to brush the sides and top of the pastry with the egg mixture. If desired scraps of pastry can be rolled out and cut in decorative shapes and placed on top.
- Bake for 20-25 minutes or until golden brown and puffed.
- Let cool slightly before slicing.
- Serve with sliced fruit.

246. Nutty Cheddar Crackers Recipe

Serving: 12 | Prep: | Cook: 20mins | Ready in:

Ingredients

- 1-1/2 cups flour
- 1/4 cup butter
- 1/2 cup chopped walnuts
- 1/4 teaspoon worcestershire sauce
- 4 ounces shredded cheddar cheese
- 8 tablespoons cold water

Direction

- Heat oven to 375.
- Lightly grease cookie sheets.
- Spoon flour into measuring cup and level off.
- In medium bowl combine flour and butter then cut in until mixture resembles coarse crumbs.
- Stir in walnuts, Worcestershire and cheese.
- Add water 1 tablespoon at a time while tossing and mixing lightly with a fork.
- Keep adding water until dough is just moist enough to form a ball when pressed together.
- On a lightly floured surface roll dough to 1/8".
- Cut into desired shapes and place 1" apart on greased cookie sheets.
- Bake 10 minutes.
- Immediately remove from cookie sheets and cool on wire rack.

247. Nutty Mushroom Camembert Appetizer Recipe

Serving: 4 | Prep: | Cook: 20mins | Ready in:

Ingredients

- 1/2 cup walnut pieces
- One 8-ounce wheel of ripe Camembert in its wooden box, at room temperature
- 1 tablespoon walnut oil
- 3/4 pound wild mushrooms, trimmed, caps thinly sliced
- salt and freshly ground pepper
- 1 shallot, minced
- 2 tablespoons chopped flat-leaf parsley
- 2 large sage leaves, minced
- Sourdough toasts, for serving

Direction

- Preheat the oven to 350°.
- Spread the walnut pieces on a baking sheet and toast in the oven for about 7 minutes, until lightly browned.
- Lower the oven temperature to 300°.
- Remove the Camembert from the box and unwrap it.
- Put the cheese back in the bottom half of the box and set it on a baking sheet.
- Bake for about 10 minutes, until soft.
- Meanwhile, in a large skillet, heat the walnut oil.
- Add the mushrooms and season with salt and pepper.
- Cover and cook over moderate heat, stirring occasionally, until softened, about 5 minutes.
- Uncover and cook, stirring, until lightly browned, 3 minutes longer.
- Add the shallot and cook until softened, 2 minutes.
- Stir in the parsley and sage; season with salt and pepper.
- Invert the Camembert onto a platter.
- Stir the walnuts into the mushrooms and spoon over the cheese.
- Serve with the toasts.

248. Olive Cheese Balls Recipe

Serving: 12 | Prep: | Cook: 17mins | Ready in:

Ingredients

- 2 cups shredded sharp natural cheddar cheese (8
- ounces)
- 1 1/4 cups Gold Medal all-purpose flour
- 1/2 cup butter or margarine, melted
- 48 small pimiento-stuffed olives, drained and patted
- dry

Direction

- Stir together cheese and flour in large bowl. Stir in butter thoroughly. (If dough seems dry, work with hands.)
- Mould 1 teaspoon dough around each olive; shape into ball. Place 2 inches apart on ungreased cookie sheet.
- Cover and refrigerate at least 1 hour but no longer than 24 hours.
- Heat oven to 400F. Bake 15 to 20 minutes or until light brown.

249. Olive Stuffed Cheese Balls Recipe

Serving: 20 | Prep: | Cook: 15mins | Ready in:

Ingredients

- 1 cup shredded sharp cheddar cheese
- 2 tablespoons unsalted butter

- 1/2 cup all-purpose flour
- Dash cayenne (I like a good dash!)
- 20 medium green olives, or olives of your choice

Direction

- In large bowl with mixer*, cream together cheese and butter
- Blend in flour and cayenne on low
- Wrap a teaspoonful of dough around each olive, covering completely
- Place on cookie sheet
- Bake at 375 or 400 degree oven for 15 minutes
- Makes about 20 balls
- *Can mix these by hand
- NOTE: Olive lovers, please refrain from eating before they are baked :)

250. Onion Cheese Dip Recipe

Serving: 20 | Prep: | Cook: 30mins | Ready in:

Ingredients

- 2 cups mayonaise
- 2 cups grated swiss cheese
- 2 packages frozen chopped onions, thawed and drained well
- 4-5 drops hot sauce (add more if you like or leave it out)

Direction

- Mix all ingredients together.
- Place in glass baking dish.
- Bake 30 minutes at 350 degrees.

251. Onion Fig And Gorgonzola Mini Puffs Recipe

Serving: 8 | Prep: | Cook: 30mins | Ready in:

Ingredients

- 1 24 ct package mini puff pastry shells
- 1 med-large white onion, finely sliced
- 3/4 cup fresh figs, diced (you may sub dried, but steam or soak first to plump)
- 1 tbsp balsamic vinegar
- 1/2 cup crumbled gorgonzola
- salt and pepper to taste
- butter or oil for pan

Direction

- Bake pastry shells according to package's directions. Remove "tops" and allow to cool.
- Meanwhile, heat a large heavy skillet with butter or oil over medium heat. Add onions and figs and season to taste with salt and pepper. Allow to cook 10-15 minutes without browning.
- Once onions begin to turn golden, add vinegar and continue cooking 20-30 additional minutes, until sticky and caramelized.
- Preheat oven to 350 degrees.
- Carefully stuff mini shells with onion and fig mixture. If desired, stuff a large crumble of bleu cheese in as well. Top with small crumbles of gorgonzola.
- Bake shells another 5-7 minutes until pastry is golden and cheese is all lovely and oozy.
- Serve immediately or allow to cool to room temp before serving.

252. Oven Fried Mozzarella Sticks Recipe

Serving: 4 | Prep: | Cook: 10mins | Ready in:

Ingredients

- 2 sprays olive oil cooking spray, divided
- 8 oz canned tomato sauce
- 2 tsp ground oregano, divided
- 3 slice reduced-calorie wheat bread, torn
- 1 tsp dried thyme

- 8 oz part-skim mozzarella cheese, cut into 8 finger-like strips
- 2 Tbsp honey mustard

Direction

- Preheat oven to 400ºF. Coat a baking sheet with cooking spray.
- In a small saucepan, combine tomato sauce and 1 teaspoon of oregano; set pan over low heat and simmer 10 minutes.
- Meanwhile, in a food processor, combine bread, remaining teaspoon of oregano and thyme; process until mixture resembles fine crumbs. Place crumbs in a shallow bowl. (Tip: Use the ends of the loaf of bread for the bread crumbs since those slices are often uneaten.)
- Coat cheese sticks with honey mustard. Transfer cheese to bread crumb mixture and turn to coat. Arrange cheese on prepared baking sheet and lightly coat with cooking spray.
- Bake until golden brown, about 4 to 5 minutes. Serve with warmed tomato sauce on the side. Yields 2 cheese sticks and about 1/4 cup of sauce per serving.

253. Oyster Parmesan Cheese Bake Recipe

Serving: 6 | Prep: | Cook: 15mins | Ready in:

Ingredients

- 2 pints oysters, freshly shucked without liquor
- 1/4 c butter
- 1 T lemon juice
- 1 clove garlic, minced
- 1/4 c seasoned bread crumbs
- 1 c parmesan cheese,shredded

Direction

- Place oysters in the bottom of a shallow baking dish. Melt butter and add garlic and lemon juice, pour over oysters. Sprinkle with bread crumbs and parmesan cheese.
- Bake at 375 degrees for 15 minutes
- Serve warm with hot sauce if desired.

254. Parmesan Artichoke Dip Recipe

Serving: 6 | Prep: | Cook: 30mins | Ready in:

Ingredients

- 4 cloves garlic
- 6 slices pickled jalapeno pepper (or to taste)
- 8 oz. cream cheese, softened
- 4 oz. mayonnaise
- 8 oz. shredded parmesan
- 8 oz. jar artichoke hearts
- 8 oz. crab meat (optional)

Direction

- Preheat oven to 350 degrees (F).
- Mince garlic and jalapeno slices in food processor.
- Add cream cheese, mayonnaise and parmesan and mix well.
- Add artichokes (and crab meat if you're using it) and pulse a few times until mixed but leave some chunks.
- Pour into baking dish and bake at 375 degrees for approximately 20 minutes, or until bubbly and golden brown.
- Let sit for 10 minutes before serving. Dip will firm up as it sits.
- Enjoy!

255. Parmesan Balls Recipe

Serving: 6 | Prep: | Cook: 26mins | Ready in:

Ingredients

- 1 ¼ cups flour, plus up to 3 tablespoons more if necessary
- 1 cup loosely packed grated parmesan cheese
- ½ teaspoon salt
- ½ teaspoon freshly ground white pepper
- ½ teaspoon dry mustard
- ½ cup melted butter

Direction

- In the bowl of the food processor, mix the flour, parmesan cheese, salt, pepper and dry mustard.
- Add the butter and work it in using the pulse button so the mixture forms crumbs.
- Press a few crumbs together with your fingers.
- If it's sticky, add 2 to 3 tablespoons more flour.
- Butter a baking sheet.
- Turn the crumbs into a bowl, press them into balls 1- inch in diameter and place them on the baking sheet.
- Chill in the refrigerator for 30 minutes.
- Heat the oven to 350 degrees.
- Bake the cheese balls until lightly browned, 26 to 28 minutes.
- They keep well in an airtight container, or they can be frozen.

256. Parmesan Black Pepper Crackers Recipe

Serving: 4 | Prep: | Cook: 20mins | Ready in:

Ingredients

- 8 tbls. unsalted butter
- 3/4 cup plus 2 tbls. flour
- 1 cup parmesan cheese, freshly grated
- 1/4 tsp. black pepper, freshly ground

Direction

- Cook time does not include chill time.
- Preheat oven to 375
- Cream butter in mixer until smooth and fluffy
- Add flour, cheese, and pepper and mix at low speed until combined
- Form dough into disk, wrap in plastic, and chill at least 2 hours
- Before rolling, let dough sit out 15-30 minutes
- On a well-floured surface with a floured rolling pin, roll out dough into a rectangle a little less than 1/4 inch
- Dough is delicate so push back any cracks with your fingers
- Transfer dough to a cookie sheet
- Prick surface all over with fork
- With a pizza cutter, cut dough into 1 1/2 inch squares
- Bake 15-20 minutes, until golden brown
- Run pizza cutter along cuts again
- Cool

257. Parmesan Breadsticks Recipe

Serving: 8 | Prep: | Cook: 10mins | Ready in:

Ingredients

- 1 3/4 C all purpose flour
- 1/2 C parmesan cheese
- 1 tsp fresh or dried herbs (rosemary)
- 1 tsp salt
- 1/2 tsp pepper
- 1/2 tsp dry yeast
- 3/4 C warm water
- 3 tbsp semolina flour or cornmeal
- 1 tsp olive oil

Direction

- Mix 3/4 C flour with cheese, herbs, salt and yeast
- Blend in water.
- Add the 1 C flour to form soft dough.
- Dust the work surface.
- Knead the dough on it for 10 mins. until elastic

- Divide into 2 portions and cover with damp towel and rest for 10 mins
- Sprinkle two 8 by 6 inch waxed paper sheet with 1 tbsp. of semolina on each and pat dough pieces into 5 by 3 inch rectangles.
- Sprinkle 1 tbsp. of semolina on each again.
- Brush with oil and cover with towel.
- Let it stand for 30 mins.
- Cut each into 10 equal strips.
- Leave it to rise, for 10 mins. uncovered.
- Pre heat oven to 200 degrees.
- Twist and turn and stretch them to make each of them longer.
- Place on the cooking sheet and bake for 10 mins.

258. Parmesan Cheese Crisps Recipe

Serving: 4 | Prep: | Cook: 10mins | Ready in:

Ingredients

- 6 Tablespoons melted unsalted butter
- 1/8 teaspoon garlic powder
- 1/8 teaspoon ground cumin
- 1/4 teaspoon paprika
- 3/4 teaspoon ground tumeric
- 1/2 cup finely grated parmesan cheese
- 12 6 inch corn tortillas
- salt

Direction

- Preheat oven to 375 degrees F. In a small bowl, combine butter and spices. Brush the top of each tortilla with butter mixture and sprinkle with Parmesan cheese and salt.
- Cut the tortillas into wedges and place them on a baking sheet and bake 10 to 15 minutes until crisp.
- Once they are crisped, take them out of the oven and transfer the chips onto a wire rack to cool. Let them cool for a few minutes before serving or storing.
- Makes about 8 dozen chips.

259. Parmesan Cheese Straws Recipe

Serving: 36 | Prep: | Cook: 7mins | Ready in:

Ingredients

- 2/3 cup REAL parmesan cheese
- 1/2 cup butter, softened
- 1 cup all-purpose flour
- 1/4 teaspoon salt
- 1/4 teaspoon red pepper (more or less, to taste)
- 1/4 cup milk
- pecan halves (optional)

Direction

- Position knife blade in food processor bowl; add cheese and butter. Process until blended.
- Add flour, salt, and red pepper to cheese mixture; process about 30 seconds or until mixture forms a ball, stopping often to scrape down sides.
- EITHER --
- Divide dough in half; roll each portion into a 1/8-inch-thick rectangle, and cut into 2- x1/2-inch thick strips.
- OR --
- Shape dough into 3/4-inch balls; flatten each ball to about 1/8-inch thickness.
- Place strips or rounds of dough onto ungreased baking sheets; brush dough with milk.
- Top with pecan halves, if desired.
- Bake strips at 350 degrees for 7 minutes AND/OR bake rounds for 10 minutes or until lightly browned.
- Transfer to wire racks to cool.
- Yield: 5 dozen cheese straws or 3 dozen cheese wafers.

260. Parmesan Cheese Twists Recipe

Serving: 12 | Prep: | Cook: 10mins | Ready in:

Ingredients

- 1 sheet frozen puff pastry
- 1 egg
- 1 tbsp water
- 1/4 cup grated Parmesean cheese
- 1 tbsp parsley
- 1/2 tsp oregano

Direction

- Thaw pastry 30 minutes. Preheat oven to 400 degrees
- Mix egg and water. Mix cheese parsley and oregano
- Unfold pastry-roll to 14 x 10 rectangle
- Cut in 1/2 lengthwise. Brush with the egg mixture
- Top rectangle with cheese.
- Place other rectangle egg side down.
- Roll gently with rolling pin
- Cut cross wise into 28 strips.
- Twist place on greased sheets-press ends down
- Bake 10 minutes

261. Parmesan Chicken Tenders Recipe

Serving: 10 | Prep: | Cook: 15mins | Ready in:

Ingredients

- 4 tablespoons plus 1/2 cup extra-virgin olive oil
- 1 cup buttermilk
- 1 1/2 pounds chicken tenders (about 18)
- 3 large garlic cloves, minced
- 1/2 teaspoon salt
- 3 tablespoons balsamic vinegar
- Freshly ground black pepper
- 1 1/4 cups freshly grated Parmesan
- 3/4 cup Italian-style seasoned bread crumbs

Direction

- Preheat the oven to 500 degrees F.
- Brush 1 tablespoon of oil over each of 2 heavy large lined baking sheets.
- Place the buttermilk in a large bowl. Add the chicken tenders and stir to coat. Let stand at least 15 minutes and up to 30 minutes.
- Meanwhile, mash the garlic with the salt in a medium bowl.
- Whisk in the vinegar and then the remaining 1/2 cup of oil.
- Season the vinaigrette, to taste, with pepper. Transfer the vinaigrette to a small serving bowl.
- Stir the Parmesan and bread crumbs in a pie dish. Remove the chicken tenders from the buttermilk and dredge them in the bread crumb mixture to coat completely, pressing to adhere.
- Arrange the coated chicken tenders on the prepared baking sheets, spacing evenly.
- Drizzle the remaining 2 tablespoons of oil over the chicken tenders and bake until they are cooked through and golden brown, about 12 - 15 minutes.
- Transfer the chicken tenders to a platter and serve the vinaigrette alongside for dipping.

262. Parmesan Chicken Wings Recipe

Serving: 4 | Prep: | Cook: 45mins | Ready in:

Ingredients

- 2 tablespoons chopped parsley
- 2 teaspoons paprika
- 1 teaspoon dried oregano

- 1/2 teaspoon dried basil
- 1/4 teaspoon salt
- 1/4 teaspoon freshly ground pepper
- 1/2 cup butter melted
- 1 pound chicken wings disjointed and tips removed

Direction

- Preheat oven to 350.
- In a paper bag combine cheese, parsley, paprika, oregano, basil, salt, and pepper.
- Toss to mix.
- Pour melted butter in a shallow bowl.
- Dip chicken pieces into butter then place in paper bag and shake to coat.
- Place chicken on foil lined baking sheet and bake 45 minutes then serve hot.

263. Parmesan Crisps Recipe

Serving: 4 | Prep: | Cook: 10mins | Ready in:

Ingredients

- 1/2 cup grated Parmesan

Direction

- Preheat oven to 400 degrees F.
- Pour a heaping tablespoon of Parmesan onto a silicone or parchment lined baking sheet and lightly pat down.
- A silicone baking sheet is highly recommended.
- I used a cookie sheet with Foil/Pam, worked great!
- Repeat with the remaining cheese, spacing the spoonfuls about a 1/2 inch apart.
- Bake for 3 to 5 minutes or until golden and crisp. Cool.

264. Parmesan Mustard Chicken Wings Recipe

Serving: 2 | Prep: | Cook: 40mins | Ready in:

Ingredients

- 1 stick (1/2 cup) unsalted butter
- 2 tablespoons dijon-style mustard
- 1/8 teaspoon cayenne
- 1 cup dried bread crumbs
- 1/2 cup freshly grated Parmesan
- 1 teaspoon ground cumin
- 20 chicken wings, wing tips cut off and discarded and the wings
- halved at the joint

Direction

- In a shallow dish whisk together the butter, the mustard, and the cayenne. In another shallow dish combine well the bread crumbs, the Parmesan, the cumin, and salt and black pepper to taste. Dip the chicken wings, a few at a time, in the butter mixture, letting the excess drip off, coat them with the crumb mixture, and arrange them without touching in a greased shallow baking pan. Bake the chicken wings in the lower third of a preheated 425F oven for 40 minutes. (If extra-crisp chicken wings are desired, turn the wings after 30 minutes.)

265. Parmesan Puffs With Marinara Recipe

Serving: 30 | Prep: | Cook: 35mins | Ready in:

Ingredients

- 1/2 cup milk
- 1/4 cup butter or margarine
- 1/2 cup Gold Medal® all-purpose flour
- 2 eggs
- 3/4 cup freshly grated parmesan cheese

- 1 cup marinara sauce, heated
- Variation
- Add 1 tablespoon chopped fresh basil, oregano or parsley (or 1 teaspoon dried) to the flour to create herbed Parmesan Puffs with Marinara.

Direction

- 1. Heat oven to 375°F. Grease cookie sheet
- 2. Heat milk and butter to boiling in 1 1/2-quart saucepan. Stir in flour; reduce heat to low. Stir vigorously about 1 minute or until mixture forms a ball; remove from heat
- 3. Beat in eggs, one at a time, and beating until smooth after each addition. Stir in cheese. Drop dough by rounded teaspoonfuls 2 inches apart onto cookie sheet.
- 4. Bake about 15 minutes or until puffed and golden brown. Serve warm with marinara sauce for dipping.
- Do-Ahead Tip
- You can prepare these puffs ahead. Cool puffs, wrap tightly and freeze. When ready to serve, place in muffin cups and heat in a 350°F oven for 8 to 10 minutes or until hot.

266. Parmesan Rounds Recipe

Serving: 24 | Prep: | Cook: 12mins | Ready in:

Ingredients

- 3/4 cup grated parmesan cheese
- 1/2 cup flour
- 1/8 tsp red pepper
- 1/4 cup butter, softened
- 2 tbls cold water
- 2 tbls finely chopped walnuts
- 1 tbl parsly flakes

Direction

- Combine parmesan cheese, flour, and red pepper; cut in butter with a pastry blender until mixture resembles coarse meal.
- Sprinkle cold water (1 tbsp. at a time) evenly over surface; stir with a fork until dry ingredients are moistened.
- Shape dough into 1 1/2 inch thick log and set aside.
- Combine walnuts and parsley in a shallow pan; roll log in mixture to coat evenly.
- Cut log with a serrated knife into 1/4 inch slices; place on ungreased baking sheet.
- Bake at 375 for 12 minutes or until lightly browned; cool on a wire rack.
- Store crackers in a tightly covered container.
- These crackers will freeze well. Yield is 2 dozen.

267. Parmesan Thins Recipe

Serving: 20 | Prep: | Cook: 10mins | Ready in:

Ingredients

- 1/2 cup all-purpose flour
- 5 tbsp. unsalted butter, softened
- 1 egg yolk
- 1 tsp. sugar
- 2/3 cup grated parmesan cheese
- pinch of salt (don't add too much salt, as the Parmesan is already salty)
- pinch (about 1/4 tsp.) of ground mustard

Direction

- Put the flour in a medium bowl. Add softened butter and work the dough with the fork until flour is well incorporated and starts to come together.
- Add the egg yolk, sugar, Parmesan, salt and mustard powder to the flour/butter mix. Work them in with the fork, until comes together nicely.
- Shape the mixture into a log. Roll it between the palms of your hands to help shape it. Wrap

the log in foil or saran wrap and chill in the fridge for 10 minutes.

- Preheat the oven to 400F. Cut the log into thin slices with a sharp knife (about 1/4 inch thick).
- Arrange on a baking sheet lined with parchment. Dip a fork in flour and flatten the crackers with the fork prongs to give them a pretty ridged pattern.
- Bake for 10 minutes, or until the crackers are crisp and lightly golden.
- Serve on their own, or with your favourite dip. Also great with soups. This recipe makes about 20 crackers.

268. Parmesan Treats For Dogs Recipe

Serving: 100 | Prep: | Cook: 15mins | Ready in:

Ingredients

- 500 g wheat wholemeal
- 160 g freshly grated parmesan
- 125 ml water
- 100 ml olive oil
- 2 eggs

Direction

- Mix everything to a dough and roll out about 5 mm thick.
- With a help of a knife cut it in small cubes.
- Bake for 15 minutes on 200°C.

269. Parmesan And Thyme Crackers Recipe

Serving: 24 | Prep: | Cook: 25mins | Ready in:

Ingredients

- 1/4 pound (1 stick) unsalted butter, at room temperature
- 4 ounces freshly grated Parmesan (about 1 cup)
- 1 1/4 cups all-purpose flour
- 1/4 teaspoon kosher salt
- 1 teaspoon chopped fresh thyme leaves (I use a little more)
- 1/2 teaspoon freshly ground black pepper

Direction

- Place the butter in the bowl of an electric mixer fitted with a paddle attachment and mix until creamy.
- Add the Parmesan, flour, salt, thyme and pepper and combine.
- Dump the dough on a lightly floured board and roll into a 13-inch long log.
- You may have to add a little bit of water to the dough as you form it as this dough is pretty crumbly.
- Wrap the log in plastic wrap and place in the freezer for 30 minutes to harden (or leave in fridge overnight, if you want to get a head start on this recipe).
- Meanwhile, preheat the oven to 350 degrees F.
- Cut the log crosswise into 1/4 to 1/2-inch thick slices.
- Place the slices on a sheet pan and bake for 22 minutes.

270. Parmesan And Thyme Stuffed Mushroom Caps Recipe

Serving: 12 | Prep: | Cook: 35mins | Ready in:

Ingredients

- What you'll need
- 25 small-medium button mushrooms or 8 large flat field mushrooms
- 1 small-medium onion (finely diced)
- 1 clove of garlic

- 10-15 sprigs of fresh thyme (about 1 tbsp chopped)
- 1 tbsp chopped fresh parsley
- 3.5 oz butter
- 2/3 cup of bread crumbs
- 1/3 cup of freshly grated parmesan cheese
- extra virgin olive oil
- sea salt flakes
- black pepper corn

Direction

- Preheat oven 350 F
- Pull the stalk out of the centre of the mushroom caps and remove any excess stalk flesh left in the cap.
- Finely chop the removed stalks.
- In a heavy based fry pan, soften the onion in the butter and approx. 3 tbsps. Of olive oil over medium heat for approx. 5 minutes.
- Add the garlic and the chopped mushroom stalks and cook a further 5 minutes.
- Add the thyme and remove from the heat.
- Add the bread crumbs to a large mixing bowl season with a little salt and pepper and add the contents of the pan, stir well.
- Add the parmesan cheese and the parsley, mix well.
- Using a teaspoon fill the mushroom caps with the mix, for the buttons you can overfill them and press the stuffing into a small mound sitting atop the mushrooms, for the field mushrooms just stuff them until the mix is level with the top of the mushroom.
- Place the stuffed mushrooms in the fridge for 15-20 minutes, place on a lightly oiled oven proof tray and bake for 15-20 minutes until golden.
- Serve the buttons on a canapé platter.
- Serve the field mushrooms with a spinach salad to the side.

271. Pea Guacamole In A Parmesan Basket Recipe

Serving: 1 | Prep: | Cook: 10mins | Ready in:

Ingredients

- For the parmesan basket:
- 75g/2¾oz parmesan, grated
- For the pea guacamole:
- 150g/5½oz peas, cooked in boiling water and refreshed in iced water
- 50g/1¾fl oz Greek yoghurt
- pinch dried chilli flakes
- 1 tbsp chopped fresh mint
- 1 tbsp chopped fresh coriander
- salt and freshly ground black pepper

Direction

- Preheat the oven to 200C/400F/Gas 6.
- To make the parmesan basket, place a sheet of greaseproof paper onto a baking sheet.
- Place the grated parmesan cheese in a pile onto the paper.
- Place into the oven to bake for eight minutes, until the cheese has melted into a flat round.
- Remove from the oven and allow to cool for one minute, until the cheese round begins to become firm.
- Carefully shape the parmesan round into a basket shape by pressing it over the back of a dariole mould, leave to cool and set.
- To make the pea guacamole, place the peas and yoghurt into a bowl and mash together to a paste.
- Add the chilli flakes and herbs and mix well.
- Season, to taste, with salt and freshly ground black pepper.
- To serve, place the parmesan basket in the centre of a plate and spoon in the pea guacamole.

272. Pear Walnut And Gorgonzola Bruschetta Recipe

Serving: 6 | Prep: | Cook: 15mins | Ready in:

Ingredients

- 6 slices rustic Italian bread
- 12 walnuts, finely chopped
- 6 ounces gorgonzola OR other meltable blue cheese
- 2 bosc pears
- olive oil

Direction

- Preheat oven to 425 degrees F.
- Slice the bread thinly into 1/2" thicknesses.
- Brush bread slices with olive oil.
- Place bread on a rack in a hot oven and toast until browned.
- Reduce oven temperature to 325 degrees F.
- Remove the rind from the cheese.
- Lay the toasted bread in an ovenproof dish.
- Cover bread with thinly sliced cheese.
- Garnish with walnuts.
- Put bread back into a medium hot oven until cheese melts.
- Core and cut the pears into small cubes.
- Garnish the bruschetta with pear cubes as soon as it comes from the oven.
- Serve.

273. Pear And Gouda Stuffed Chicken Breasts With Caramelized Onion Sauce Recipe

Serving: 6 | Prep: | Cook: 30mins | Ready in:

Ingredients

- 8 slices thick-cut bacon, diced to 1/4"
- 3 whole chicken breasts, split in half lengthwise
- 3 bosc pears, diced in 1/4" cubes (skin on)
- 1 T. fresh rosemary, finely chopped
- 6 slices smoked gouda cheese (approx. 6 oz.)
- 3 medium yellow onions, in 1/4" slices
- 1 t. salt
- 3 T. brown sugar
- 2 T. balsamic vinegar
- rosemary sprigs for garnish

Direction

- 1. Preheat oven to 400 degrees.
- 2. Render fat from bacon: In large saucepan, fry bacon over medium-low heat until crisp. Remove bacon to paper towels, reserving liquid in pan.
- 3. While bacon is cooking, pound chicken breasts between two sheets of plastic until approx. 3/8" uniform thickness.
- 4. Add pears and rosemary to reserved fat in pan. Cook over medium-high heat until slightly softened and golden-brown, approx. 5 minutes.
- 5. Remove pear-rosemary mixture from pan, using slotted spoon and reserving liquid in pan. Mix pears with bacon.
- 6. Lay out chicken breasts with smallest end at bottom. Top with 1 slice Gouda cheese, then 1/6 of pear-rosemary-bacon mixture, leaving approx. 2" at bottom.
- 7. Roll chicken jelly-roll fashion, tucking in sides. Secure with toothpicks on side.
- 8. Lightly brown top and bottom of chicken in reserved liquid in pan over medium-high heat, approx. 2 minutes per side.
- 9. Place chicken breasts, top side up, in 13" X 9" pan, reserving liquid in pan. Bake at 400 degrees for 15 to 18 minutes or until internal temperature registers 160 degrees.
- 10. Meanwhile, cook onions in reserved liquid in pan, scraping any browned portions from bottom of pan, over medium-high heat until golden brown (onions may start to stick to bottom of pan -- this is okay). Lower heat and keep warm until chicken is done.

- 11. Remove chicken from oven and drain liquid. Tent chicken with foil.
- 12. Deglaze onions over medium-high heat using chicken liquid. Reduce to approx. 3/4 cup. Add brown sugar and stir until smooth and glossy.
- 13. Remove onion sauce from heat and stir in balsamic vinegar.
- 14. Place chicken breasts on serving dish and cover with onion sauce. Garnish with additional rosemary sprigs.

274. Pecorino Romano Crostini With Apples And Fig Jam Recipe

Serving: 6 | Prep: | Cook: 15mins | Ready in:

Ingredients

- 6 dried figs, halved
- 1/2 cup simple syrup, recipe follows
- 2 tablespoons brandy
- 1/4 cup chopped toasted hazelnuts
- 24 baguette slices
- olive oil, for drizzling
- 1/2 cup grated Pecorino Romano
- 1 large apple (Granny Smith or Braeburn), thinly sliced into 24 slices
- 1/4 pound chunk Pecorino Romano, for shaving 24 pieces
- Simple syrup:
- 1/2 cup water
- 1 cup sugar

Direction

- For simple syrup: In a saucepan combine water and sugar over medium heat. Bring to a boil, reduce heat and simmer for 5 minutes, until the sugar has dissolved. Take pan off heat and cool the syrup. Any extra cooled syrup can be saved in an airtight container in the refrigerator.
- Preheat the oven to 375 degrees F.
- Place a small saucepan over medium heat. Add the figs, simple syrup, and brandy. Bring the mixture up to a simmer. Turn off the heat and let sit for 10 minutes. Place the fig mixture and the hazelnuts in a food processor and blend, pulsing a few times, until pureed. Set aside.
- Place the baguette slices on a heavy baking sheet. Drizzle with olive oil. Top each slice with 1 teaspoon grated Pecorino Romano. Bake until the bread is toasted and the cheese is melted and golden, about 7 minutes.
- Top each slice of toast with 2 teaspoons of fig jam, a slice of apple and a piece of shaved Pecorino Romano. Transfer the toasts to a serving platter and serve.

275. Peppery Panko Crusted Parmesan Chicken Wings Recipe

Serving: 24 | Prep: | Cook: 70mins | Ready in:

Ingredients

- 2 cups Italian-style panko bread crumbs
- 1 cup finely shredded or grated parmesan cheese
- 2 teaspoons black pepper
- 1 1/2 cups all-purpose flour seasoned with salt and black pepper
- 2 eggs, beaten
- 12 whole chicken wings, split at the joint
- ranch dressing or other sauce for serving, optional

Direction

- Preheat oven to 425 degrees.
- Line a baking sheet with foil and coat with non-stick spray.
- Using 2 shallow plates, combine the bread crumbs, cheese and 2 teaspoons black pepper

on one and place the seasoned flour on the other.

- Place the beaten eggs in a bowl.
- Dredge each chicken wing in the seasoned flour, shake off any excess, dip in the egg mixture and then roll in the bread crumbs -- patting the crumb mixture to adhere.
- Set on the prepared baking sheet.
- Repeat with all the chicken wings.
- Spray the chicken wings lightly with non-stick cooking spray.
- Bake for 40 minutes or until the wings are cooked through.
- Remove from oven and serve with dipping sauce, if desired.

276. Phyllo Turnovers With Shrimp And Ricotta Filling Recipe

Serving: 15 | Prep: | Cook: 25mins | Ready in:

Ingredients

- 3 tablespoons butter
- 1 tablespoon canola oil
- 1/3 cup chopped celery stalk
- 1/3 cup chopped green pepper
- 2/3 cup chopped green onions
- 2 dashes hot sauce, such as Tabasco
- 1 teaspoon salt
- 2 tablespoons all-purpose flour
- 1 pound large shrimp - peeled, deveined and chopped
- (approx. 1cm x 1cm) or Bigger if You Like
- 1/2 cup ricotta cheese
- 1/3 cup milk
- 1 (16 ounce) package frozen phyllo dough, thawed
- 1/2 cup butter

Direction

- Melt 3 tablespoons butter in a large skillet over medium heat, and add the canola oil.
- Stir in the celery and peppers; cook until tender, about 5 minutes.
- Add the green onions, hot sauce, and salt; cook and stir until onions are wilted, about 3 minutes.
- Stir the flour, shrimp, ricotta cheese, and milk into the pepper mixture; cook and stir until the shrimp turn pink, about 3 minutes.
- Remove from heat and cool.
- Preheat oven to 425 degrees F (220 degrees C).
- Melt 1/2 cup butter in a small saucepan over medium heat.
- Remove from heat and keep warm.
- Stack two sheets of phyllo on top of each other, and cut into 3 strips about 3 inches by 12 inches.
- Brush the top of each strip with melted butter, and place a teaspoon of the shrimp mixture at one end.
- Fold phyllo dough over the filling, working back and forth from side to side to make a triangle.
- Seal the end closed with a little water or butter. Place triangle on an ungreased baking sheet.
- Repeat with remaining phyllo sheets and filling.
- Bake in preheated oven until tops are golden brown and flaky,
- 10 to 15 minutes. Cool on a wire rack.

277. Phyllo Wrapped Crab And Brie Recipe

Serving: 15 | Prep: | Cook: 25mins | Ready in:

Ingredients

- 1/2 pound crabmeat
- 1 tablespoon butter
- 2 tablespoons chopped sweet red pepper
- 1/4 teaspoon Old Bay Seasoning

- 1/4 teaspoon salt
- 1/4 teaspoon pepper
- 2 teaspoons minced parsley
- Tabasco to taste (optional)
- 1/2 pound brie, cut into thin slices
- 15 sheets phyllo (1/2 pound)
- 3/4 cup clarified butter

Direction

- Melt butter; add red pepper and sauté until tender. Add the crab, heat through and season with salt, pepper Old Bay and Tabasco. Spread slices of Brie over crab. Keep over low heat without stirring until Brie softens enough to be stirred without breaking lumps of crab. Set aside and allow mixture to cool.
- Preheat oven to 375 degrees F.
- Remove 5 sheets of phyllo and cut in half lengthwise. For each packet, lay out 1 strip phyllo with the short end toward you, and brush with butter. Place about 1 1/2 teaspoons filling in corner of strip. Fold over to make a triangle shape and roll triangle over triangle till you reach the end and brush with butter. Repeat until all ingredients are used. Bake 20 to 25 minutes until crisp and golden. The triangles can be made ahead and frozen before baking.
- Serve hot.

278. Pies Recipe

Serving: 8 | Prep: | Cook: 1mins | Ready in:

Ingredients

- 1 package pie sheets
- 3 eggs
- 200 ml oil
- 200g cream cheese
- 200g salted cheese
- 50g sour cream
- pepper
- dill
- 1 egg yolk for smear the pie

Direction

- Heat the oven.
- Mix in a bowl, eggs, cream cheese, salted cheese, sour cream, pepper, and dill. Set aside.
- Smear an oven tray, with a little oil.
- Take each pie sheet, and stretch it, then oil it delicate with a brush.
- Put cheese mix, on each sheet, then roll.
- Use the egg yolk, to give a beautiful colour to the pies.
- Bake.

279. Portobellos With Provolone Bacon And Spinach Recipe

Serving: 3 | Prep: | Cook: 15mins | Ready in:

Ingredients

- 3 portobello mushrooms, cleaned, stems removed
- 4 ounces fresh spinach (1/2 a bag) chopped
- 3 slices thick-sliced bacon, chopped
- 1/2 medium red onion, finely diced
- 1/4 red bell pepper, finely diced
- 2 cloves garlic, minced
- 1/2 cup provolone cheese, finely diced
- Hot Shot, a hefty sprinkle
- shredded mozzarella cheese

Direction

- In skillet, sauté bacon until nearly crisp. Add onion, red pepper, garlic and sauté until soft. Add spinach and Hot Shot and continue cooking until spinach is just wilted. Transfer to bowl and mix in provolone well.
- Mound mixture into mushrooms, cover with shredded mozzarella, and bake at 450 until cheese is golden brown.
- Can also do on grill!

280. Pot Nachos Recipe

Serving: 4 | Prep: | Cook: 10mins | Ready in:

Ingredients

- 1 can black beans drained but not rinsed.
- 1 can Yellow corn Drained
- 3 to 5 Tomatoes- your choice
- Sliced jalapenos (can be omitted)
- 2 chicken breast cooked and sliced
- salsa (either homemade or store bought)
- 4 potatoes Baked and salted
- Sheredded Cheese- Both yellow and white
- sour cream
- chives

Direction

- Slice the potatoes (thin) and arrange on a plate
- Sprinkle a thin layer of cheese over these potatoes
- Add another layer a little bit smaller that the first to create a layer effect.
- Add a small layer of black beans and top of with Shredded Cheese.
- Add another layer of potatoes- stacked a little bit smaller again.
- Add your Chicken neatly down the potatoes. Then the rest of the cheese.
- Place in oven for about 10 mins until cheese is melted.
- Add your Salsa, Yellow Corn, black beans, tomatoes, and jalapenos.
- Top with Sour Cream and chives. Enjoy!!

281. Potato Dippers With Jalapeno Cheddar Dip Recipe

Serving: 8 | Prep: | Cook: 30mins | Ready in:

Ingredients

- potatoes
- 4 russet potatoes
- 2 tbls. olive oil
- 1/2 tsp. garlic powder
- 1 tsp. chili powder
- Dip
- 1/3 cup sour cream
- 1/3 cup mayonnaise
- 1/4 cup cheddar cheese, shredded
- 1/4 cup tomato, finely chopped
- 2 jalapenos, finely chopped
- 2 scallions, finely sliced for garnish

Direction

- Potatoes
- Preheat oven to 450
- Line large baking sheet with foil
- Spray with cooking spray
- Cut potatoes into thin slices
- Add potatoes, oil, and chili and garlic powder to bowl.
- Coat all potatoes
- Bake for 30 minutes turning over half way through
- Dip
- Mix all dip ingredients except scallions into mixing bowl
- Top with scallions

282. Potato Gratin With Porcini Mushrooms And Mascarpone Cheese Recipe

Serving: 8 | Prep: | Cook: 30mins | Ready in:

Ingredients

- 4 ounces dried porcini mushrooms*
- 1 cup boiling water
- 2 tablespoons (1/4 stick) butter
- 2 tablespoons extra-virgin olive oil

- 1/4 cup plus 2 tablespoons grated parmesan cheese
- 1 1/2 cups mascarpone cheese** (from about 1 1/2 seven-ounce containers)
- 1 cup whipping cream
- 3 garlic cloves, chopped
- Pinch of freshly grated nutmeg
- 2 1/2 pounds russet potatoes (about 5 large), peeled, cut crosswise into 1/8-inch-thick slices

Direction

- Place porcini and 1 cup boiling water in medium bowl.
- Place small bowl atop mushrooms to keep submerged. Let soak 20 minutes.
- Drain and coarsely chop mushrooms.
- Melt butter with oil in medium skillet over medium heat.
- Add mushrooms and sauté until beginning to brown, about 3 minutes.
- Sprinkle with salt and pepper.
- Remove from heat. Whisk 1/4 cup Parmesan and next 4 ingredients in small bowl; season with salt and pepper.
- DO AHEAD: Mushrooms and cheese mixture can be prepared 1 day ahead. Cover separately and chill.
- Preheat oven to 325°F. Butter wide shallow 2-quart baking dish. Arrange 1/4 of potato slices in bottom of dish.
- Sprinkle lightly with salt and pepper. Scatter 1/4 of mushrooms over.
- Repeat. Spread half of cheese mixture over, shaking dish to settle. Repeat with remaining potatoes and mushrooms in 2 layers each; spread remaining cheese mixture over. Sprinkle 2 tablespoons Parmesan over.
- Place gratin dish on rimmed baking sheet.
- Bake gratin until top is brown and sauce is bubbling at edges, about 1 hour 15 minutes.
- Let gratin rest 15 minutes before serving.
- DO AHEAD: Can be made 2 hours ahead. Let stand at room temperature. Tent loosely with foil and rewarm in 300°F oven 20 minutes.
- *Available in the produce section of many supermarkets and at specialty foods stores and Italian markets.
- **Italian cream cheese; sold at many supermarkets and at Italian markets

283. Potato Nachos Recipe

Serving: 12 | Prep: | Cook: 12mins | Ready in:

Ingredients

- 8 medium red potatoes
- 1 envelope dry ranch salad dressing
- 1 (12 ounce) jar pickled jalapeno pepper slices, drained
- 8 ounces cheddar cheese, shredded
- 8 ounces monterey jack cheese, shredded
- 2 cups sour cream
- 6 to 8 green onions, thinly sliced (including tops)

Direction

- Cook potatoes in boiling, salted water just until tender. Drain and cool slightly.
- Cut potatoes into 1/4 inch thick slices. Arrange in single layer on greased rimmed baking sheet or sheets. (You may need more than one.)
- Sprinkle potato slices with dry salad dressing mix. Top each with a jalapeno slice and both cheeses.
- Bake at 350 degrees for 10 to 15 minutes or until cheese is melted.
- Top with sour cream and green onions.
- Salsa can be served on the side if desired.

284. Potato Skin Nachos Recipe

Serving: 32 | Prep: | Cook: 72mins | Ready in:

Ingredients

- 4 large baking potatoes, scrubbed well
- 1/4 tsp chili powder
- 1/4 tsp salt
- 1 (8 oz) jar taco sauce
- 1 and 1/2 cups shredded Monterey Jack or cheddar cheese
- 2 jalapeno peppers, seeded and finely chopped (be sure to wash hands well after handling jalapenos!)
- 1 clove garlic, minced
- 2 Tbl minced fresh cilantro

Direction

- Preheat oven to 400F. Bake potatoes in the oven for 1 hour. Remove, leaving oven on, allow potatoes to cool until they can be easily handled.
- Halve the potatoes lengthwise, and scoop out pulp, leaving shells 1/2 inch thick. Halve each shell again lengthwise, then halve each crosswise.
- Arrange skins, flesh side up, on an ungreased baking sheet. Sprinkle with chili powder and salt. Bake, uncovered, for 10 minutes or until heated through.
- Combine taco sauce, cheese peppers garlic, and cilantro in a small bowl. Spoon the mixture onto the hot potato skins.
- With oven rack 4 inches from heat, broil the skins for 1-2 minutes or until cheese is melted.

285. Potato Skins With Cheddar And Bacon Recipe

Serving: 4 | Prep: | Cook: 60mins | Ready in:

Ingredients

- •4 medium baking potatoes, scrubbed
- •7oz (200g) bacon, rind removed, cut into sticks
- •2 shallots, finely chopped
- •scant ½ cup whole milk
- •2 tbsp butter
- •¾ cup shredded cheddar cheese
- •2 tbsp chopped parsley
- •salt and freshly ground black pepper

Direction

- Preheat the oven to 400°F (200°C). Prick the potato skins all over with a fork.
- Bake in the oven for about 45–50 minutes, until tender. Reduce the oven temperature to 350°F (180°C).
- . Meanwhile, cook the bacon in a frying pan over medium-high heat about 4 minutes until golden.
- Add the shallots and cook until they soften, about 1 minute more.
- Slice off the top third of each potato, horizontally. Using a spoon, scoop out the flesh into a large bowl.
- Reserve the hollowed-out skins and place in a lightly oiled baking dish.
- Mash the potato with a potato masher.
- Add the milk and butter, and beat until smooth. Stir in the Cheddar and bacon mixture along with the parsley.
- Season with salt and pepper.
- . Spoon the mixture back into the potato skins and bake for 20–25 minutes, or until the filling is heated through and golden on top. Serve hot with extra chopped parsley sprinkled on top, if desired.

286. Praline Topped Brie Recipe

Serving: 10 | Prep: | Cook: 20mins | Ready in:

Ingredients

- 1 13 to 15oz round of Brie or camembert cheese
- 1/2 c orange marmalade
- 2 T brown sugar, packed

- 1/3 c coarsley chopped pecans

Direction

- Preheat oven to 350 degrees. Place the round of cheese in a shallow ovenproof serving dish or pie plate. In a small bowl, stir together orange marmalade and brown sugar. Spread on top of cheese. Sprinkle with pecans.
- Bake about 15 minutes for smaller round, about 20 minutes for larger round, or till cheese is slightly softened and topping is bubbly.
- Serve with toasted baguette slices and fresh fruit.

287. Provolone Tomato Bruschetta Recipe

Serving: 6 | Prep: | Cook: 10mins | Ready in:

Ingredients

- 12 pieces of bread, sliced into bite size pieces.
- 2 tomatoes, sliced
- 1/3 cup of olive oil
- seasonings-I use oregano, italian seasoning, garden mix
- 12 slices provolone cheese
- 6 sage leaves, optional

Direction

- Preheat oven to 350
- Mix seasonings with olive oil
- Place bread onto pan and lightly cover with oil mixture
- Top with slice of cheese and tomato
- Lightly cover with more oil
- If want to sprinkle chopped sage leaves on top
- Bake for about 10 minutes, or until cheese melts

288. Pulled Pork BBQ Nachos Recipe

Serving: 4 | Prep: | Cook: 20mins | Ready in:

Ingredients

- your favorite tortilla chips
- 2 cups leftover pulled pork
- 1/2 yellow onion, finely diced
- 1/2 can black beans, rinsed and drained
- 8 oz. shredded cheddar
- 1/2 c. prepared coleslaw
- 1/4 c. seeded, chopped, fresh, red, ripe tomatoes
- 4 green onions, sliced, including the green tops

Direction

- Warm pulled pork n microwave. Set aside.
- Take a large round pizza pan and spread a layer of tortilla chips, top with some of the cheese, sprinkle with half of the black beans, then half of the pork, then more cheese. Add the rest of your chips, cheese, rest of the black beans, rest of the pork, and finish off with the remaining cheese.
- Bake at 350 for 15 minutes or until nicely melted throughout.
- Top with dollops of coleslaw, sprinkle with tomatoes, finish off with the green onions.

289. Pumpkin And Cheddar Souffle Recipe

Serving: 8 | Prep: | Cook: 15mins | Ready in:

Ingredients

- 8 mini pumpkins
- 4 large eggs
- 4 tsp flour
- 1/4 tsp baking powder
- 3 oz Cabot cheddar (ex: habanero)
- salt and pepper to taste

Direction

- Bake uncut pumpkins in 1/4 inch water in a 350F oven about 40 minutes and cool
- Remove tops with a paring knife, remove seeds, pulp leaving a 1/4 inch shell
- Place 4 cups of pumpkin flesh in a bowl
- Separate eggs
- Stir yolks into pumpkin with combined flour and baking powder
- Stir in cheese
- Beat whites stiff and fold into mixture
- Place into pumpkins and bake 12 to 15 mins or puffed and set

290. Quiche Appetizers Recipe

Serving: 0 | Prep: | Cook: 45mins | Ready in:

Ingredients

- 16 Ritz crackers, crushed
- 2 Spanish onions, chopped and sauteed
- 2 cans mushrooms, chopped fine
- 1/2 c. cooked ham, chopped
- 8 oz. cheddar cheese, grated
- 8 eggs, beaten
- salt and pepper

Direction

- Mix all ingredients and bake at 375 degrees in small greased muffin tins for 20 to 30 minutes until a pick comes out clean. They can also be made in small tart pans.

291. Quick Holiday Cheese Dip Recipe

Serving: 10 | Prep: | Cook: 15mins | Ready in:

Ingredients

- 1 stick butter
- 1 tablespoon minced garlic
- 1 cup sliced green onions
- 1 cup sour cream
- 8 oz. cream cheese, softened
- 1 teaspoon cracked black pepper
- 1 teaspoon dried parsley
- 1/4 cup Frank's hot sauce
- 2 (8 oz) packages shredded cheddar cheese(any variety)
- 4 oz. shredded parmesan cheese
- 1 small can chopped black olives

Direction

- Sauté garlic in butter until lightly browned.
- Mix together cream cheese, garlic butter, green onions, sour cream, pepper, 8 oz. of the shredded cheddar, Parmesan cheese, and hot sauce.
- Spoon into casserole or oven proof serving dish.
- Spread black olives and remaining cheese over top.
- Sprinkle with parsley and bake at 350 degrees for 15 minutes or until lightly browned.
- Serve with assorted chips, crackers, or chunks of toasted French or Italian bread.
- * As an added treat, spread bread with garlic butter and run under broiler until lightly browned before serving with cheese dip.

292. RICOTTA CALZONES WITH RED PEPPERS SPINACH AND GOAT CHEESE Recipe

Serving: 6 | Prep: | Cook: 12mins | Ready in:

Ingredients

- Dough
- 4 cups bread flour (22 ounces), plus additional for dusting work surface

- 2 1/4 teaspoons instant yeast (1 envelope)
- 1 1/2 teaspoons table salt
- 2 tablespoons extra-virgin olive oil
- 1 1/2 cups water , plus 1 tablespoon (12 1/2 ounces), 105 degrees
- Filling
- 10 ounces whole-milk ricotta
- 8 ounces shredded fresh mozzarella (2 cups)
- 1 1/2 ounces grated parmesan cheese (about 3/4 cup)
- 1 large egg yolk
- 1 tablespoon minced fresh oregano leaves
- table salt
- 1/8 teaspoon ground black pepper
- 2 tablespoons olive oil
- 2 medium red bell peppers , cut into 1/2 inch by 2-inch strips
- 3 medium cloves garlic , pressed through garlic press or minced (about 1 tablespoon)
- 1/4 teaspoon red pepper flakes
- 1 pound spinach , washed, dried, and stems trimmed (about 4 cups)
- 8 ounces goat cheese , crumbled
- extra-virgin olive oil for brushing shaped calzones
- kosher salt for sprinkling

Direction

- Note:
- In addition to standard kitchen tools, to make this recipe you will need a standing mixer or food processor, parchment paper, and a baking stone. The stone must heat for an additional 30 minutes once the oven has come up to temperature; if your oven heats slowly, begin heating it about an hour into the dough's first rise. Leftover calzones must be refrigerated; to reheat, heat the oven with the baking stone just as you did when making the recipe, then set the calzones on the hot stone for about 10 minutes. A simple tomato sauce is a nice accompaniment to the calzones.
- 1. FOR THE DOUGH (See below for food processor procedure): In bowl of standing mixer, whisk flour, yeast, and salt to combine. Attach bowl and dough hook to mixer; with mixer running at medium-low speed, add olive oil, then gradually add water; continue to mix until mixture comes together and smooth, elastic dough forms, about 10 minutes. Lightly spray large bowl with non-stick cooking spray; form dough into ball, transfer it to bowl, cover bowl with plastic wrap lightly sprayed with non-stick cooking spray, and let rise in warm spot until doubled in size, 1 1/2 to 2 hours.
- 2. FOR THE FILLING: Combine ricotta, mozzarella, Parmesan, egg yolk, oregano, 1/4 teaspoon salt, and black pepper in medium bowl, cover with plastic wrap and refrigerate until needed.
- 3. Heat 1 tablespoon extra-virgin olive oil in 10-inch non-stick skillet over high heat until oil begins to smoke. Stir in red bell peppers and 1/8 teaspoon salt; cook until slightly softened and spotty brown, about 5 minutes, stirring only 2 or 3 times. Clear centre of pan; add 1 tablespoon extra-virgin olive oil, 1 tablespoon minced or pressed garlic, and red pepper flakes to clearing and mash with back of spoon until fragrant, about 10 seconds, then stir into red peppers. Immediately stir in spinach and 1/8 teaspoon salt off heat; continue to stir until spinach is wilted, about 1 minute. Transfer mixture to paper towel-lined plate and cool to room temperature; once cooled, pat with paper towels to absorb excess moisture and set aside until needed.
- 4. Adjust oven rack to lowest position, set baking stone on oven rack, and heat oven to 500 degrees. Line baking sheet with parchment paper and spray parchment lightly with non-stick cooking spray. Turn risen dough out onto lightly floured work surface. Divide dough in half, then cut each half into thirds. Gently reshape each piece of dough into ball. Transfer to baking sheet and cover with plastic wrap lightly sprayed with non-stick cooking spray. Let dough rest at least 15 minutes but no more than 30 minutes.
- 5. Cut eight 9-inch squares of parchment paper. Working with one piece of dough at a time and keeping other pieces covered, roll

dough into 9-inch round. Set round onto parchment square and cover with another parchment square; roll out another dough ball, set dough round on top of first, and cover with parchment square. Repeat to form stack of 3 rounds, covering top round with parchment square. Form second stack of 3 with remaining dough balls and parchment squares.

- 6. Remove top parchment square from first stack of dough rounds and place rounds with parchment beneath on work surface; if dough rounds have shrunk, gently and evenly roll out again to 9-inch round. Place scant 1/2 cup cheese filling in centre of bottom half of dough round. Using small spatula, spread/press filling in even layer across bottom half of dough round, leaving 1-inch border uncovered. Spread 1/6 of pepper mixture over the cheese and then sprinkle with 1 ounce goat cheese. Fold top half of dough over filling, leaving 1/2 inch border of bottom layer uncovered. With fingertips, lightly press around silhouette of cheese filling and out to edge to lightly seal dough. Face seam of calzone toward you. Beginning at left end of seam, place left index finger diagonally across edge and with right thumb and index finger gently pull bottom single layer of dough gently over tip of resting index finger and gently press into dough (double thickness) to seal. Remove index finger from fold and rest in new imprint. Repeat process, working to your right, until calzone is fully sealed. With very sharp paring knife or razor blade, cut 5 slits, about 1 1/2 inches long, diagonally across top of calzone, making sure to cut through only top layer of dough and not completely through calzone. With pastry brush, brush top and sides of calzone with extra-virgin olive oil and lightly sprinkle with kosher salt.
- 7. Using scissors, trim excess parchment paper; slide calzones on parchment onto pizza peel or rimless baking sheet, then slide calzones with parchment onto hot baking stone, spacing them evenly apart. Bake until golden brown, about 11 minutes; use pizza peel or rimless baking sheet to remove calzones with parchment to wire rack. Cool 5 minutes, remove parchment, and serve. While first batch bakes, form second batch, and bake after removing first batch.
- FOOD PROCESSOR METHOD
- 8. Made in a food processor, the calzone dough bakes up with slightly less chew than we like, but it offers an alternative method for making the dough if you do not own a standing mixer. The quantity of dough is too large to be made in any food processor that does not have at least an 11-cup bowl.
- 9. In a food processor, pulse flour, yeast, and salt to combine, about five 1-second pulses. While pulsing, add olive oil through feed tube, then gradually add water; continue pulsing until dough forms ball, then process until smooth and elastic, about 30 seconds. Turn dough out onto lightly floured work surface and knead by hand a few turns to form smooth, round ball. Lightly spray large plastic container or bowl with non-stick cooking spray; transfer dough to container, cover container with plastic wrap lightly sprayed with non-stick cooking spray, and let rise in warm spot until double in size, about 1 1/2 to 2 hours.
- 10. Continue with recipe from step 2.
- Note: Making Calzones
- 1. With fingertips, press dough ball into 5-inch circle. With floured rolling pin, roll outward from centre in all directions until dough forms 9-inch circle. If dough sticks, dust flour under it.
- 2. Place scant 1/2 cup cheese filling in centre of bottom half of dough round. Using small spatula, spread/press filling in even layer across bottom half of dough round, leaving 1-inch border uncovered.
- 3. Fold top half of dough over cheese-covered bottom half, leaving 1/2-inch border of bottom layer uncovered.
- 4. With fingertips, lightly press around silhouette of cheese filling and out to edge to lightly seal dough.

- 5. Beginning at one end of seam, place index finger diagonally across edge and gently pull bottom layer of dough over tip of index finger; press into dough to seal. Repeat until calzone is fully sealed.
- 6. With very sharp paring knife or razor blade, cut 5 slits, about 11/2 inches long, diagonally across top of calzone, making sure to cut through only top layer of dough and not completely through calzone.

293. Ricotta Pie Recipe

Serving: 10 | Prep: | Cook: 90mins | Ready in:

Ingredients

- 1 - pre-made frozen crust. We like Pillsbury Deep-Dish but any deep pie crust works
- 5 eggs-beaten
- 1/2 cup Parmesan or Romano cheese-grated plus extra to sprinkle on top
- 1 pound ricotta cheese, excess liquid drained off. If you use Sorrento (east coast USA) or Precious (west coast) it is not watery and does not need draining.
- 1 cup pepperoni cut into 1/2" cubes, about 3/4 of a stick.
- 1 cup shredded mozzarella cheese
- 1/2 teaspoon fresh ground black pepper
- 2 tablespoons fresh parsley-chopped

Direction

- Preheat oven to 400F
- In a large bowl, mix all filling ingredient except 1 tablespoon eggs and reserved grated cheese
- Pour filling into frozen pie crust and smooth top
- Mix reserved egg with tablespoon water to create egg wash
- Brush top with reserved egg wash
- Sprinkle top with reserved grated cheese
- Bake for 10 minutes at 400F then reduce oven to 350F and bake until top has puffed out and browned, about 1 hour more.
- Cool to room temp and serve or move to refrigerator and chill

294. Ricotta And Roasted Tomato Crostini Recipe

Serving: 24 | Prep: | Cook: 25mins | Ready in:

Ingredients

- 7-8 plum tomatoes
- 2 tbsp olive oil
- ½ tsp ground black pepper
- ¼ tsp salt
- 1-2 baguettes
- 2 cups ricotta
- 3 tsp balsamic vinegar
- 1/3 cup chopped fresh basil

Direction

- Preheat oven to 400°F. Line baking sheets with parchment paper, or lightly grease.
- Slice tomatoes crosswise into ¼" rounds.
- In bowl, toss together tomatoes, oil, pepper and salt.
- Place in single layer on prepared baking sheets. Bake in centre of oven for 15 minutes. Set aside.
- Turn oven to BROIL.
- Cut baguettes into ½" slices, cutting at an angle.
- Place on a wire rack set over a baking sheet. Broil 6-7 minutes, flipping slices ½ way through.
- Spread each toast with some ricotta. Top with a tomato slice, a drizzle of vinegar, and a pinch of basil.

295. Romano Shrimp Stuffed Mushrooms Recipe

Serving: 5 | Prep: | Cook: 15mins | Ready in:

Ingredients

- 20 Large fresh mushrooms (2-2 1/2 inch diameter)
- 1 4 1/2 ounce can shrimp, drained, rinsed, and broken up
- 1 4 ounce container whipped cream cheese with chives
- 1/2 teaspoon worcestershire sauce
- Dash garlic powder
- Dash bottled hot pepper sauce
- Grated romano cheese

Direction

- Remove the stems from mushrooms.
- Sinner the mushroom caps in boiling water for 2 minutes.
- Drain. Invert caps on paper towelling.
- Cool,
- Meanwhile, combine the shrimp, cream cheese, Worcestershire sauce, garlic powder, and hot pepper sauce.
- Spoon shrimp mixture into mushroom caps.
- Place in shallow baking pan.
- Sprinkle with Romano Cheese.
- Cover and chill at least 3 hours.
- Before serving, uncover and bake in a 400 degree oven for 15 minutes.

296. Romanos Macaroni Grill Hot 7 Layer Dip Recipe

Serving: 10 | Prep: | Cook: 10mins | Ready in:

Ingredients

- 1 can of refried beans
- 1 can of black beans, drained
- 1 package of taco seasoning mix
- 1/2 cup of sour cream
- 1 cup of salsa
- 1 can (4oz.) of Diced green chiles
- 2 tablespoons diced jalepenos
- 1 cup of shredded cheese
- 2 large green onions
- 1 pack of chips

Direction

- Preheat oven to 375° F.
- Combine refried beans, black beans and seasoning mix in medium bowl. Spread bean mixture in ungreased 8-inch-square baking dish. Spread sour cream over bean mixture. Top with salsa, chilies, jalapeños and cheese; cover.
- Bake for 20 minutes. Uncover; bake for an additional 10 minutes or until cheese is melted and dip is bubbly. Garnish with green onions. Serve with chips.
- Serves 10

297. SAUSAGE CHEESE BALLS Recipe

Serving: 100 | Prep: | Cook: 25mins | Ready in:

Ingredients

- 3 cups Original Bisquick® mix
- 1 pound bulk pork sausage
- 4 cups shredded cheddar cheese (16 ounces)
- 1/2 cup grated parmesan cheese
- 1/2 cup milk
- 1/2 teaspoon dried rosemary leaves, crushed
- 1 1/2 teaspoons chopped fresh parsley or 1/2 teaspoon parsley flakes
- barbecue sauce or chili sauce, if desired

Direction

- 1. Heat oven to 350°F. Lightly grease bottom and sides of jelly roll pan, 15 1/2x10 1/2x2x1 inch.

- 2. Stir together all ingredients, using hands or spoon. Shape mixture into 1-inch balls. Place in pan.
- 3. Bake 20 to 25 minutes or until brown. Immediately remove from pan. Serve warm with sauce for dipping.

298. SUPER NACHO Recipe

Serving: 6 | Prep: | Cook: 30mins | Ready in:

Ingredients

- 2 cans refried beans
- 2 lbs. ground chuck
- 2 env. taco mix
- 1 can chopped green chili peppers
- 1 (10 oz.) block monterey jack cheese with Jalepeno peppers
- 1 (10 oz.) block Longhorn or colby cheese
- 2 bottles taco sauce (1 hot and 1 mild) OR 2 milds
- 1 sm. can ripe pitted olives
- 2 bunches green olives
- 2 ripe avocados
- 1 pt. sour cream
- garlic powder
- onion salt
- salad dressing
- coriander
- chili powder
- 1 lemon
- Doritos

Direction

- Spread refried beans on dish. Brown ground chuck with 1 bunch of onions. Add taco mix with water as per directions on package. Simmer and drain water and grease from mixture. Spread beef mixture on top of beans. Sprinkle on chili peppers. Shred both kinds of cheese and place on top of peppers. Drizzle taco sauce on top of cheeses. Bake at 350 degrees for 30 minutes. Chop green onions and slice olives to use as garnish

299. Salmon Cheddar Bake Recipe

Serving: 8 | Prep: | Cook: 35mins | Ready in:

Ingredients

- 14oz salmon, cooked and flaked
- 8-9 slices bread, crusts trimmed
- 1 ½ cups grated cheddar cheese
- 6 eggs
- ¾ cup low fat milk
- ½ teaspoon each salt and pepper
- ¼ cup green onions sliced
- 1 tablespoon better, melted

Direction

- Pre-heat oven 350f.
- Arrange bread in a spiral pattern in a greased 9 inch pie plate arranging the edges to form a crown.
- Sprinkle ½ cup cheese over the bread.
- Whisk together eggs, milk salt and pepper until well combined.
- Stir in salmon, green onions and remaining 1 cup of cheese. Pour over bread.
- Bake at 350f for 35-40 minutes or until center is set. Check it after 25 minutes to be safe, but mine took 45 minutes!

300. Salmon And Jalapeno Nachos Recipe

Serving: 4 | Prep: | Cook: 10mins | Ready in:

Ingredients

- 6 ounces tortilla chips

- 2-3 tablespoons seeded, minced jalapenos
- 1 cup flaked, cooked salmon, skin removed
- 3 tablespoons feta cheese
- 2/3 cup chopped sweet onions
- 1/2-3/4 cup shredded monterey jack cheese

Direction

- Preheat oven to 400 degrees.
- Spread a double layer of tortilla chips in a baking dish.
- Sprinkle with jalapeno, salmon, feta and onions.
- Top with Monterey Jack cheese.
- Bake for 10 minutes, or until cheese is melted.

301. Salted Cheese Recipe

Serving: 6 | Prep: | Cook: 1mins | Ready in:

Ingredients

- 150g bread crumbs
- 100g butter
- 200 g cow cheese
- 2 eggs
- 50 ml sour cream
- salt
- black pepper
- 2 tomatoes
- 50g parmesan
- french parsley

Direction

- Mix bread crumbs with melted butter.
- Chill.
- Mix cheese, sour cream, eggs, salt, and pepper.
- Pour on bread and bake.
- After it is cold, put tomatoes slices (peeled before you cut them), parmesan, and French parsley above.

302. Sausage Cheese Balls Recipe

Serving: 40 | Prep: | Cook: 18mins | Ready in:

Ingredients

- 1 lb. sausage (like Jimmy Dean)
- 4 c. sharp cheddar, grated (about 16 oz.)
- 1 c. baking mix (like Bisquick)

Direction

- Mix all ingredients well.
- Shape into 1 inch balls.
- Place on ungreased cookie sheet.
- Bake 15-18 minutes, or until golden brown.
- Serve warm.
- Makes approximately 40 balls.

303. Sausage And Cheese Balls Recipe

Serving: 30 | Prep: | Cook: 20mins | Ready in:

Ingredients

- 2 cups biscuit mix
- 1 lb. ground sausage meat
- 1 cup finely grated cheddar cheese

Direction

- Mix all ingredients together in a medium bowl. Roll into bite-size balls. Place on a cookie sheet and bake at 350 F for 15 to 20 minutes.

304. Sausage And Parmesan Puffs Recipe

Serving: 16 | Prep: | Cook: 20mins | Ready in:

Ingredients

- 1 package Pillsbury crescent rolls
- 1 egg
- 1 tablespoon milk or cream
- 1 (1 pound) package Bob Evans® Original Recipe sausage Roll, well chilled
- 6 tablespoons grated parmesan cheese, divided
- 1/2 tsp sugar
- salt/pepper/hot sauce to taste

Direction

- Preheat oven 400 degrees F. Use each crescent roll triangle but roll into strips. In small bowl, beat egg with milk until well blended. Brush top of each crescent with the egg/milk mixture and sprinkle each with 1 tablespoon of cheese.
- Divide the uncooked sausage into 6 equal portions. Shape each portion into a log the same length as the crescent strips. Place one sausage log in the middle of each crescent roll. Fold edges of the crescent up to enclose sausage and pinch together tightly. Brush tops with remaining egg glaze. Chill 15 minutes.
- Bake for 15-20 minutes or until sausage is cooked and pastry is lightly browned. Refrigerate leftovers.

305. Sausage Cheese Balls Recipe

Serving: 15 | Prep: | Cook: 25mins | Ready in:

Ingredients

- 3 cups Original Bisquick® mix
- 1 pound bulk pork sausage
- 4 cups shredded cheddar cheese (16 ounces)
- 1/2 cup grated parmesan cheese
- 1/2 cup milk
- 1/2 teaspoon dried rosemary leaves
- 1/2 teaspoon parsley flakes
- barbecue sauce or chili sauce, if desired

Direction

- Heat oven to 350°F. Lightly grease bottom and sides of jelly roll pan, 15 1/2x10 1/2x2x1 inch.
- Stir together all ingredients, using hands or spoon. Shape mixture into 1-inch balls. Place in pan.
- Bake 20 to 25 minutes or until brown. Immediately remove from pan. Serve warm with sauce for dipping.

306. Sausage Cheese Balls Recipe

Serving: 84 | Prep: | Cook: 22mins | Ready in:

Ingredients

- 3 cups Original Bisquick® mix
- 1 pound bulk pork sausage
- 4 cups shredded cheddar cheese (16 ounces)
- 1/2 cup grated parmesan cheese
- 1/2 cup milk
- 1/2 teaspoon dried rosemary leaves
- 1/2 teaspoon parsley flakes
- barbecue sauce or chili sauce, if desired

Direction

- 1. Heat oven to 350°F. Lightly grease bottom and sides of jelly roll pan, 15 1/2x10 1/2x2x1 inch.
- 2. Stir together all ingredients, using hands or spoon. Shape mixture into 1-inch balls. Place in pan.
- 3. Bake 20 to 25 minutes or until brown. Immediately remove from pan. Serve warm with sauce for dipping.
- High Altitude (3500-6500 ft.) Heat oven to 375°F. Decrease Bisquick to 2 1/2 cups; stir in 1/2 cup Gold Medal® all-purpose flour. Bake 25 to 30 minutes.
- Do-Ahead Tip

- Want to make these savoury cheese balls ahead? Your options are many! You can:
- Cover and refrigerate unbaked balls up to 24 hours. Bake as directed.
- Cover and freeze unbaked balls up to 1 month. Heat oven to 350°F. Place frozen balls on ungreased cookie sheet. Bake 25 to 30 minutes or until brown.
- Bake as directed; cover and freeze up to 1 month. Heat oven to 350°F. Place frozen balls on ungreased cookie sheet. Bake 10 to 12 minutes or until heated through.
- Bake as directed; cover and freeze up to 1 month. Place 6 frozen balls on microwavable plate. Loosely cover with waxed paper. Microwave on High 45 seconds to 1 minute or until heated through.
- Success
- It's true. You don't need to cook the sausage before using it when making this recipe

307. Savory Baked Brie Recipe

Serving: 1 | Prep: | Cook: 15mins | Ready in:

Ingredients

- 14 oz Brie (I buy these at Sam's. It is larger and cheaper than most grocery stores or specialty stores)
- 1-16 ounce jar of roasted red peppers
- 1 bunch fresh basil

Direction

- In a fire baker or on an oven proof plate or dish, warm the brie in the oven for about 15 minutes at 300 degrees. Be careful not to get the brie too hot or it will rupture and the cheese will ooze everywhere. It will still taste fine but the presentation isn't so good.
- Julienne the red peppers and basil.
- Spread the peppers and basil over the top and serve with toast points or your favourite crackers.

308. Savory Cheese Puffs Recipe

Serving: 32 | Prep: | Cook: | Ready in:

Ingredients

- 4 tablespoons unsalted butter (best quality)
- 1/4 cup whole milk
- 1/2 teaspoon sea salt
- 1/2 cup all-purpose flour, sifted
- 1/8 teaspoon baking powder
- 2 eggs
- 1/2 cup grated Gruyère (I used sharp white cheddar)
- parmigiano-reggiano, grated, for sprinkling

Direction

- Preheat the oven to 400 degrees.
- Bring the butter, milk, 1/4 cup water, salt to a boil. Remove from the heat and add the sifted flour and baking powder. Stir well, and return to medium heat. Cook, stirring constantly, until the mixture pulls away from the sides of the pan and forms a ball, about 2 minutes.
- Place the cheese and the mixture in the bowl of a mixer fitted with a paddle, and beat until just warm. Add the eggs slowly as the mixer runs, until dough is smooth and shiny. (Alternatively, stir to cool by hand and beat in eggs with a wooden spoon.)
- Transfer to a pastry bag, and pipe in 1-inch mounds using a No. 4 tip, or drop with a teaspoon, on a sheet pan lined with parchment. (At this stage, the puffs can be frozen and then stored in a plastic bag. They do not have to be thawed before baking, but 11/2 to 2 minutes should be added to the cooking time.) Sprinkle with parm cheese and bake for 15 minutes; when puffs are golden brown, reduce to 375 degrees and cook 2 to 3 minutes more. Serve hot or at room temperature. May be reheated.

309. Savory Mexican Cheesecake Recipe

Serving: 24 | Prep: | Cook: 1hours | Ready in:

Ingredients

- 2 packages (8 ounces each) cream cheese, room temp
- 1-1/4 cups sour cream, divided
- 2 tablespoons organic taco seasoning
- 3 cage free eggs, room temp
- 1 1/2 cups (6 ounces) shredded sharp cheddar cheese
- 1 small can (4 ounces) fire roasted green chilies, chopped
- 1 cup homemade salsa, drained
- to serve: organic tortilla chips and/or crudites

Direction

- Preheat oven to 350°. In a large bowl, beat cream cheese, 1/2 cup sour cream and taco seasoning until smooth. Add eggs; beat on low speed just until combined. Stir in cheddar cheese and chilies.
- Transfer to a greased 9-in. springform pan lined with parchment paper to fit bottom and place on a baking sheet. Bake at 350° for 30-35 minutes or until center is almost set. Take out of oven, spread remaining sour cream evenly over top and then bake 5-8 minutes longer or until topping is set.
- Cool on a wire rack for 10 minutes. Carefully run a knife around edge of pan to loosen; cool 1 hour longer. Refrigerate overnight.
- Just before serving, spread salsa over cheesecake. Serve with tortilla chips or vegetables. .

310. Savory Parmesan Bites Recipe

Serving: 32 | Prep: | Cook: 30mins | Ready in:

Ingredients

- 1 pkg. (8 oz.) cream cheese, softened
- 1 cup grated parmesan cheese, divided
- 2 cans (8 oz. each) refrigerated crescent dinner rolls
- 1 cup chopped red peppers
- 1/4 cup chopped fresh parsley

Direction

- HEAT oven to 350°F. Beat cream cheese and 3/4 cup Parmesan with mixer until well blended.
- SEPARATE crescent rolls into 8 rectangles; press perforations together to seal. Spread each with 3 Tbsp. cream cheese mixture. Top with peppers and parsley. Fold 1 long side of each dough rectangle over filling to centre; fold again to enclose filling. Cut each into 4 squares. Place, seam-sides down, on baking sheet. Sprinkle with remaining Parmesan.
- BAKE 13 to 15 min. or until golden brown.

311. Seafood Nachos Recipe

Serving: 6 | Prep: | Cook: 8mins | Ready in:

Ingredients

- 30 baked tortilla chips
- 1 pkg. (8 oz) imitation crabmeat, chopped
- ¼ cup reduced-fat sour cream
- ¼ cup reduced fat mayonnaise
- 2 Tbsps. finely chopped onion
- ¼ tsp. dill weed
- 1 cup (4 oz.) shredded reduced-fat cheddar cheese
- ¼ cup sliced ripe olives
- ¼ tsp. paprika

Direction

- Arrange the tortilla chips in a single layer on an ungreased baking sheet.
- In a bowl, combine the crab, sour cream, mayonnaise, onion and dill; spoon about 1 Tbsp. onto each chip. Sprinkle with the cheese, olives and paprika.
- Bake at 350 degrees for 6-8 minutes or until the cheese is melted. Yield:
- 6 servings.

312. Sesame Cheddar Turnovers Recipe

Serving: 12 | Prep: | Cook: 40mins | Ready in:

Ingredients

- Pastry: 8 oz. cream cheese
- 1/2 cup butter
- 1 1/2 C flour
- Filling: 8 oz. (2 C) shredded sharp cheddar
- 2 beaten eggs
- 1 TBS grated onion
- 1 tsp. prepared mustard (try Dijon)
- 1/4 tsp. hot pepper sauce
- 1/8 tsp. salt
- Topping: 1 egg beaten with 1 tsp. water
- sesame seeds

Direction

- Make dough: Blend all ingredients well until crumbly.
- Form into a ball and wrap; chill at least 1 hour.
- Make filling: Mix all ingredients well; chill while rolling dough.
- Roll out chilled dough 1/8" thick. Cut out 3" circles or cut into squares, re-rolling scraps.
- Place a spoonful of filling on the centre of each circle or square, fold in half to make crescents or triangles, and seal the edges well with a fork.
- Brush top with egg and sprinkle generously with sesame seeds.
- Bake on ungreased sheets at 400° 15-20 minutes or until golden brown.
- Can be served warm or at room temperature.
- Can be frozen after cooling and reheated straight from the freezer at 325° for 10-15 minutes if desired.
- Makes about 4 dozen.

313. Slow Baked Bacon Parmesan Cheese Snacks Recipe

Serving: 20 | Prep: | Cook: 120mins | Ready in:

Ingredients

- Waverly crackers (your choice on number of crackers)
- parmesan cheese
- Hickory bacon slices, cut in half

Direction

- Mound the Parmesan cheese on the cracker.
- Sprinkle with cayenne, (optional).
- Wrap in one half bacon slice.
- Place in a broiler pan or pan with sides and rack.
- Bake at 200 degrees for 2 hours.
- Leave in pan to drain.
- Some kind of delicious!

314. Smoked Cheddar Stuffed Mushrooms Recipe

Serving: 8 | Prep: | Cook: 30mins | Ready in:

Ingredients

- cooking spray

- 1/4 cup minced shallots (about 1 large)
- 1 garlic clove, minced
- 40 medium button mushrooms (about 1 pound)
- 1/4 cup dry breadcrumbs
- 2 tablespoons chopped fresh parsley
- 1/2 teaspoon salt
- 1/2 teaspoon freshly ground black pepper
- 2 ounces smoked cheddar cheese, diced
- 1 teaspoon olive oil
- 1 teaspoon water

Direction

- Preheat oven to 400°.
- Heat a small non-stick skillet over medium-high heat.
- Coat pan with cooking spray.
- Add minced shallots and minced garlic; sauté 2 minutes or until tender.
- Place shallot mixture in a medium bowl.
- Remove stems from mushrooms; chop stems.
- Add chopped mushroom stems, breadcrumbs, chopped parsley, salt, freshly ground black pepper, and smoked cheddar cheese to shallot mixture; toss with a fork until blended. Add olive oil and 1 teaspoon water; stir well to combine.
- Spoon about 1 teaspoon filling into each mushroom cap.
- Arrange mushrooms, filling side up, on a baking sheet.
- Bake at 400° for 20 minutes or until filling begins to brown and cheese melts.
- Serve warm.

315. Smoked Gouda And Pineapple Stuffed Jalapenos Recipe

Serving: 24 | Prep: | Cook: 30mins | Ready in:

Ingredients

- 24 fresh jalapeno peppers
- 16 ounces cream cheese softened
- 3/4 pound smoked gouda cheese shredded
- 2 tablespoons real bacon bits
- 1 cup canned crushed pineapple in juice, drained and juice reserved

Direction

- Preheat oven to 350.
- Cut a slice off the stem end of each pepper, and use a sharp paring knife or pepper corer to scoop out the veins and seeds from the peppers.
- Mix cream cheese, Gouda cheese, bacon, pineapple and 1 teaspoon of reserved pineapple juice or as needed to make a workable filling, in a bowl until thoroughly blended.
- Using a small spoon stuff the hollow peppers with the cheese mixture.
- Place a rack onto a baking sheet.
- Stand peppers stem sides up into rack and bake in preheated oven until the peppers are softened and the filling is hot and bubbly - about 30 minutes.

316. Smoked Sausage Cheddar Beer Dip Recipe

Serving: 0 | Prep: | Cook: 12mins | Ready in:

Ingredients

- 2 Tablespoons unsalted butter
- 1/2 finely chopped green onion
- 1 pound smoked sausage, diced (Bryan or your favorite brand)
- 2 Tablespoons Dijon mustard
- 1 8-ounce package cream cheese
- 1 12-ounce bottle dark beer
- 1 pound shredded sharp white cheddar cheese
- 1/2 teaspoon ground cayenne pepper

Direction

- Melt the butter in a medium-size saucepan over medium-high heat. Add the onion, and sauté for 2 minutes. Add the sausage and cook until it is no longer pink in colour and is cooked through - approximately 8 to 10 minutes. Drain off fat. Add the mustard, cream cheese, and beer, stirring until the cream cheese is melted. Remove from the heat and stir in the cheddar cheese, a little at a time, until melted. Add the cayenne pepper. May serve in a dip bowl or bread bowl with crackers or bread crumbs for dipping.
- To prepare ahead, make dip and place in a 1 quart baking dish that has been sprayed with non-stick cooking spray. Then refrigerate for up to 3 days. When ready to use, bring the dip to room temperature. Bake in 350* oven for 20-25 minutes. Serve warm.

317. So Tried True Hot Beef Cheese Dip Recipe

Serving: 10 | Prep: | Cook: 30mins | Ready in:

Ingredients

- 1 pound lean ground beef
- 1/2 cup chopped onion, (optional)
- black pepper to taste
- 1 teaspoon cumin
- 2 teaspoons chili powder
- 1 can rotel
- I pound Velveeta cheese
- .

Direction

- In a skillet, brown ground beef, onion, salt and pepper to taste
- Drain well, and set aside
- In medium saucepan, slowly melt chunks of Velveeta, cumin, chili powder, Rotel, stirring frequently
- (I place cheese, Rotel, cumin, chili powder in a Pyrex bowl, and microwave)
- Combine meat mixture with melted cheese Rotel mixture*
- Place in casserole dish
- Place dish in oven, bake at 350 degrees until thoroughly hot
- Remove from oven
- Serve with Fritos Corn Chips, or Scoops
- *At this point, can serve, but it is better if heated in the oven

318. Southern Pimiento Cheese Spread

Serving: 8 | Prep: | Cook: 40mins | Ready in:

Ingredients

- 1-1/2 cups shredded cheddar cheese
- 1 jar (4 ounces) diced pimientos, drained and finely chopped
- 1/3 cup mayonnaise
- Assorted crackers

Direction

- Combine cheese, pimientos and mayonnaise. Refrigerate for at least 1 hour. Serve with crackers.
- Nutrition Facts
- 2 tablespoons: 116 calories, 11g fat (4g saturated fat), 21mg cholesterol, 144mg sodium, 1g carbohydrate (0 sugars, 0 fiber), 4g protein.

319. Southwestern Cheese Dip Recipe

Serving: 0 | Prep: | Cook: 15mins | Ready in:

Ingredients

- 8 oz (2 cups) Shredded cheddar cheese

- 8 oz (2 cups) Shredded mozzarella cheese
- 2 cups mayonnaise
- 2 small (or med) Chopped onions
- 3 chopped tomatoes
- 2 small cans of Sliced black olives
- 4 - 6 dashes of Tabasco sauce (or to taste)
- 1 small Bird pepper (or pepper of choice)
- 1 large bag of tortilla chips

Direction

- Combine all ingredients together in a large bowl. Ensure mayonnaise and pepper is evenly distributed.
- Place in a casserole sized baking pan and bake at 350 degrees until bubbly and slightly browned around the edges.
- Serve immediately with Tortilla chips.

320. Speedy Fiesta Chicken Nachos Recipe

Serving: 4 | Prep: | Cook: 10mins | Ready in:

Ingredients

- 1 - can Premium Chunk chicken breast (12.5-ounces)
- 1 - bag tortilla chips, 8-ounces
- 1 - teaspoon taco seasoning mix
- 2 - cups colby-Jack cheese,
- shredded jalapenos,
- sliced sour cream salsa guacamole

Direction

- Preheat oven to 350°F.
- Spread chips on ovenproof platter or jelly roll pan.
- Top chips with chicken. Sprinkle chicken with taco seasoning, then top with cheese.
- Bake 10 minutes or until cheese is melted.
- Serve nachos with your favourite toppings: sliced jalapenos, sour cream, salsa and guacamole

321. Spicy Baked Feta Recipe

Serving: 4 | Prep: | Cook: 10mins | Ready in:

Ingredients

- 1 (8 ounce) slice feta cheese
- 2 teaspoons olive oil (optional)
- 2 tablespoons crushed red pepper flakes, or as needed
- 1 pinch dried oregano
- (garlic is Good in This Too!)

Direction

- Preheat an oven to 300 degrees F (150 degrees C).
- Place the feta in an ovenproof baking dish.
- Drizzle with olive oil.
- Cover liberally with pepper flakes, and sprinkle with oregano.
- Bake, uncovered, in the preheated oven until feta is soft, about 10 minutes.

322. Spicy Cheddar Dollars Recipe

Serving: 8 | Prep: | Cook: 15mins | Ready in:

Ingredients

- 1 1/2 sticks butter, softened
- 1 1/2 cups cheddar cheese, grated
- 1 cup flour
- 1 cup crispy rice cereal
- 1t hot sauce
- 1t worcestershire sauce
- 1t cayenne
- 1T dry parsley flakes, or 2T fresh and finely chopped
- dash of kosher salt and fresh ground pepper

Direction

- Mix butter with hot sauce and Worcestershire until creamy and combined.
- Add cheddar cheese, and mix completely.
- Add flour, salt, pepper, cayenne, parsley and rice cereal and mix with dough hook on stand mixer, or by hand, as you do bread, until thoroughly combined.
- Roll dough into about 1 1/2 inch balls and place on cookie sheet.
- Press dough with fork tines in crisscross pattern, to flatten.
- Bake at 350 for about 15 minutes until edges and bottoms are just starting to brown.
- Let cool on cookie sheet
- ***please note, this dough should be similar to sugar cookie dough, or even play dough...slightly tacky and thick, you'll need to roll them in your hands to get them to the ball stage...if the dough doesn't seem to fit this consistency, try adding a bit more cereal and/or refrigerate it. I don't recommend adding more flour, because they will taste too pasty, then. :) ***

323. Spicy Spinach Cheese Dip Recipe

Serving: 5 | Prep: | Cook: | Ready in:

Ingredients

- 1 (10 oz) package frozen spinach, thawed, drained and chopped
- 10 oz monterey jack cheese, shredded
- 1 (4 oz) can green chiles, liquid removed and diced
- 1 (14.5 oz) can peeled tomatoes (whole), liquid removed and chopped
- 1 onion, diced
- 1 (8 oz) package of softened cream cheese
- 1 cup half-and-half
- 2 tbsp vegetable oil
- 1 tbsp red wine vinegar
- salt and pepper (to taste)

Direction

- Preheat oven to 400 degrees F.
- In oil, sauté onion over medium heat until softened, around 4 minutes. Add in chiles, and tomatoes, and allow them to cook for 2 minutes.
- Place the mixture in a large bowl and mix in spinach, cheese, cream cheese, vinegar and cream. Next, season with salt and pepper (to taste). Spoon the mixture into shallow baking dish (for example, a 9 inch pie plate or quiche dish).
- Bake until the dip is bubbly and the top is slightly browned, around 35 minutes.

324. Spinach And Muenster Quiche Bites Recipe

Serving: 32 | Prep: | Cook: 30mins | Ready in:

Ingredients

- 1 10oz package frozen chopped spinach
- 2 T olive oil
- 1 c sliced fresh mushrooms
- 1/2 c chopped onion
- 1/2 c chopped red pepper
- 6 large eggs
- 1/4 t ground white pepper
- /14 t nutmeg
- 1/4 t salt
- 2 8-oz ;ackages muenster cheese, grated

Direction

- Preheat oven to 350
- In large skillet, heat oil over med heat
- Add mushrooms, onions, red pepper, spinach, and seasonings
- Cook until veggies are soft
- Drain in paper towel lined colander

- Whisk eggs in large bowl
- Stir in spinach mixture
- Add cheese
- Pour into lightly greased 9x13 baking dish
- Bake 25-20 minutes or until lightly browned
- Cool for 10 minutes
- Cut into squares and serve
- ** Great with fresh fruit as a side

325. Spinach Artichoke Dip Hot And Delicious Recipe

Serving: 0 | Prep: | Cook: 1hours10mins | Ready in:

Ingredients

- 1 Can of artichoke hearts
- 1 Small package of Frozen whole leaf spinach
- 16oz cream cheese
- 6 cloves garlic Crushed or minced
- 1/2 Cup Mayo
- 1/4 Cup Ramano cheese
- 1/4 Cup parmesan cheese
- 1/2 Teaspoon pepper
- 1/2 Teaspoon garlic salt
- 8 oz Mozzarella
- 1/2 Teaspoon basil
- 1/3 Cup sour cream
- 2 Tablespoon butter
- olive oil
- 2 large Bags of your Favorite Nacho chips

Direction

- Cook the Spinach in a covered pot add 2 tablespoons Butter and Olive Oil. Salt and pepper the spinach to taste. Crush 3 cloves of garlic and add to the spinach. Continue cooking for about 5-10 min covered.
- While you cook the spinach combine in a bowl Cream cheese, 3 Cloves garlic Minced/Crushed, All cheeses, Garlic Salt, Pepper, Basil, Sour Cream, And Mayo.
- Pre-Heat oven to 350
- Dice up your artichoke hearts into strips and separate leaves.
- Do not drain oils from spinach. Add whole pot to the mixing bowl with other ingredients. Stir then add your artichoke and stir lightly. Find a baking dish to accommodate the dip and grease it with olive oil. Move Dip to the baking dish. Top with mozzarella lightly. Cook covered for 15 min then remove cover Stir and continue cooking for 10-15 min.
- Top should brown lightly and serve Hot!

326. Spinach Artichoke And Asiago Squares Recipe

Serving: 12 | Prep: | Cook: 20mins | Ready in:

Ingredients

- 2 cups jarred marinated artichokes, drained
- 1 cup frozen chopped spinach, thawed and squeezed
- 1/2 cup chopped onion
- 1 clove chopped garlic
- 2 Tbsp. lemon juice
- 1 Tbsp. chopped fresh oregano
- 4 large eggs
- 1/4 cup dry breadcrumbs
- 1/2 lb. grated asiago cheese

Direction

- Preheat oven to 350 °F. Grease and line with parchment paper (to make it easy to get them out!) an 8-inch square pan, so that the paper hangs over the sides.
- In a food processor, pulse artichokes, spinach, onion, garlic and oregano until finely chopped but not puréed. Pulse in eggs, then pulse in breadcrumbs and Asiago cheese. Scrape the mixture into a prepared pan and spread to level. Bake for 20 to 25 minutes until set.
- Cool to room temperature before slicing into squares and store refrigerated. Makes 1 8-inch square pan. Cuts into 25 squares.

327. Spinach And Feta Mini Strudels Recipe

Serving: 20 | Prep: | Cook: 30mins | Ready in:

Ingredients

- 1 tbsp olive oil
- 1 small onion, finely chopped
- 2 cloves garlic, finely chopped
- 1/2 lb feta cheese, crumbled
- 2 10oz/300 g pkg frozen chopped spinach, defrosted and squeezed dry
- 2 eggs
- 3 tbsp chopped fresh dill
- 1/2 tsp pepper
- pinch of nutmeg
- 1 pkg phyllo pastry (20 sheets)
- 1/2 cup dry breadcrumbs
- 1/3 cup melted butter or olive oil

Direction

- Prepare filling by heating oil in a small skillet and cooking onions and garlic until tender and fragrant.
- Place cheese, spinach, eggs, dill, nutmeg and pepper in a large mixing bowl. Add the onions and garlic and combine well. Reserve.
- Open package of phyllo pastry and lay out on counter. Cover with plastic wrap and then a damp tea towel. Have breadcrumbs at hand. Combine butter and water and have a pastry brush ready.
- Arrange one sheet of pastry on work surface. Brush with butter and sprinkle with a bit of the breadcrumbs. Repeat with 4 more layers. *You could also use olive oil and spray it from an oil atomizer.*
- Arrange 1 cup (125 mL) cheese mixture down one long edge of pastry. Roll up lengthwise tucking in ends as you roll. Transfer to a baking sheet and score the top of the pastry with horizontal slashes into 10 to 20 pieces depending how thick you would like them to be. Don't cut all the way through the strudels just the top layers of phyllo. Repeat until 4 rolls are made. Brush with any extra butter.
- Bake in a 200 °C (400 °F) oven for 20 to 25 minutes until well browned. Slice through and serve warm or at room temperature.
- Makes 45 to 50 pieces
- Wrap whole or half strudels and freeze for up to 2 months. Reheat thawed strudels for 10 minutes at 350F and they will crisp up again beautifully.

328. Spinach And Feta Squares Recipe

Serving: 10 | Prep: | Cook: 50mins | Ready in:

Ingredients

- 3 (10 oz.) pkg. frozen chopped spinach, defrosted and well
- drained
- 1/2 lb. feta cheese, crumbled
- 7 eggs
- 1/2 lb. Apollo filo leaves
- 1/4 c. fresh Italian parsley, chopped
- 1 bunch scallions, sliced and sauteed in oil until soft
- 1/4 lb. or more melted butter
- 2 tsp. salt
- pepper to taste

Direction

- Preheat oven to 375 degrees. Bring dough to room temperature.
- Beat eggs well. Add spinach, cheese, parsley, scallions, salt and pepper. Brush sides and bottom of 9x13 inch pan with melted butter. Carefully place 1 sheet of dough in pan with dough extending up sides and ends. Brush with butter.
- Add another piece of dough. Repeat using 10-12 pieces of dough; save 3 sheets for top.

- Add spinach mixture. Top with 3 pieces of dough buttering each layer. Fold dough from bottom layers down onto top layers. Brush with butter. Cut 3 slits in top. Bake for 50 minutes. This is delicious to serve to a crowd.

329. Starry Night Baked Brie Recipe

Serving: 8 | Prep: | Cook: 25mins | Ready in:

Ingredients

- 1 wheel of Brie (the bigger the better)
- 1 Pillsbury pie crust at room temperature
- Cute mini star cookie cutters

Direction

- Unwrap the Brie and cover it with the pie crust.
- Trim the excess dough carefully from the edges, smooth out the dough and close up any open seams.
- Roll out the remaining dough and decorate the pastry covered Brie with the cut-out shapes.
- Bake in an oven proof dish at 375 degrees for 25 minutes or until the top is golden brown.

330. Strawberry Patch Nachos Recipe

Serving: 4 | Prep: | Cook: 15mins | Ready in:

Ingredients

- 24 (about 4oz) light or baked tortilla chips
- 1 1/2 cups fresh fruit such as halved grapes, sliced bananas and berries
- 1/4 cup SMUCKER'S creamy natural peanut butter OR JIF creamy peanut butter
- SMUCKER'S Strawberry sugar Free preserves OR SMUCKER'S Low sugar preserves
- ground cinnamon

Direction

- PLACE half the tortilla chips on a serving platter.
- COVER with half the fresh fruit
- PLACE the peanut butter in a resealable food storage bag; microwave on HIGH (100 % power) 20 seconds. Knead until thinned.
- Cut a small corner from the resealable bag.
- Squeeze the bag to drizzle half the peanut butter over the chips.
- Spoon dabs of preserves over tortilla chips.
- Repeat process with remaining chips, fruit, peanut butter and preserves.
- Sprinkle with cinnamon.
- Serve immediately! Enjoy

331. String Cheese Sticks With Dipping Sauce Recipe

Serving: 4 | Prep: | Cook: 10mins | Ready in:

Ingredients

- 2-1/4 cups original Bisquick
- 2/3 cup milk
- 1 pkg (8 ounces) plain or smoked string cheese
- 1 tablespoon butter or margarine, ..melted
- 1/4 teaspoon garlic powder
- 1 can (8 ounces) pizza sauce, heated

Direction

- Preheat oven to 450 degrees F.
- Stir Bisquick and milk until a soft dough forms; beat 30 seconds with a spoon.
- Place dough on surface sprinkled with Bisquick; gently roll in Bisquick to coat.
- Shape into a ball; knead 10 times
- Roll dough 1/4 inch thick.

- Cut into 8 - 6 x 2 inch rectangles
- Roll each rectangle around 1 piece of cheese, pinch edge into roll and seal; seal ends...roll on surface to completely enclose cheese sticks. Place seam sides down on ungreased cookie sheet.
- Bake 8 to 10 minutes or until golden brown;
- Mix butter and garlic powder, and brush over warm cheese sticks, before removing from cookie sheet.
- Serve warm with pizza sauce for dip or you can use a ranch dip

332. Stuffed Peppers Recipe

Serving: 10 | Prep: | Cook: 35mins | Ready in:

Ingredients

- 1 lb bacon, cooked and crumbled
- 2 (8oz) pkgs cream cheese, softened
- 1 (8oz) pkg shredded cheddar cheese
- 1 large handful shredded mozzarella cheese
- 1/2 bottle CHOLULA hot sauce
- 10 ancient sweet peppers or 6 (red, orange or yellow) bell peppers

Direction

- Cut off top, butterfly or cut in half and deseed peppers. Mix together the rest of the ingredients. Fill peppers with cheese mixture. Bake @ 400° for 30-40 mins. Peppers with feel soft if poked with fork when done. Allow to cool a few minutes and enjoy.

333. Sundried Tomato And Mozzarella Piccolo Regalo Recipe

Serving: 56 | Prep: | Cook: 25mins | Ready in:

Ingredients

- 1 package frozen phyllo (filo) dough (1 box makes 2 batches) -- if you aren't comfortable with phyllo, croissants and puff pastry dough may make interesting alternatives, but I haven't tried them
- 1 jar sundried tomatoes packed in olive oil
- 1 jar premade pesto (optional, for dipping; I like Classico)
- 1/2 stick butter
- 1 pastry brush
- 1 package good mozzarella cheese, shredded (I recommend Sargento)

Direction

- Set oven to 325
- Melt butter in microwave, about 40 seconds
- On a clean, flat, smooth surface, roll out thawed phyllo dough (if you're like me and forgot to thaw it, pop it in the microwave for 30 seconds).
- Take off 2-3 sheets of dough (they're very thin), and cut in half. Keep the unused portions of phyllo under plastic wrap and a damp towel.
- Brush melted butter along phyllo and fold in half. Be careful not to use too much butter, it will make it hard to fold
- Brush interior with more butter
- On a separate plate, slice one sundried tomato fairly thin. Depending on how much tomato you care for, more can be added. Place sliced tomato in centre of dough.
- Spread mozzarella cheese carefully atop tomato slices
- Roll phyllo up (like a burrito), and place on a greased cookie pan, seam-side down
- Repeat as necessary
- Bake at 325 for 20-25 minutes, or until golden brown
- Serve with premade pesto, if desired

334. Super Nachos Recipe

Serving: 6 | Prep: | Cook: 15mins | Ready in:

Ingredients

- 1 pound chorizo casings removed
- 2 teaspoons chili powder
- 2 teaspoons cumin
- Pinch of salt
- 1-2 small cans refried beans or bean dip-warmed
- 1 12-ounce bag corn tortilla chips I use the assorted
- 1 1/4 pounds Monterey Jack grated with or without jalapenos peppers
- 2 cans of jalapeno pepper rings drained thoroughly
- 1 large onion, chopped
- 2 tomatoes, chopped
- 1 6-ounce can black olives, chopped

Direction

- Brown the sausage in a medium skillet. Drain. When cool enough to handle, put in food processor and pulse to a fine consistency. Return to pan. Add the chili powder, cumin and salt. Rewarm and set aside.
- Spread a thin layer of refried beans or bean dip over the bottom of a platter or shallow, heat-proof bowl. Then spread a layer of chips over the beans, top with a layer of cheese, sausage, onion, tomato, peppers and olives. Repeat until all the ingredients are used. I try to get 4 layers.
- Bake at 375° for 15 minutes. Serve warm with sour cream and Guacamole Dip, if desired.

335. Sweet And Spicy Pinwheels Recipe

Serving: 52 | Prep: | Cook: 15mins | Ready in:

Ingredients

- ½ cups Bottled cheese spread (Cheez Whiz)
- 2 teaspoons Chopped And Seeded Canned Chipotle pepper
- ¼ teaspoons Each Of salt And pepper
- 2 teaspoons Packed brown sugar
- 1 package (397g Package) puff pastry, Thawed But Cold
- 1 whole egg
- 1 Tablespoon water

Direction

- Note: double the above ingredients if using 2 sheets of puff pastry.
- Preheat oven to 375°F.
- In a bowl mix together the cheese spread, chipotle pepper, salt, pepper and sugar.
- On a lightly floured surface, roll out the pastry sheet to 14 x 11 inches. Spread mixture evenly over the pastry. Starting at the long end, roll up and then put in the fridge for 1 hour or freezer for 45 minutes.
- Remove from the fridge and trim ends. Cut into 1/2-inch slices and place cut side down on a parchment paper-lined cookie sheet. Brush tops lightly with egg and water mixture. Bake 15-17 minutes till golden. So yummy!

336. Taco Sandwich Recipe

Serving: 0 | Prep: | Cook: 5mins | Ready in:

Ingredients

- tortilla
- Shredded cheese
- pepperoni slices

Direction

- Lay one tortilla down on microwaveable safe plate.
- Place pepperoni slices all around tortilla.
- Sprinkle shredded cheese all over tortilla me pepperoni.

- Place 2nd tortilla over first.
- Place in microwave for approximately 30-45 seconds or until cheese is melted.
- Cut in half and enjoy.

337. Tinks Sausage Cheese Balls Recipe

Serving: 18 | Prep: | Cook: 15mins | Ready in:

Ingredients

- 2 pkg bulk sausage un -cooked
- 16 ounces sharp cheddar cheese
- 1- 1/2 cups all-purpose baking/ biscuit mix like (Bisquick) or any brand you like ......
- 1/2 cup finely chopped onion..
- 1/2 teaspoon garlic powder.....

Direction

- Preheat oven to 375 degrees F.
- Shred cheese and mix all ingredients in a large bowl, until all is mix well.
- Form into 1 inch balls.
- Place on ungreased baking sheet
- Bake 15 minutes until golden brown
- Makes 6 dozen
- Note from Tink;...... sausage - cheese balls can be frozen uncooked.........
- And if you want a firmer texture add extra 3 cups of the baking mix and extra 2 cups of the cheese to the above ingredients.........myself I like the recipe as is but I do like to sometimes add more cheese to it anyway.........

338. Tomato Basil And Parmesan Tartlets Recipe

Serving: 48 | Prep: | Cook: 10mins | Ready in:

Ingredients

- 4 (2.1 oz.) pkgs frozen mini phyllo shells
- 12 oz. reduced-fat cream cheese, at room temperature
- 1 (8 oz.) pkg shredded mozzarella cheese
- 1/2 cup grated parmesan cheese
- 2 large eggs, slightly beaten
- 1 cup oil-packed sundried tomatoes, chopped and drained
- 1 cup fresh basil, chopped
- 2 cloves garlic, minced
- black pepper

Direction

- Preheat oven to 350. Divide the frozen phyllo shells between two rimmed baking sheets.
- Set the baking sheets aside.
- Place cream cheese, mozzarella cheese, Parmesan cheese, eggs, sundried tomatoes, basil and garlic in bowl of a large mixer or a food processor. Blend on low speed of mixer or pulse of food processor until ingredients come together and are well combined.
- Season with black pepper.
- Place 1 teaspoon of mixture in each phyllo shell.
- Bake until cheese bubbles and the shells are crisp and brown. 8-10 minutes.
- Remove from oven and serve warm.
- Can be made earlier in the day and reheated in preheated 350 oven for 3-4 minutes.

339. Tomato Cheese Appetizer Delights Recipe

Serving: 16 | Prep: | Cook: 20mins | Ready in:

Ingredients

- 2 packages crescent dinner roll dough
- 8 ounces cream cheese softened
- 1 cup salad dressing
- 1 package ranch salad dressing mix
- 3 cups chopped tomatoes
- 2 cups pepper jack cheese grated finely

Direction

- Spread crescent rolls on cookie sheet and press together to make a flat crust.
- Bake at 350 for 15 minutes.
- In medium bowl mix together cream cheese, salad dressing and ranch dressing mix.
- Spread onto cooled crust then cover with tomatoes and sprinkle grated cheese on top.
- Place under broiler just long enough to melt cheese then remove.
- Cool and cut into squares and refrigerate until serving.

340. Tomato Mozzarella Tart With Prosciutto Recipe

Serving: 6 | Prep: | Cook: 35mins | Ready in:

Ingredients

- flour for dusting work surface
- 1 (1.1 lb) box frozen puff pastry (pepperidge farm,thawed in the box in the refrigerator overnight)
- 1 large egg, beaten
- 1 oz parmesan cheese, freshly grated (1/2 cup)
- 1 lb roma tomatoes (3-4 medium), cored and cut crosswise into 1/4 in thick slices
- salt
- 2 garlic cloves, minced
- 2 tbs EVOO
- ground black pepper
- 8 oz low-moisture WHOLE-milk mozzarella shredded (2 cups)
- 2 tbs coarsely chopped basil
- 2 oz thinly sliced prosciutto

Direction

- Adjust an oven rack to the lower middle position and heat oven to 425.
- Dust work surface with flour and unfold both pieces of puff pastry onto the work surface.
- Brush some of the beaten egg along one edge of the sheet of pastry.
- Overlap with the second sheet of pastry by one inch and press down to seal the pieces together.
- With a rolling pin, smooth out the seam.
- The rectangle should measure 18 by 9 inches.
- Use a pizza wheel or knife to cut a one inch strip from the long side of the dough. Cut another one inch strip from the same side.
- Cut a one inch strip from the short side of the dough. Repeat on same side.
- Transfer large sheet of dough to a parchment lined baking sheet and brush with more beaten egg.
- With pizza wheel of knife, trim any excess dough from the corners.
- Sprinkle the dough with the Parmesan.
- Using a fork, uniformly and thoroughly poke holes in the bottom of the shell.
- Bake form 15 minutes, then reduce the oven temperature 350 and continue to bake until golden brown and crisp, 15-17 minutes longer.
- Transfer to a wire rack and increase the oven temp to 425.
- While the shell bakes, place the tomato slices in a single layer on 2 layers of paper towels and sprinkle evenly with 1/2 tsp. of salt; let stand for 30 minutes.
- Place 2 more layers of paper towels on top of the tomatoes and press firmly to dry the tomatoes.
- Combine the EVOO, the garlic, a pinch of salt and pepper in a small bowl and set aside.
- Sprinkle the mozzarella evenly over the bottom of the warm (or cool, if made ahead) baked shell. Follow with the prosciutto.
- Shingle the tomato slices width-wise on top of the cheese (about 4 slices per row); brush the tomatoes with the garlic oil.
- Bake until the shell is deep golden brown and the cheese is melted, 15-17 minutes.
- Cool on a wire rack for 5 minutes, sprinkle with the basil, slide on to a cutting board, cut into pieces and serve!!!

341. Truffle Filled Baked Brie Recipe

Serving: 12 | Prep: | Cook: 30mins | Ready in:

Ingredients

- 1 small wheel of brie cheese
- 4 oz cream cheese softened
- truffle oil (I used the black truffle oil which I was told was more intense in flavor than the white oil))
- 1 small can of mushroom pieces (drained) or if you can afford a jar of truffles use them
- 1 sheet of puff pastry

Direction

- Chill cheese well.
- Remove top rind.
- Cut cheese in half horizontally
- Soften cream cheese and mix with truffle oil to taste
- Spread the cream cheese over the bottom half of brie.
- Place drained mushrooms across the cheese evenly
- Place top half over cheese, and place some mushrooms over that
- Enclose the whole cheese in puff pastry and seal well
- Bake in a 400F oven until puffed and golden about 30 minutes
- Let cheese set about 10 minutes before cutting into wedges with a sharp knife.
- May serve as is or with assorted crackers

342. Tuna And Cheese Dip Recipe

Serving: 8 | Prep: | Cook: 30mins | Ready in:

Ingredients

- 2 cans solid white tuna, drained and shredded
- 1 stalk celery, diced
- 1/2 small onion, diced
- 1/2 cup mayonnaise (more if you like more mayo)
- 2 cups shredded Velveeta cheese
- 1 bread bowl
- potato chips

Direction

- In a large mixing bowl, mix 1st 4 ingredients
- Fold in cheese
- Pour into baking dish and cover with foil
- Bake @ 350 for 30 minutes
- While tuna is in the oven, cut hole into bread bowl.
- Slice bread that was removed from bowl into pieces and set aside
- Remove tuna from oven and pour into bread bowl
- Arrange bread pieces and chips around bowl.

343. Turkey Nachos Recipe

Serving: 6 | Prep: | Cook: 5mins | Ready in:

Ingredients

- 2 cups diced cooked chicken or turkey
- 1/2 cup FRANK'S® REDHOT® buffalo wing sauce or FRANK'S® REDHOT® Original cayenne pepper sauce
- 1 (10 oz.) bag tortilla chips
- 2 cups shredded Cheddar or Jack cheese
- blue cheese or ranch salad dressing
- sour cream

Direction

- 1. Toss chicken with Buffalo Wing Sauce.
- 2. Layer chicken mixture with chips and cheese in baking dish or on pizza pan.
- 3. BAKE at 350°F for 5 min. until hot and cheese melts. Serve with blue cheese dressing,

sour cream and additional Buffalo Wing Sauce.

344. Unos Nachos Recipe

Serving: 8 | Prep: | Cook: 10mins | Ready in:

Ingredients

- tortilla chips
- 1 can chili with beans
- chunky salsa
- Jalapeños
- cheddar cheese
- sour cream

Direction

- Preheat oven to 350.
- Place tortilla chips on oven-safe platter.
- Cover chips with can of chili
- Slice Jalapeños into rings and scatter on top of chili.
- Cover with cheddar cheese.
- Bake at 350 until cheese is melted and nachos are heated (5-10 minutes).
- Top with Sour Cream and Salsa.

345. Vegetable Medley Nacho Platter Recipe

Serving: 4 | Prep: | Cook: 17mins | Ready in:

Ingredients

- 1 bag of multigrain corn chips
- 1/2 lb of lean ground beef, cooked
- 14 grape tomatoes,cut in half
- 1/2 small onion, chopped
- 1 medium carrot, grated
- 4 asparagus spears
- 1/2 red bell pepper, chopped
- 1 tsp minced garlic
- 1 1/2 cups of grated cheddar cheese, divided
- 2 tsp low sodium taco seasoning
- 1/2 tbsp canola oil
- 1 tsp dried parsley
- pinch of salt and pepper

Direction

- Preheat oven to 350° F
- Cook beef in skillet until cooked through (approx. 7 min)
- Drain liquid and mix in taco seasoning, put in a bowl and set aside
- In the same skillet, add the oil, carrot, asparagus, pepper, onion and garlic
- Cook on med/high heat for around 3 minutes
- Line cookie sheet with foil and parchment paper (for easy clean up)
- Spread corn chips on sheet
- Sprinkle half of the cheese on top
- Spread meat and veggies (except the tomatoes) on top
- Sprinkle the rest of the cheese on top
- Place tomatoes and parsley on top of the cheese
- Bake in the oven for 10 minutes (until cheese has melted)

346. Venison Cheddar Jalapeno Smoked Sausage Recipe

Serving: 40 | Prep: | Cook: 120mins | Ready in:

Ingredients

- 1 cup cold water
- 3 tablespoons curing mixture (e.g., Morton® Tender Quick®)
- 2 teaspoons mustard seed
- 1 teaspoon garlic powder
- 1 teaspoon coarse ground black pepper
- 2 teaspoons liquid smoke flavoring

- 3 pounds lean ground venison
- 1 cup shredded cheddar cheese
- 2 jalapeno peppers, seeded and minced

Direction

- Stir the water, curing mixture, mustard seed, garlic powder, black pepper, and liquid smoke in a large bowl until the curing mixture has dissolved. Mix in the ground venison, Cheddar cheese, and jalapeno peppers; mix until evenly blended and somewhat sticky, about 3 minutes. Divide the mixture in half, and roll each half into 2 inch thick logs. Wrap each log tightly with aluminum foil (we use casings,) and refrigerate for 24 hours.
- Preheat an oven to 300 degrees F (150 degrees C). Line a baking sheet with aluminum foil, then remove the foil from the sausage logs (we don't remove the casings,) and place them onto the baking sheet.
- Bake in the preheated oven until the internal temperature reaches 170 degrees F (75 degrees C), 1 1/2 to 2 hours. Cool the sausages on a rack until they have cooled to room temperature. Dab occasionally with a paper towel to absorb excess grease. Slice thinly to serve.

347. Vidalia Onion Cheese Dip Recipe

Serving: 4 | Prep: | Cook: 25mins | Ready in:

Ingredients

- 3 large Vadalia onions, coarsely chopped
- 2 Tbsp. margarine
- 8-ounces sharp cheddar cheese, grated
- 1 cup mayonnaise
- 1/2 teaspoon Tabasco sauce
- 1 clove garlic, minced or a few shakes of garlic powder
- tortilla chips or crackers

Direction

- Preheat oven to 375 degrees. Sauté onions in margarine. Mix cheese, mayonnaise, garlic and Tabasco sauce. Stir in onions. Put in buttered casserole and cook 25 minutes. Serve hot with tortilla chips or crackers.

348. Warm Blue Cheese Bacon Garlic Dip Recipe

Serving: 6 | Prep: | Cook: 40mins | Ready in:

Ingredients

- 7 slices bacon, chopped
- 2 cloves garlic, minced
- 8 ounces cream cheese, softened
- 1/4 cup half and half
- 4 ounces blue cheese, crumbled
- 2 tabs chopped fresh chives
- 3 tabs chopped smoked almonds

Direction

- 1- Cook bacon in a large skillet over medium-high until almost crisp, about 7 minutes.
- 2- Drain excess fat from skillet. Add garlic and cook until bacon is crisp, about 3 minutes.
- 3- Preheat oven to 350 degrees. Beat cream cheese until smooth. Add half and half and mix until combined. Stir in bacon mixture, blue cheese, and chives.
- 4- Transfer to a 2- cup ovenproof serving dish and cover with foil. Bake until thoroughly heated, about 30 minutes. Sprinkle with chopped almonds.
- 5- May be prepared 1 day in advance. Keep refrigerated, if going to a party. Bake it there.

349. Warm Blue Cheese Dip Recipe

Serving: 10 | Prep: | Cook: 30mins | Ready in:

Ingredients

- 8 slices hickory smoked bacon,diced
- 2 cloves garlic,minced
- 8 oz cream cheese,softened
- 1/4 c heavy cream
- 4 oz crumbled blue cheese (1 c)
- 2 Ths chopped fresh chives
- 2 Tbs chopped almonds
- chopped fresh parsley
- crackers,French bread and/or fresh vegetables

Direction

- Preheat oven to 350 degrees. In non-stick skillet, cook bacon over medium-high heat for about 8 mins or till nearly crisp.
- Drain bacon; wipe skillet dry. Return bacon to skillet; add garlic and cook over medium heat till bacon is crisp, about 3 mins, making sure garlic doesn't burn. Drain on paper towels.
- With mixer on medium speed, beat cream cheese until smooth. Add cream; beat well. Fold in bacon, garlic, blue cheese and chives.
- Transfer to 2 cup baking dish. Sprinkle top evenly with almonds. Bake until heated through and browned on top, 25-30 mins.
- Sprinkle with parsley. Serve with crackers, bread and/or vegetables.

350. Warm Broccoli N Cheddar Dip Recipe

Serving: 1 | Prep: | Cook: 30mins | Ready in:

Ingredients

- 1 envelope vegetable soup mix
- 1 container (16 oz.) sour cream
- 1 pkg. (10 oz.) broccoli or spinach, chopped, thawed and squeezed dry
- 1 cup (4 oz.) shredded cheddar cheese

Direction

- Preheat oven to 350F
- In 1 quart casserole dish, combine vegetable soup mix, sour cream, broccoli or spinach and 3/4 cup cheese
- Top with remaining 1/4 cup cheese
- Bake uncovered for 30 minutes or until heated through
- Serve with your favourite dippers

351. Warm Crab Parmesan Dip Recipe

Serving: 8 | Prep: | Cook: 45mins | Ready in:

Ingredients

- 1 (6 ounce) can crabmeat, drained and flaked
- 1 (8 ounce) package cream cheese, softened
- 1 cup mayonnaise
- 1 1/2 cups grated parmesan cheese
- 1 cup sour cream
- 4 cloves garlic, peeled and crushed

Direction

- Preheat oven to 350 degrees F (175 degrees C).
- In a small baking dish, mix the crabmeat, cream cheese, mayonnaise, Parmesan cheese, sour cream and garlic.
- Bake uncovered in the preheated oven 45 minutes, or until bubbly and lightly browned.
- Serve with blue or corn tortilla chips.

352. Warm Cranberry Walnut Brie Recipe

Serving: 8 | Prep: | Cook: 15mins | Ready in:

Ingredients

- 1 (8 oz) round brie cheese
- 2 Tb dried cranberries
- 1 tsp chopped fresh thyme
- 1 tsp chopped walnuts,toasted
- crackers (Triscuits,etc)

Direction

- Preheat oven to 350 degrees.
- Using serrated knife, remove topmost rind from cheese; discard rind.
- Place cheese, cut side up in a small ovenproof baking dish; sprinkle with cranberries and thyme. Top evenly with nuts.
- Bake at 350 for 15 mins or till cheese is soft and warm. Serve with crackers.

353. Warm Fruited Brie In Crust Pastry Recipe

Serving: 24 | Prep: | Cook: 35mins | Ready in:

Ingredients

- 1 pkg (15 oz.) refrigerated all-ready pie-crust
- 2 lb. wheel brie cheese,about 8 in. in diameter
- 2 apples, cored and sliced
- 1 cup seedless grapes
- 1/2 pint raspberries or strawberries
- 1 cup apple juice
- 1 Tbsp. cornstarch

Direction

- Preheat oven to 400 degrees F
- On large baking sheet, unfold one piecrust
- Place Brie in centre of piecrust
- Turn under edge of piecrust to within 1/2 in. of cheese and decoratively flute edge
- Remove Brie and set aside
- Prick piecrust with a fork to prevent from puffing while baking
- Place baking sheet on centre rack of oven and bake for 10 min.
- Remove from oven
- Lightly flour a wooden board, marble slab or other work surface
- Unfold 2nd piecrust and place on floured board
- With a leaf cookie cutter or tip of paring knife, cut out 4 -2 in. long oval-shaped leaves; mark veins on leaves with back of knife
- Place leaves on baking sheet; bake 5 min. or until golden brown
- Transfer to wire rack to cool
- Lower oven temperature to 350 F
- Place Brie on fluted piecrust
- Arrange apple slices around top edge of cheese; place grapes and berries in the centre
- Return fruit-topped Brie to oven and bake 10 min.
- Meanwhile, in small saucepan, blend apple juice and cornstarch
- Bring mixture to boil over moderate high heat and cook, stirring constantly for 1 min. or until mixture is clear and thick.
- Remove saucepan from heat.
- Remove Brie from oven and arrange pastry leaves on top
- Brush leaves and fruit with apple juice glaze
- Allow to stand 15 min., until cheese softens
- Carefully transfer to a serving board
- Cut into wedges to serve
- Makes 24 wedges

354. Warm Salsa Cheese Dip Recipe

Serving: 10 | Prep: | Cook: 40mins | Ready in:

Ingredients

- 1 can chili, no beans   I prefer Hormel brand (15oz)
- 1 jar of your favorite salsa (16oz)
- 1 (8 ounce) package cream cheese, softened
- 2 cups colby Jack shredded cheese   (or can use 1 cup mozzarella and 1 cup sharp cheddar, for a different taste, your preference)
- If you like your dip a bit more chunky
- Can add -
- 1 small green pepper, chopped
- 1 small onion, chopped
- 1 small can sliced black olives, drained

Direction

- Preheat oven to 350.
- Combine all ingredients in a mixing bowl.
- Spoon into a casserole dish. Cover with foil.
- Bake covered for 30 minutes.
- Remove cover and bake 5 -10 minutes more or until bubbly
- Serve with nachos or corn chips.

355. Warm Tomato And Feta Bruschetta Recipe

Serving: 21 | Prep: | Cook: 15mins | Ready in:

Ingredients

- 1 8 oz. loaf of Sour Dough or French bread (baguette)
- 1/3 cup Italian dressing
- 1 lb plum tomatoes, seeded and chopped
- 1/4 cup chopped red onion
- 1/2 tbsp minced garlic
- 1 4 oz pkg crumbled feta cheese
- 3/4 cup fresh shredded parmesan cheese

Direction

- Preheat oven to 375.
- Cut bread into 1/2 inch thick slices. Brush one side of each slice with Italian dressing. Place in preheated oven until lightly toasted (about 5 minutes).
- Meanwhile in a medium bowl combine tomatoes, onion, garlic and feta and remaining Italian dressing.
- Spoon mixture onto each toast slice and sprinkle with shredded parmesan.
- Return to oven for 7-10 minutes or until toppings are heated through. Serve immediately.
- **You can increase or decrease the amount of Italian dressing added to the tomato mixture according to your tastes. I have also found that the "basil and sun dried tomato" flavored feta works extremely well in this recipe. **

356. Wild Mushrooms Tarts With Gruyère, Herb Salad & Balsamic Glaze Recipe

Serving: 8 | Prep: | Cook: | Ready in:

Ingredients

- double recipe of: http://www.simplyrecipes.com/recipes/all_butter_crust_for_sweet_and_savory_pies_pate_brisee/
- ~
- Filling:
- 1 1/2 pounds wild mushrooms, cleaned
- 3 tablespoons olive oil
- 1 clove garlic, chopped
- 1 teaspoon fresh thyme leaves, chopped
- 3/4 cup fresh whole milk ricotta
- 2 tablespoons crème fraîche
- 2 large organic egg yolks
- 1/2 pound Gruyère, grated (I used emmentaler swiss)
- 1/4 cup freshly grated parmigino-reggiano
- 1 bunch scallions, chopped
- salt and pepper, to taste
- ~
- To serve:

- organic baby lettuce mix
- herbs (such as parsley, tarragon, dill, chervil & chives), cleaned
- fresh lemon juice, evoo
- Balsamic glaze or aged-balsamic reduction

Direction

- Preheat the oven to 400'F.
- Roll the pastry to 1/8 inch thickness on a floured surface. Cut out shapes or make a large rectangular tart. Place on a parchment lined baking tray. Keep chilled until ready to use.
- Tear the mushrooms/slice into pieces. Heat the olive oil in a large sauté pan and add the mushrooms (you can do this in batches). Add the garlic, scallions and thyme and sauté until the mushrooms are tender and a little crispy. Season with salt and pepper. Reserve.
- Mix the ricotta and the crème fraiche with egg yolks. Season with salt and pepper. Spread the ricotta mixture on the pastry leaving a half an inch border. Sprinkle cheeses on top and then the mushrooms.
- Bake for 25 minutes. Or until bubbly in the centre with a golden crust around the edges.
- To serve:
- Mix the herbs with greens in a bowl and toss with a squeeze of lemon and a touch of olive oil. Season with salt and pepper.
- Cut the tart into pieces (if you're making a large one). Drizzle the balsamic reduction on the plate, place the wild mushroom tarts on top and finish with the salad.

357. Zahras Zesty Parmesan Potato Wedges Recipe

Serving: 8 | Prep: | Cook: 45mins | Ready in:

Ingredients

- 8 Medium Size russet potatoes Sliced into Wedges with Skins
- 1/2 Tsp salt
- 1 Tsp garlic pepper seasoning or 1/2 Tsp Garlic & 1/2 TSP Pepper
- 2 Tbsp parmesan cheese
- 1/2 Cup olive oil or canola oil

Direction

- Preheat oven to 350 degrees F.
- Line a baking sheet with foil and lightly brush with the olive or canola oil, to prevent wedges from sticking to the baking sheet.
- Mix 1/2 olive or canola oil with salt, garlic and pepper.
- Place potato wedges onto prepared baking sheet.
- Sprinkle with Parmesan Cheese.
- Bake in preheated oven for 45 minutes or until tender.
- Serve warm with your favourite condiments. Simply delicious. :-)
- Bon appetit....

358. Zucchine Ripiene Con Ricotta Recipe

Serving: 6 | Prep: | Cook: 15mins | Ready in:

Ingredients

- 6 medium zucchini (about 2 lbs.),
- halved lengthwise
- 7 tbsp. extra-virgin olive oil
- 3 cloves garlic, finely chopped
- 1 yellow onion, finely chopped
- 2 medium tomatoes, cored, seeded,
- and chopped
- 2 cups homemade or store-bought ricotta
- 3⁄4 cup grated pecorino
- 3⁄4 cup fresh bread crumbs
- 3 tbsp. finely chopped flat-leaf parsley leaves
- 2 tsp. dried mint, crumbled
- 2 tsp. chopped fresh oregano
- 2 egg yolks, beaten

- kosher salt and freshly ground black pepper,
- to taste

Direction

- Using a small spoon, scoop out and discard pulp from each zucchini half, leaving a 1/4" rim around the edges. Heat 3 tbsp. of the olive oil in a 10" skillet over medium heat.
- Add garlic and onions; cook, stirring occasionally, until translucent, about 6 minutes. Add tomatoes and cook, stirring occasionally, until soft, about 4 minutes more.
- Remove from the heat and set aside.
- In a medium bowl, stir together the ricotta, 1/4 cup of the pecorino, 1/4 cup of the bread crumbs, the parsley, mint, oregano, and egg yolks.
- Fold in the onion mixture and season with salt and pepper. Set the filling aside.
- Arrange an oven rack about 7" from the broiler element and heat. Rub the insides of the zucchini with 2 tbsp. of the olive oil and season lightly with salt. Place zucchini cut side up on a foil-lined baking sheet and broil for 5 minutes.
- Remove baking sheet from oven and fill each zucchini half with enough of the ricotta mixture that it mounds slightly but doesn't spill over the edges of the zucchini.
- Sprinkle each stuffed zucchini with the remaining pecorino and bread crumbs and drizzle with the remaining olive oil.
- Broil until the zucchini are soft and the tops are lightly browned, 10–15 minutes.

359. Zucchini Quiche With Feta Cheese Recipe

Serving: 4 | Prep: | Cook: 45mins | Ready in:

Ingredients

- 2 sheets frozen ready-rolled shortcrust pastry, thawed (partially)
- 1 small zucchini
- 60g Greek feta cheese,
- 4 eggs
- 1/4 cup finely grated parmesan cheese
- 1 tablespoon finely chopped fresh chives
- 2 garlic cloves, crushed
- 1/4 teaspoon dried chili flakes

Direction

- Preheat oven to 190°C fan-forced.
- Cut the zucchini into ribbons and crumble the feta.
- Place a baking tray in oven. Use pastry to line base and side of a 4cm-deep, 24cm (base), loose-based fluted flan tin, trim it to fit. Prick the base (you can use a fork).
- Freeze until firm. Place tin on hot baking tray in oven. Bake until golden (about 10-15Min). Remove from oven. Reduce oven temperature to 170°C fan-forced.
- Using a 2.5cm-deep, 11.5cm x 34cm (base), loose-based fluted tart pan.
- Arrange zucchini and feta in pastry case.
- Make egg mix. Stir in chives, garlic and chilli. Pour over zucchini mixture. Bake for 35 minutes or until golden and just set. Serve.

360. Baked Mozzarella Ritz Recipe

Serving: 152 | Prep: | Cook: 18mins | Ready in:

Ingredients

- 1 packade (8 oz.) kraft low-moisture part-skim mozzarella cheese
- 60 Ritz crackers
- 1 cup marinara sauce

Direction

- Preheat oven to 325 degrees Fahrenheit. Cut cheese crosswise into 15 slices. Cut each slice in half.

- Top each 30 crackers with 1/2 cheese slice; cover with remaining cracker. Place on 15x10x1-inch baking pan.
- Bake 7 min. or until cheese begins to melt. Serve with marinara sauce.

361. Beef And Cheese Dip Recipe

Serving: 8 | Prep: | Cook: 30mins | Ready in:

Ingredients

- 2 small jars dried beef,minced
- 16 ounces cream cheese
- 8 ounces sour cream
- 1/4 cup chopped red bell pepper
- 1/4 cup chopped green bell pepper
- 1/4 cup chopped green onions
- 1 cup chopped pecans

Direction

- Combine all ingredients except pecans, transfer to baking dish. Top with pecans. Bake at 300 for 30 minutes.
- Serve with assorted crackers chips.

362. Brie Recipe

Serving: 4 | Prep: | Cook: 10mins | Ready in:

Ingredients

- 1 brie wheel
- 1tbsp of maple sryup
- 2 tbsp of strawberry jam
- handful of sliced almonds

Direction

- Heat oven to 400
- Line tray with foil
- Put cheese on tray and poke several times with fork.
- Put into oven for 10mins or till puffing up (may only be 5-8mins depending on the oven)
- Sauce
- Combine the maple syrup and jam and microwave for 20-30 seconds till jam is melted. Stir.
- Drizzle the sauce over top the cheese once it's transferred to a plate. Sprinkle with almonds.
- Enjoy

363. Crescent Wrapped Brie Recipe

Serving: 12 | Prep: | Cook: 24mins | Ready in:

Ingredients

- 1 (8 ounce) can of refrigerated cresent dinner rolls
- 1 (8 ounce) round natural brie cheese
- 1 egg beaten

Direction

- Heat oven to 350 degrees f.; unroll roll; separate crosswise into 2 sections, pat dough and firmly press perforations to seal; forming 2 squares. Place 1 square on ungreased cookie sheet, place brie cheese on centre of dough.
- With small cookie cutter or canapé cutter, cut 1 shape from each corner of remaining square; set cut-outs aside.
- Place remaining square on top of cheese round. Press dough evenly around cheese; press to seal completely; brush with beaten egg.
- Top with cut-outs; brush with additional beaten egg
- Bake at 350 degrees F for 20 to 24 minutes or until golden brown, cool 15 minutes serve warm, with crackers and jalapeno jelly or chutney.
- Servings 12

364. Jerk Chicken Nachos Recipe

Serving: 6 | Prep: | Cook: 7mins | Ready in:

Ingredients

- 6 cups tortilla chips
- 3 cups diced cooked chicken
- 1 cups shredded cheese
- 2 tbsp jamaican jerk rub, divided
- 1 small red bell pepper
- 1 lime
- 2 tbsp smipped fresh cilantro
- 1/4 cup sour cream

Direction

- Preheat oven to 425 degrees. Arrange chips slightly overlapping on baking
- Combine chicken, cheese and 1 tbsp. of jerk rub, mix gently
- Sheet sprinkle chicken mixture evenly over tortilla chips.
- Bake 5-7 minutes or until cheese is melted
- Meanwhile, dice pepper. Cut lime in half, squeeze juice into bowl.
- Mix with remaining jerk rub and pepper.
- Mix in snipped cilantro
- Spoon over warmed chips
- Serve with sour cream, salsa and lime pieces

365. Veggies Nachos Recipe

Serving: 64 | Prep: | Cook: 2mins | Ready in:

Ingredients

- 1 cup diced tomatoes
- 1/4 cup diced green pepper
- 2 Tbs. chopped green olives
- 2 Tbs. chopped black olives
- 2 Tbs. chopped green chiles
- 2tsp. white vinegar
- 1/4 tsp. garlic powder
- fresh ground black pepper-to taste
- 8 corn tortillas
- 1/4 cup shredded,cheddar cheese

Direction

- Combine first 8 ingredients
- Cut each tortilla into 8 pie shapes (64 nachos)
- Spoon about 1 1/2 tsp. of vegetables on each nacho
- Divide cheese evenly over vegetables
- Broil, 6" from flame' for 1-2 minutes, until cheese is melted.

Index

A

B

C

D

E

R

S

T

V

W

Z

L

Conclusion

Thank you again for downloading this book!

I hope you enjoyed reading about my book!

If you enjoyed this book, please take the time to share your thoughts and post a review on Amazon. It'd be greatly appreciated!

Write me an honest review about the book – I truly value your opinion and thoughts and I will incorporate them into my next book, which is already underway.

Thank you!

If you have any questions, **feel free to contact at:** *author@friesrecipes.com*

Peggy Ervin

friesrecipes.com

Made in United States
Troutdale, OR
12/14/2024